SCHOOL OF AMERICAN RESEARCH PRESS

ARROYO HONDO ARCHAEOLOGICAL SERIES

DOUGLAS W. SCHWARTZ
GENERAL EDITOR

ARROYO HONDO ARCHAEOLOGICAL SERIES

1
The Contemporary Ecology of Arroyo Hondo, New Mexico
N. Edmund Kelley

2
Prehistoric Pueblo Settlement Patterns: The Arroyo Hondo, New Mexico, Site Survey
D. Bruce Dickson, Jr.

3
Pueblo Population and Society: The Arroyo Hondo Skeletal and Mortuary Remains
Ann M. Palkovich

4
The Past Climate of Arroyo Hondo, New Mexico, Reconstructed from Tree Rings
Martin R. Rose, Jeffrey S. Dean, and William J. Robinson

5
The Faunal Remains from Arroyo Hondo Pueblo, New Mexico: A Study in Short-Term Subsistence Change
Richard W. Lang and Arthur H. Harris

6
Food, Diet, and Population at Prehistoric Arroyo Hondo Pueblo, New Mexico
Wilma Wetterstrom

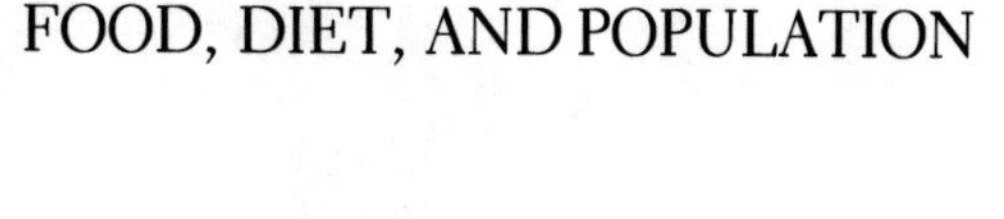

FOOD, DIET, AND POPULATION

The publication of this volume
was made possible by a grant from the
NATIONAL SCIENCE FOUNDATION

FOOD, DIET, AND POPULATION AT PREHISTORIC ARROYO HONDO PUEBLO, NEW MEXICO

Wilma Wetterstrom

With Additional Reports:

Ethnobotanical Pollen
Vorsila L. Bohrer

Artifacts of Woody Materials
Richard W. Lang

SCHOOL OF AMERICAN RESEARCH PRESS
ARROYO HONDO ARCHAEOLOGICAL SERIES, Volume 6

SCHOOL OF AMERICAN RESEARCH PRESS
Post Office Box 2188
Santa Fe, New Mexico 87504

Library of Congress Cataloging in Publication Data

Wetterstrom, Wilma.
Food, diet, and population at prehistoric Arroyo Hondo Pueblo, New Mexico.

(Arroyo Hondo archaeological series ; v. 6)
Bibliography: p.
Includes index.
1. Arroyo Hondo Site (N.M.) 2. Pueblo Indians—Food. 3. Pueblo Indians—Population. 4. Indians of North America—New Mexico—Food. 5. Indians of North America—New Mexico—Population. I. Title. II. Series.
E99.P9W44 1986 978.9″53 86-13869
ISBN 0-933452-16-0

Manufactured in the United States of America. Library of Congress Catalog Number 86-13869. ISBN 0-933452-16-0. First edition.

Contents

List of Illustrations

List of Tables

Foreword
Douglas W. Schwartz

PART 1
Food, Diet, and Population
at Prehistoric Arroyo Hondo Pueblo, New Mexico
Wilma Wetterstrom

Acknowledgments
Introduction

1. THE FOODS OF ARROYO HONDO PUEBLO
The Plant Foods
Archaeological Plant Remains
The Arroyo Hondo Plant Remains
Cultivated Plants
Wild Plants
Other Potential Plant Foods

Animal Foods
Mammals
Birds

2. MAKING A LIVING IN A MARGINAL ENVIRONMENT
Arroyo Hondo Pueblo's Territory
Farm Lands
Plant Collecting
Hunting Territories
Arroyo Hondo's Population
Arroyo Hondo's Bounty: Estimating the Resources
Maize
Other Crops
Wild Plants: Weedy Annuals
Other Wild Plants
Animal Resources of the Arroyo Hondo Area
The Sum of Arroyo Hondo's Foods

3. LEAN TIMES IN A MARGINAL ENVIRONMENT
Reconstructing the Prehistoric Climate
Contemporary Rainfall
Dendroclimatology and Prehistoric Rainfall
Temperature Past and Present
Life During Lean Times
Minor Food Shortages at Arroyo Hondo Pueblo
Major Food Stresses
Responses to Major Food Stresses
Food Resources and a Small Population
Food Distribution and Individual Diets
Dietary Implications of Lean Times
The Young Child's Diet

4. DIET, DEATH, AND DEMOGRAPHY
Diet and Health
Demographic Effects
Demographic Effects on Growing Populations
Effect of a One-Year Drought
Long-Range Effects
Time Range of Effects
Implications of an Adult Population Decline
The Effects of Migration

Testing the Hypothesis
Archaeological Evidence of Food Stress
Faunal Evidence for Food Stress
Demographic Structure
Skeletal Indicators of Nutritional Stress
Archaeological Evidence of Population Dips
Summary and Conclusions

Appendixes
A. Energy Requirements of the Arroyo Hondo Pueblo Population
B. Protein Requirements of the Arroyo Hondo Pueblo Population
C. The Calorie Content of Arroyo Hondo Foods
D. Food Plant Remains Found at Arroyo Hondo Pueblo

PART 2
Additional Reports

I. THE ETHNOBOTANICAL POLLEN RECORD AT ARROYO HONDO PUEBLO
Vorsila L. Bohrer

Acknowledgments
Introduction
Historic Changes in Vegetation
Field and Laboratory Methods
Ethnobotanical Pollen
Ethnobotanical Pollen at Arroyo Hondo
Cheno-ams
Beeweed
Squash
Jimsonweed
Buckwheat
Sunflower
Pincushion Cactus
Cholla
Prickly Pear
Cattail
Some Interpretations from Ethnobotanic Pollen
Two Shallow Basins in Plaza A
Pollen from Turkey Dung Samples

Appendixes
A. Pollen Counts for Each Numbered Sample
B. Data on Pollen Samples from Arroyo Hondo Pueblo
C. Descriptions of Ethnobotanical Pollen
Notes

II. ARTIFACTS OF WOODY MATERIALS FROM ARROYO HONDO PUEBLO
Richard W. Lang

Twine
Unspun Strands and Bark Strips
Bark Sheets
Fiber Cloth
Basketry
Wooden Objects
Specimens from Component I
Specimens from Component II
References
Index

ILLUSTRATIONS

Fig. i. Reconstruction of Arroyo Hondo Pueblo about A.D. 1330 (drawing by Rachel Conine).
Fig. ii. Schematic plan of Arroyo Hondo Pueblo, Component I (drawing by Richard W. Lang).
Fig. iii. Schematic plan of Arroyo Hondo Pueblo, Component II (drawing by Richard W. Lang).
1. Location of Arroyo Hondo Pueblo.
2. Site catchment territory for Arroyo Hondo Pueblo.
3. Food needs of Arroyo Hondo compared with estimated maize yields.
4. Reconstruction of spring precipitation, A.D. 1190 to 1590.
5. Reconstruction of twelve-month precipitation, A.D. 1190 to 1590.
6. Size of the adult population relative to expected population.
7. Number of births in five-year intervals as drought cohort females pass through their fertile years.
8. Size of the adult population as the offspring of the drought cohort mature.

9. The Arroyo Hondo composite life table.
10. Locations of pollen samples taken from Arroyo Hondo Pueblo.
11. Number of subsamples in cheno-am frequency classes.

TABLES

1. Summary of food plant remains found at Arroyo Hondo Pueblo.
2. Arable land within 4 kilometers of Arroyo Hondo Pueblo.
3. Population estimates for Arroyo Hondo Pueblo.
4. Potential harvest of maize.
5. Annual caloric requirements for populations of different sizes.
6. Potential harvest of beans.
7. Potential harvest of field weed seeds.
8. Potential harvest of prickly pear fruit.
9. Potential harvest of banana yucca fruit.
10. Potential harvest of pinyon nuts.
11. Estimated hare populations in the Arroyo Hondo area.
12. Potential harvest of hares and rabbits.
13. Estimated mule deer population in the Arroyo Hondo area.
14. Potential harvest of mule deer.
15. Potential harvest of wild turkeys.
16. Potential harvest of pronghorn antelope.
17. Summary of the estimated harvests of Arroyo Hondo Pueblo's food resources.
18. Potential maize harvest on canyon lands during dry periods.
19. Potential harvest of prickly pear fruit during drought periods.
20. Amino acid requirements of children and adults compared with the amino acid content of maize protein.
21. Protein, tryptophan, and lysine content of beans and various uncultivated foods.
22. Losses to the future adult population when probability of death between ages 1 and 5 is increased, MT:15–30.
23. Losses to the future adult population when probability of death between ages 1 and 5 is increased, MT:20–50.
24. Losses to the future adult population when probability of death between ages 1 and 5 is increased, MT:30–50.
25. Losses to the future adult population when probability of death between ages 1 and 5 is increased, expanding population.
26. The effect on age class mortality of increasing annual mortality during one year.
27. Arroyo Hondo composite life table.
28. Human energy requirements.
29. Energy requirements of the Arroyo Hondo population.

30. Human protein requirements.
31. Protein requirements of the Arroyo Hondo population.
32. Calorie content of plant foods.
33. Caloric value of animal foods.
34. Numbers of seeds and seedlike structures by provenience.
35. Percentages of cheno-am and arboreal pollen in modern surface samples from Arroyo Hondo Pueblo.
36. Prehistoric samples with cheno-am percentages above 40.
37. Squash pollen at Arroyo Hondo Pueblo.
38. Buckwheat pollen at Arroyo Hondo Pueblo.
39. Sunflower pollen at Arroyo Hondo Pueblo.
40. Cholla pollen at Arroyo Hondo Pueblo.
41. Diameters of cholla pollen from various locations.
42. Prickly-pear cactus pollen at Arroyo Hondo Pueblo.
43. Cattail pollen at Arroyo Hondo Pueblo.
44. Pollen counts for each numbered sample.
45. Size in micrometers of sunflower pollen.
46. Size in micrometers and sources of *Mammillaria* pollen.
47. Distribution of unknown type 1 pollen.
48. Distribution of unknown type 2 pollen.
49. Distribution of unknown type 3 pollen.
50. Distribution of asteroid polygon plant microfossil.

Foreword

Arroyo Hondo Pueblo, located about five miles south of Santa Fe, New Mexico (fig. i), was a major settlement in the northern Rio Grande region during the fourteenth and early fifteenth centuries. In 1970 it became the focus for an archaeological research project by the School of American Research that began with three central objectives: (1) to determine the characteristics of northern Rio Grande Pueblo culture as represented in the large fourteenth-century towns; (2) to determine what led to the growth and change of these pueblos; and (3) because the surface survey and preliminary test results suggested that the pueblo experienced extremely rapid growth immediately after its initial settlement, to use Arroyo Hondo and comparative ethnographic material to examine the crosscultural implications and interrelationships of rapid population growth and culture change.

Seventeen years have passed since the Arroyo Hondo project was first conceived, the site surveyed and tested, and funds obtained from the National Science Foundation to begin the major excavation. Since then a great deal has been learned about Arroyo Hondo Pueblo; additional lessons have been learned about the pursuit of a major archaeological project, including the analysis of a vast amount of data and the translation of the results into publishable form. With the publication of this sixth volume in the Arroyo Hondo Series, it seems appropriate to reflect briefly on the preliminary conclusions regarding the site's culture history and on lessons that have been learned regarding the publication of a series of this kind.

The earliest clearly identifiable farming settlements in the northern

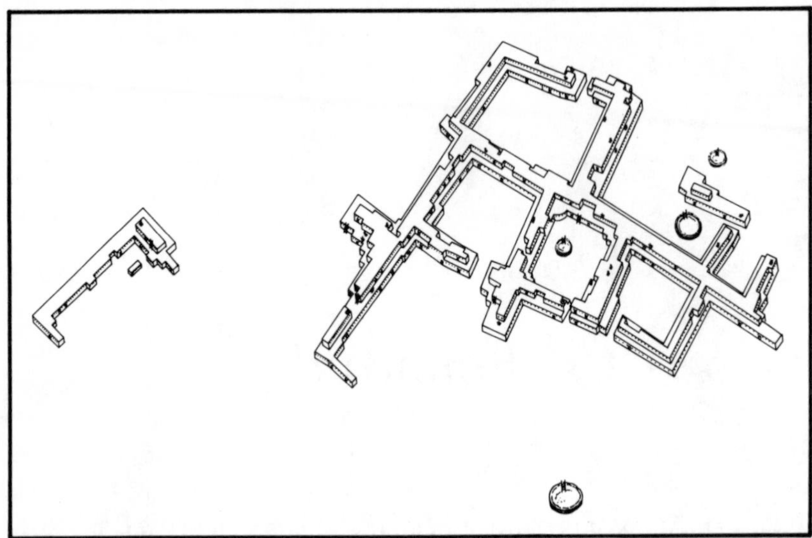

Fig. i. Reconstruction of Arroyo Hondo Pueblo about A.D. 1330 (drawing by Rachel Conine).

Rio Grande Valley date to the seventh century A.D., when average yearly precipitation began to increase. Farming conditions remained highly favorable in this high, mountain-bordered valley for several hundred years. The earliest agricultural settlements were located near the floodplains of permanent watercourses best suited for early agricultural technology. But with increases in crop yields and population size, villages began to be placed away from the rivers on the higher, adjacent piedmont. As climatic conditions improved even further, what had been substandard land now acquired a potential for greater productivity. As additional growth in regional population occurred, settlements were constructed progressively farther away from the rivers.

As this expansion of settlement locations continued in the Rio Grande, another trend was taking place over much of the Southwest. In the fourteenth century, towns that were much larger than any of their predecessors began to appear, reflecting, instead of gradual settlement growth, a quantum jump from villages of less than a hundred rooms to towns of five hundred to two thousand rooms. Point of Pines, Grasshopper, and Awatovi pueblos in Arizona and Pecos Pueblo in New Mexico are examples of such large communities. So two coinciding trends seem to account for Arroyo Hondo Pueblo: the settlement of several towns of much greater size and the expansion of settlements beyond the immediate confines of the Rio Grande Valley.

At its peak in about A.D. 1330, Arroyo Hondo Pueblo would have been an impressive settlement. With twenty-four roomblocks of one- and two-story apartments clustered around ten plazas (fig. i), its inhabitants numbered as many as one thousand. The town survived for slightly more than a century, with two separate episodes of rapid growth followed by precipitous decline.

The time of the pueblo's founding, about A.D. 1300, was one of increased precipitation after nearly fifty years of below-average moisture. A free-flowing spring and well-watered soils in Arroyo Hondo Canyon must have attracted the first settlers, who built an alignment of rooms along the edge of the 125-foot-deep gorge.

From the start, agriculture formed the basis of the pueblo's economy. The lands in Arroyo Hondo Canyon could support irrigation or floodwater farming, while the surrounding higher areas offered a less reliable opportunity for dry farming. In the arroyo, the settlers probably planted the first fields of corn, beans, and squash. These crops were supplemented by gathering seasonally available wild greens, seeds, and nuts in the pueblos' eight-square-mile territory. Among the more than ninety species of animals available, deer provided the major source of protein, while rabbits, turkeys, antelope, and bison were also significant. The inhabitants traded for painted turtles from villages just to the south, live macaws from what is now Mexico, and shells from the Pacific coast.

In the first thirty years, the pueblo prospered and grew to nearly a hundred times its original size (fig. ii). But soon after 1335, annual precipitation began to decrease, and the town's population declined dramatically. Because of disease complicated by malnutrition and iron deficiency, half of all children died before the age of five.

As times got harder the population dwindled, and many of the deserted rooms were used as refuse dumps. Ceramics from trash suggest that by 1345 the pueblo was virtually abandoned. For the next thirty years, the ruined pueblo was inhabited at most by a small, remnant population, perhaps seasonally, and at times the town may have been totally vacant. This abandonment marks the end of what is referred to as the Component I occupation of Arroyo Hondo.

Sometime during the 1370s, the phase of settlement designated as Component II began. Correlating with a second period of increased

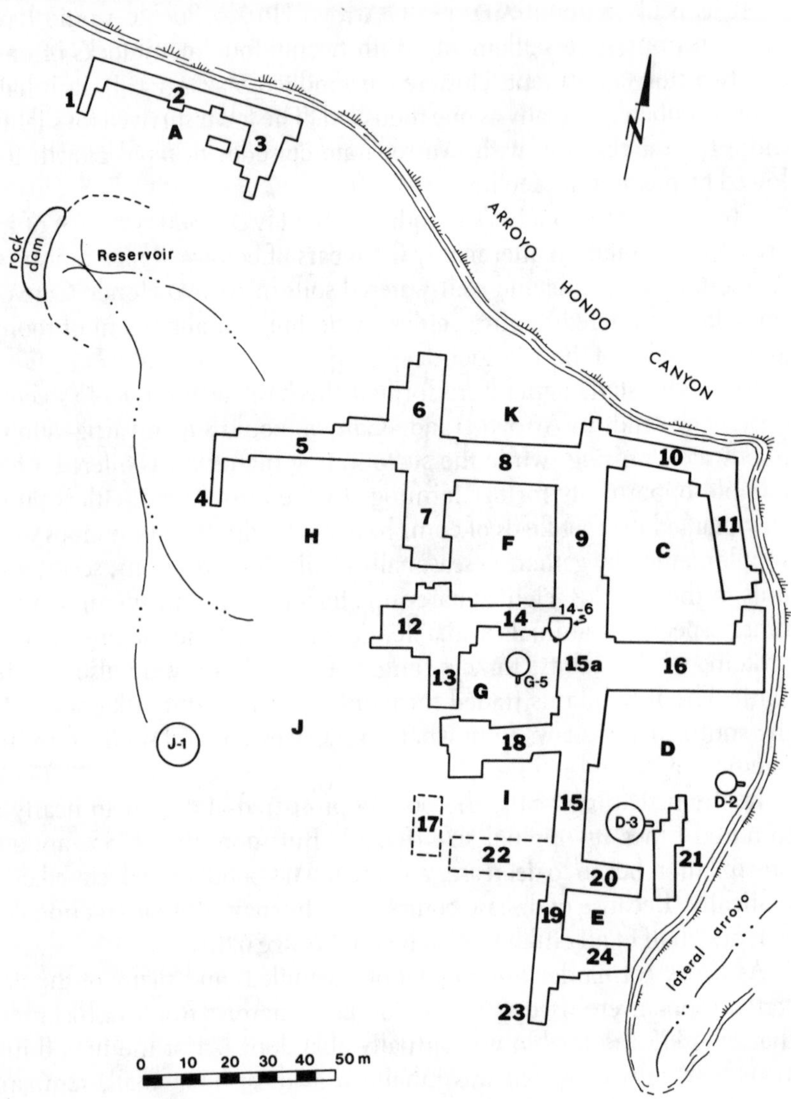

Fig. ii. Schematic plan of Arroyo Hondo Pueblo, Component I (drawing by Richard W. Lang).

moisture, a new settlement was built on top of the ruins of the earlier town. By the early 1400s, Arroyo Hondo had grown into a large village with some two hundred rooms organized in nine roomblocks around three plazas (fig. iii). The renewed growth did not continue, however, for soon after 1410 the region was again affected by drought. As before, rooms were abandoned and demolished as population declined. About 1420, a catastrophic fire destroyed a large part of the village. A few years later, the drought reached a severity unprecedented in the history of the pueblo—the lowest annual precipitation in the one thousand years represented in the dendroclimatological record. With this last misfortune, the second and final occupation of Arroyo Hondo Pueblo came to an end.

A general and progressive population decline followed the abandonment of Arroyo Hondo Pueblo in the northern Rio Grande Valley. During this late prehistoric period, most of the population again settled near the major water sources. The climax period of northern Rio Grande prehistoric settlement had passed. Then, at the time of the Spanish *entrada*, European diseases dealt another blow to the population of the region, from which they would not recover for generations.

HISTORY OF THE PROJECT

Research at Arroyo Hondo began in 1970 with test excavations, supported by the School of American Research, to determine the nature of the site and to obtain data for the preparation of a research proposal. Funds for excavation and laboratory work between 1971 and 1974 were subsequently received from the National Science Foundation (grants GS-28001 and GS-42181). A systematic program of excavation during these years covered roomblock architecture, site organization and growth, residential and plaza configuration, kiva and burial excavation, and regional survey and ecological analysis. During the course of the excavations, interim results were published in three preliminary reports (Schwartz 1971, 1972; Schwartz and Lang 1973). In 1974, upon completion of the field work, a film titled *The Rio Grande's Pueblo Past*, made with support from the National Geographic Society, illustrated the history of the project and presented some initial conclusions.

As the excavation progressed, it became clear that the amount of archaeological and ecological material being recovered and the complex-

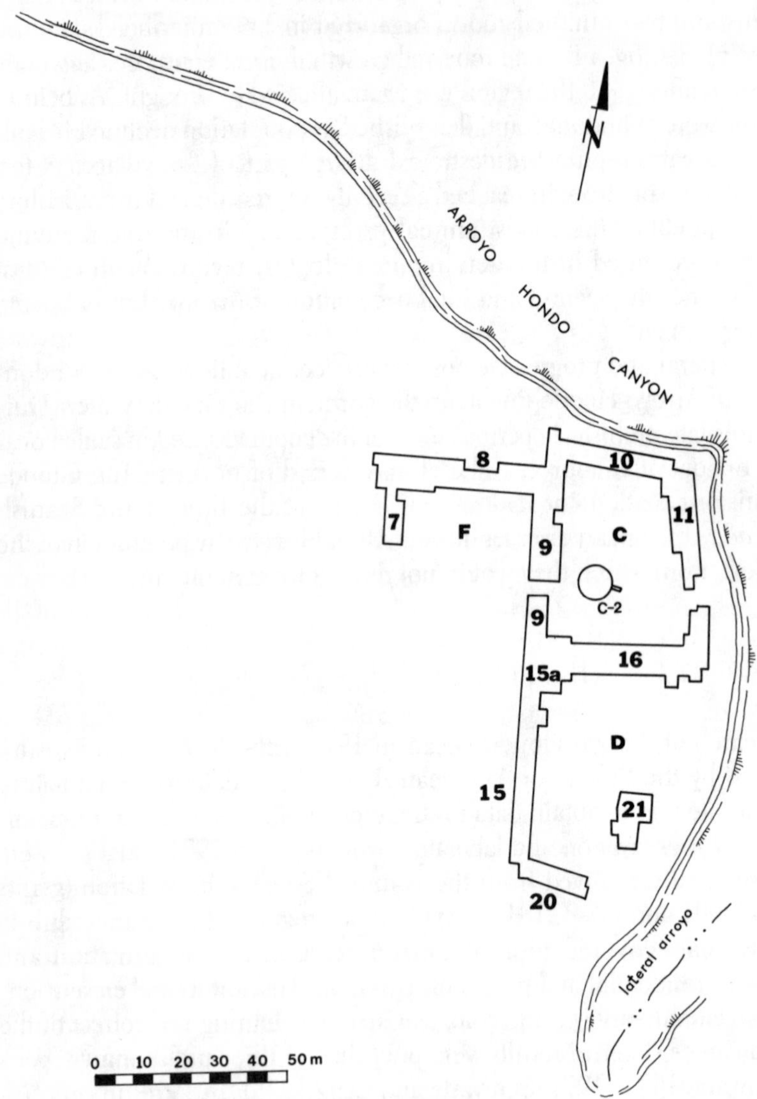

Fig. iii. Schematic plan of Arroyo Hondo Pueblo, Component II (drawing by Richard W. Lang).

ity of ideas emerging from the work could most effectively be documented by the publication of more than one summary volume. Furthermore, I felt it would be best for a number of authors to bring their special knowledge to the ongoing analysis. Midway in the project, each of the main topics was assigned to the individual who knew the most about it or who it was believed could develop the necessary expertise to compile and analyze the data. In many cases, these were people who had first become involved at the fieldwork stage and could move into analysis with firsthand knowledge of the site. Some were advanced graduate students hired to use this material for a thesis (Kelly) or dissertation (Dixon, Palkovich, Wetterstrom), others were part of the School of American Research archaeological staff (Beal, Lang) or outside experts (Rose, Dean, Robinson).

The series was planned to consist of volumes providing a comprehensive presentation of data from each major area and an analysis of those data. While each volume was planned as a contribution to the overall research design of the project, each was also designed to make its own independent contribution. A final volume was planned to synthesize the results of the project and the data volumes and to consider the broader implications of the project results: the culture history of the pueblo, its place in Rio Grande and southwestern prehistory, and the cultural consequences of rapid population growth.

A subsequent National Science Foundation grant (BNS 76-83501) provided for the publication of the data volumes. The number of volumes to be published changed as the importance and potential contribution of the various topics could be better assessed. Some, originally planned as full volumes, have developed into shorter reports or appendixes. To date, published volumes and shorter, appended reports have covered contemporary ecology, prehistoric settlement patterns, skeletal and mortuary remains, paleoclimatology, faunal remains, and artifacts of bone, shell, hide, fur, and feathers. In addition to the present volume on ethnobotany and pollen remains, a volume on architecture is forthcoming, and progress is being made on lithics and ceramics. With the completion of all these volumes, work will begin on the concluding synthesis and discussion volume.

The completion of a series of volumes of this kind over an extended period of time and by several authors involves several problems: the amount of time a researcher-author can spend on a project; the amount of money available for the support of the various elements of the work;

differences in the time taken to complete the various volumes and therefore the availability of the results to the other authors; the persistence and motivation of authors; differences in research and writing ability; and the willingness of authors to see the importance of bringing a manuscript to completion. No project of this kind can avoid these and similar problems, and unfortunately, few of these can be predicted in the initial stages of work.

In spite of delays, changes, and the great additional expense entailed, I still feel the use of a variety of specially skilled individuals as analysts and authors on different parts of the data from an excavation is the only way to proceed. While this method will always cause delay, in the long run the result will be superior. As I look back over each of the volumes that has been published, I am satisfied that they have added significantly both to the project and to Southwestern prehistory.

A project that covers two decades requires the principal investigator to keep the project moving forward, whatever the difficulties, and to recognize that a major segment of his professional life will have to be dedicated to this effort. Only the final results will determine if such an effort was worthwhile. Research efforts focusing on small sites may yield faster returns, but the amount of data and the depth of the interpretation that can emerge from work at larger sites like Arroyo Hondo justifies the extended effort. It is clear that a group research effort will, in the long run, produce a much more sophisticated understanding of what occurred at Arroyo Hondo and how it relates to the broader issues of cultural process.

ETHNOBOTANY OF ARROYO HONDO

The contribution made by Wilma Wetterstrom to our knowledge of the ethnobotany of Arroyo Hondo and our understanding of the role of food stress in the life of the pueblo is an excellent illustration of the value of group effort in archaeological research. Wetterstrom has concentrated on several key issues relating to the central problems of the project: the nature of food resources and diet, how this food was produced in a marginal environment, the effect this precarious diet had on the inhabitants, and how diet was related to the settlement's demographic structure and cultural evolution.

From the analysis of botanical remains found at the site, she begins with a discussion of the three cultivars—corn, beans, and squash—and sixteen species of wild plants that constituted the vegetable elements of the diet. Each of these is described in detail as they occurred at the site, with expanded comparative material from other archaeological and ethnographic contexts. A discussion of how much food the pueblo's occupants were able to produce and collect follows, including data on animal remains from the work of Lang and Harris. From her conclusion that the food resources of Arroyo Hondo were modest at best, she examines the effects of climate change on food resources and how life may have been conducted during major food shortages. She gives special consideration to the problem of children's diet, the effect of malnutrition on disease, and the changing demographic makeup of the settlement. Not content simply to examine the evidence for food stress and malnutrition, she then turns to an intriguing consideration of their effects throughout the culture of Arroyo Hondo Pueblo.

Douglas W. Schwartz
School of American Research

Part 1

Food, Diet, and Population at Prehistoric Arroyo Hondo Pueblo, New Mexico

Wilma Wetterstrom

Acknowledgments

This study grew out of my dissertation, submitted to the University of Michigan Department of Anthropology in 1976, and as a result has been in the making off and on for more than ten years. During this time I have received assistance, encouragement, and support from many individuals and organizations. I owe special thanks to Douglas Schwartz, who invited me to work at Arroyo Hondo Pueblo in 1972 and provided financial support in an era when graduate students excavated for no more than room, board, and experience. I appreciate the free rein he has given me to carry out this research as well as his encouragement.

Richard I. Ford, who served as my dissertation committee chairman, has been an ever-helpful critic and a source of unflagging moral support. Without his periodic encouragement and prodding I might never have made my way through a second long manuscript on Arroyo Hondo Pueblo.

Vorsila L. Bohrer, N. Edmund Kelley, Sheldon Margen, and Richard Lang generously contributed their time and expertise in reading and critiquing an early draft of the manuscript. Their many thoughtful comments and suggestions were most helpful to me in revising the text.

The staff of the School of American Research has provided support and assistance in innumerable ways. Jane Kepp, director of publications, and Laura de la Torre Bueno, editor, pored over the manuscript, questioning me on virtually every point, clarifying ambiguities, and tightening up fuzzy arguments. I am most thankful for the improvements they wrought upon the manuscript. I am especially grateful to Jane Kepp for seeing the project through from start to finish with such thoroughness, patience, and commitment to the highest standards.

I appreciate the cooperation and support I received from the Arroyo Hondo field and lab staffs during the excavations. Special thanks are due Richard W. Lang, Marshall A. Beach, and Michael P. Marshall for their help in collecting samples for flotation. I am most grateful to Ed Kelley who generously shared his knowledge of the local ecology and helped me collect and identify modern plant reference specimens.

I offer my thanks to the typists who patiently plodded through a long, tedious manuscript. Ruth Spear and Karen Chaney of MIT both did superb work on the first draft, cleaning up many spelling errors and inconsistencies. Anne Peacocke of the School of American Research completed the task. Gigi Bayliss is to be credited for the excellent maps and line drawings.

The National Science Foundation supported the excavations and provided funds for publication. I received additional assistance from an NSF dissertation improvement grant (GS-37500) and from the Horace Rackham School of Graduate Studies at the University of Michigan.

Introduction

Because food affects the health of individuals, it also affects a group's collective well-being and ultimately its birth and death rates. By influencing the health and demographic patterns of ancient peoples, foods could have played an important role in the evolution of human societies. Indeed, the shift from food collection to food producing involved some dramatic changes in diet that must have had a profound impact on prehistoric peoples. Some scholars have even suggested that the world's population mushroomed after this transition because the food supply became larger and more stable than it had been during the Paleolithic period (for example, Childe 1941; Braidwood and Reed 1957).

These common-sense examples point to the importance of food in cultural evolution, but recent research indicates that common-sense reasoning alone does not yield an adequate understanding of *how* foods influenced that evolution. For example, Cook (1971) and Cassidy (1972), in independent studies, found that diet and health actually deteriorated with the advent of agriculture, contrary to common opinion. Comparing the skeletal remains of two prehistoric groups from the American Midwest, hunter-gatherers and farmers, each researcher discovered far more evidence of nutritional stress among the farmers in her sample than among the foragers. Apparently the farmers' corn-based diet was lower in protein, vitamins, and minerals than was the hunter-gatherers' fare. Other physical anthropologists examining the remains of prehistoric agriculturists have likewise found evidence of diet-related pathologies (for example, Angel 1971; El-Najjar et al. 1976). Apparently, human populations expanded during the Neolithic period despite their diet, not because of it. These surprising conclusions illustrate the complexity of a population's relationship to its food resources, and they caution against simplistic assumptions. They also suggest the potential value of examining these relations, and they highlight how scant our knowledge is in this area and point to a need for in-depth studies.

Accordingly, a study was undertaken of an Anasazi community and its food resources and diet at a prehistoric pueblo in New Mexico. The inquiry focused on several issues: How does a community produce food in a marginal environment? How does the resulting diet affect individuals and specific groups within the community? How do their responses in turn influence the community as a whole, both biologically and culturally?

Arroyo Hondo Pueblo, located about 8 kilometers (5 miles) southeast of Santa Fe (fig. 1), flourished during the relatively short period from about A.D. 1300 to 1425. Starting from a modest nucleus, the pueblo eventually became a massive structure of twelve to fifteen hundred small rooms arranged around six plazas, all together covering 2.4 hectares (6 acres). The village's size suggests a substantial population, yet the food base was almost certainly meager and precarious. Located on a high plateau at an elevation of 2,135 m (7,000 feet) in a semiarid region, the pueblo was not well situated for either farming or foraging. The narrow Arroyo Hondo canyon, cutting through the alluvium along the northern edge of the site, offers the only relatively fertile and well-watered soils in the region. The area's single reliable source of water, the small stream flowing through the canyon, depends on runoff and springs, both of which dwindle during dry years. The climate is cool, with hard freezes occasionally striking in late May and early September, critical periods for crop development. Since the region's annual precipitation averages only 355.6 mm (14 inches), natural vegetation is a relatively sparse pinyon-juniper woodland. A variety of fruits, seeds, and nuts are found here in quantities that fluctuate along with climate, dwindling markedly during the not-uncommon droughts of two to three years' duration. In such an area, game is not especially abundant, and, like the plant resources, it is vulnerable to droughts.

Given these circumstances, the inhabitants of Arroyo Hondo Pueblo must have had to maintain a delicate balance between a sizable population and a precarious food supply. They almost certainly were a more sensitive barometer of any fluctuations in their foods than the members of a better-situated community would be. Thus, they offer an excellent opportunity to study the relations among people and foods.

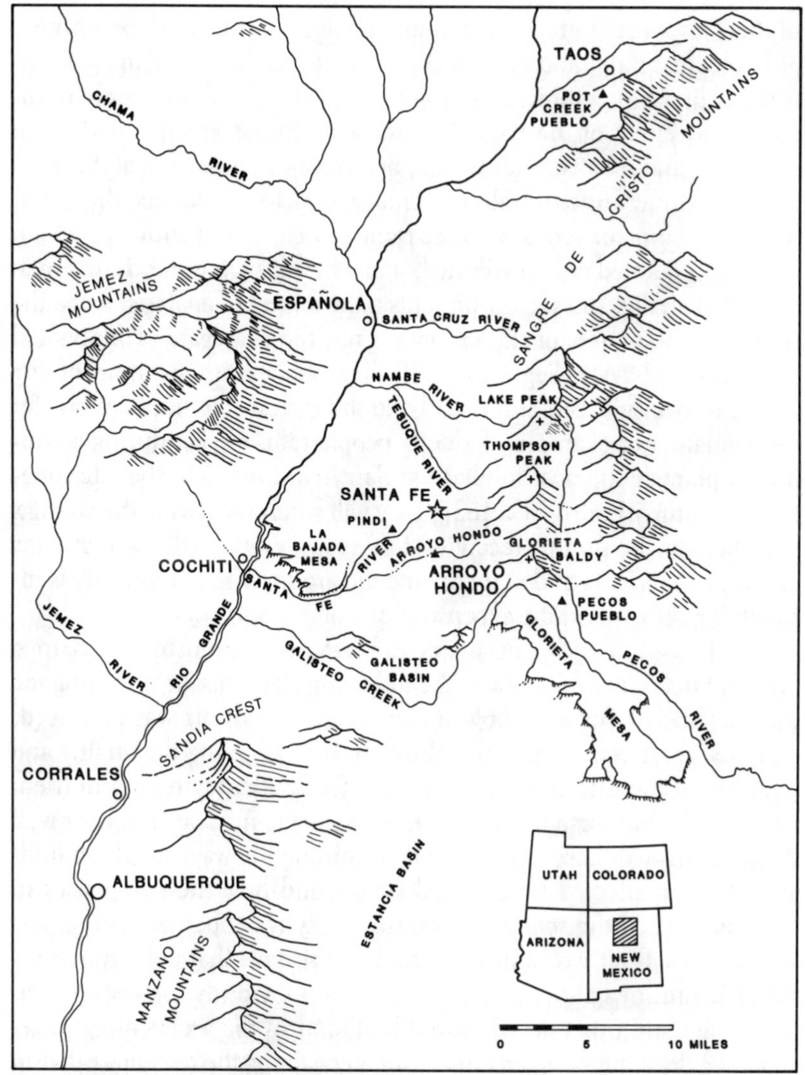

Fig. 1. Location of Arroyo Hondo Pueblo in the northern Rio Grande region.

Trying to unravel these relationships is a complex task requiring far more analysis than the obvious approach of matching numbers of people with quantities of food. At least three levels of investigation must be considered, beginning with the biochemical, physiological aspects of nutrition. Human beings differ widely in their nutrient needs as well as in their responses to food, depending on age, health, work performed, physiological state, and other factors. Foods, in turn, vary in their nutrient content, digestibility, and storability, which all ultimately influence their effect on individual consumers. Foods are also part of an ecosystem and sociocultural system, and must be considered at this level as well. Numerous cultural and ecological factors influence the quantities and kinds of foods produced and stored, the manner in which they are processed and distributed, and who ultimately eats how much of each. Finally, the society presents a third level of analysis, since the needs and responses of the group are not the aggregate of individual needs and behavior (Segraves 1977). The societal implications of any action or decision can and usually do differ from the implications for individuals. For example, if elderly people refuse to eat during a famine, (a practice that was followed at San Juan Pueblo in the late nineteenth century [Ford 1968a:162]), they will surely die, while the younger members of the group, receiving the extra rations, will have a better chance of surviving and perpetuating the group. The community is ultimately nourished at the expense of one of its components.

The task of deciphering these people-food relationships at Arroyo Hondo Pueblo involves, then, the following elements: determining the pueblo's food resources, how much of each foodstuff was produced, and how these resources varied through time; assessing the quality and quantity of the diet created from these foods; identifying the nutrient needs of the various groups within the society and assessing how well the diet satisfied these needs; and determining the ways in which individuals were affected by the food supply and how their responses in turn influenced the society. Since this study is concerned with a prehistoric society, it works under certain constraints that determine how the tasks outlined above can be carried out. Obviously, precise quantitative data and exact detail cannot be found in the archaeological record, but these are not prerequisites for ascertaining the relations between a prehistoric society and its food. It is possible through a variety of indirect means to bracket the range of food resources, the components of the diet, and the potential variation in dietary quality and quantity. The diet's possible effects on health and survival can be inferred using ethnographic data and contemporary nutrition studies; these inferences can then be tested with skeletal evidence and other archaeological data. Finally, demographic models provide a way to examine the probable impact of diet-related deaths, while the archaeological data offer a means for testing these hypotheses.

Although the task of analysis involves a wide range of problems, it can be simplified by focusing on specific segments of a society: those most sensitive to variations in food resources and those that account for the largest share of demographic variation. The most sensitive groups are obviously the best food "barometers," while the segments that account for the greatest variation in mortality are the most important for understanding the impact of food on demography. The elderly are obviously one sensitive and demographically critical group. They are more likely to succumb to starvation and malnutrition than healthy young adults, and they usually represent a large portion of a society's mortality. However, their sensitivity to nutrient deficiencies and their impact on demographic patterns does not match that of young children, who as a group are much more vulnerable to calorie and protein deficiencies and are more likely to die from malnutrition than any other segment of a population.

In contemporary nonindustrial societies, which in some respects offer a useful analogy to societies of prehistoric agriculturists, protein-calorie malnutrition (PCM) is pervasive among young children and is a major cause of death (Behar 1968; Gopalan 1975; Scrimshaw 1975). Young children in these societies are important to demographic patterns since they constitute a larger share of the total mortality than any other single group. In a sample of seven non-industrial countries, children under five represented 35 to 65 percent of all deaths in the mid-1960s (Patwardhan 1964). Moreover, young children as a class can exhibit wide ranges in their death rates, thereby having a great impact on demographic patterns and change. In the nineteenth century, for example, death rates for young children in developed countries were as high as those in contemporary underdeveloped countries, but with improvements in diet and health care, these rates had dwindled to less than 4 percent in some places by the mid-twentieth century. In short, young children are the group most sensitive to dietary changes and most likely to have a significant impact on demographic patterns.

This inquiry then, will explore the foods, diet, and population of Arroyo Hondo Pueblo, focusing particularly on young children: how they responded to variations in food resources and how their health and mortality influenced the community. Using the indirect methods outlined above, the study will analyze the possible impact of Arroyo Hondo's precarious food base. Although models and inference rather than precise quantitative measurements provide the bulk of the data, the results strongly suggest that food resources could have had a profound effect on the pueblo's population patterns, with important implications for the functioning of the community. Specifically, it appears that lean periods would have meant a deficient diet for young children, resulting in higher death rates and a skewed population profile. When the lean-period cohort reached adulthood, the community would have been faced with a shortage of productive adults, a problem that may have had consequences for food production, household structure, social organization, and intracommunity relationships. These are the possible links in one mechanism whereby food played a role in the cultural evolution of a prehistoric community.

1

The Foods of Arroyo Hondo Pueblo

The diet of a prehistoric community cannot, of course, be observed or measured directly, but it can be reconstructed and analyzed through a variety of indirect methods using archaeological, ecological, and ethnographic data. This chapter offers a summary of the community's major foods and the relative importance of each, without which it would be impossible to assess the quality of the diet and its consequences for nutrition and health, issues to be considered in detail later.

THE PLANT FOODS

The floral remains collected at Arroyo Hondo Pueblo include three cultivars—corn, beans, and squash—16 taxa of wild plants, and a number of types that could not be identified, as well as charcoal (see table 1). Corn appears to have been by far the most important food. It was found in 84 percent of all proveniences (appendix D), greatly surpassing any other taxon, and was predominant in pollen samples as well. Beans were present in only 9 percent of proveniences; however, more were probably eaten than this figure suggests, since beans have a low probability of appearing in the archaeological record. The third cultivated vegetable, squash, also preserves poorly, and it was found in only 3 percent of proveniences. It does not grow well at high altitudes (Whit-

TABLE 1.
Summary of food plant remains found at Arroyo Hondo Pueblo.

Plant	*Number of Seeds*
Corn	Large quantities of cob fragments and kernels
Beans	588
Squash	20
Chemo-ams	1,260
Purslane	3,039
Winged-pigweed	114
Bee plant	12
Sunflower	17
Ground cherry	78
Indian rice grass	518
Hedgehog cactus	62
Pincushion cactus	6
Prickly-pear cactus	2
Yucca	5
Chokecherry	3
Pinyon nut	100

NOTE: These data are based on materials excavated during 1972 and 1973.

aker and Davis 1962:144) and was most likely of limited importance in the pueblo's diet.

Wild plant remains occurred in 56 percent of Arroyo Hondo proveniences (appendix D). The most prominent were purslane *(Portulaca retusa* Engelm.), of which a total of over three thousand seeds was found in 22 percent of proveniences; chenopod *(Chenopodium* sp.) and amaranth *(Amaranthus* sp.), about twelve hundred of whose seeds altogether appeared in 43 percent of proveniences; and Indian rice grass *(Oryzopsis hymenoides* Roem S. Schult.), 500 seeds of which occurred in 7 percent of proveniences.

Several plants that do not preserve well and hence would have left only a few traces may also have been used as food at Arroyo Hondo. These include beeweed *(Cleome serrulata* Pursh.), ground cherry *(Physalis* sp.), sunflower *(Helianthus* sp.), banana yucca *(Yucca baccata* Torr.), pinyon nuts *(Pinus edulis* Engelm.), and several cacti *(Echinocereus triglochidiatus* Engelm., *Mammilaria* sp., and *Opuntia* sp.).

Archaeological Plant Remains

Direct evidence of Arroyo Hondo's foods comes from the archaeological plant remains. These offer a wealth of information, but they also pose special problems that impede attempts to reconstruct the diet. The most serious of these obstacles is the skewing caused by differential preservation: plant materials with hard, dry seeds and those with waste products tend to be overrepresented; while moist, fleshy foods and those with no waste often leave few traces or none at all. Another difficulty is the eclectic nature of the plant record. The remains of food are not always easy to distinguish from the traces of fuels, construction materials, dye plants, fibers, and incidentals that also appear among the floral remains.

Both of these problems can be largely overcome, however, in reconstructing the Arroyo Hondo diet. Careful analysis of the remains' archaeological context often resolves the question of function, and it also sheds light on the relative importance of various foods. Some of the skewing in the plant record can be corrected by considering the probability of a plant's being preserved and how it became preserved.

Two other sources of information also help to correct the biases in the plant record and illuminate the composition of the Arroyo Hondo diet. First, the pollen samples from the pueblo complement the macrofloral remains and compensate for some of their limitations (see Bohrer, this volume). Pollen as an analytical tool has its shortcomings, but these rarely coincide with those of the macroflora. For example, while the pollen record favors species that produce profuse pollen and disperse it over great distances, it also documents any plants that leave pollen in the pueblo, regardless of their chances of being preserved in charred form. Traces of pollen may in fact be the only clue that certain plants, such as fleshy stems, were used there. Pollen grains can also be valuable in verifying that a particular plant preserved in the form of a charred seed was in fact useful to the site's inhabitants. In addition, the specific functions of a plant are sometimes suggested by the pollen record. For example, pollen found in a mealing bin suggests that the plant from which it came was ground and used for flour.

Ethnographic information from the Southwest is another powerful, complementary set of data. The modern lifeways of the native southwestern peoples are by no means a perfect mirror of the past, particularly because the Spaniards introduced many new foods and practices.

However, information about the oldest and most traditional foods they use today can offer insights into the diet of their prehistoric ancestors. A knowledge of indigenous plants presently regarded as food alerts the archaeologist to plants that leave no macrofloral remains and helps in sorting out incidentals, medicinals, and others not eaten. The ethnographic sources sometimes also suggest the context in which an item should or should not be found if it served a particular function. A sacred tea used in ceremonies in a kiva, for example, should not turn up in a household hearth. Ethnographic literature also offers a wealth of information on processing and cooking techniques that can be essential in deciphering ancient food habits.

The Arroyo Hondo Plant Remains

Floral remains were systematically collected at Arroyo Hondo Pueblo throughout the 1972, 1973, and 1974 field seasons. Wherever plant material was seen, it was retrieved with trowels or screens and saved. Since much of the material preserved at archaeological sites is not visible, sediment samples were also collected throughout the pueblo for flotation retrieval of plant remains.

In 1972, sampling was geared to maximum coverage of the site. An average of 4 liters of sediment samples was taken from each natural level in the rooms, from all features such as burial pits and hearths, and from test pits and trenches. Areas that were exceptionally rich in plant remains were sampled more extensively. Sampling in 1973 and 1974 was more selective: sediments were collected only from hearths, middens, and other areas that contained plant remains. These again averaged 4 liters, except where deposits were particularly rich.

The flotation procedure was simple and effective. The sediment sample was slowly poured into a large tub of water and stirred. After several minutes, the silt settled and the surface of the water was skimmed with a large kitchen strainer. A woven fabric with a mesh of 22 threads per centimeter was set over the strainer to assure that all specimens, including those less than 1 millimeter in diameter, were recovered. Dipping was repeated with additional pieces of fabric until the water surface was nearly devoid of material. When dry, the sample was carefully brushed from the fabric and transferred to a plastic bag. Sludge samples were periodically taken from the bottom of the tub to check for specimen loss, which appeared to be very slight.

Most of the macrofloral materials from the Arroyo Hondo site were processed and analyzed by the author, the bulk of them at the Ethnobotanical Laboratory of the University of Michigan Museum of Anthropology during the academic years 1972–73 and 1973–74. Each sample was weighed and then sifted through a graded set of geological sieves, which separated the remains into different size classes for examination. The large particles were then scanned by eye; the smaller ones with a dissecting binocular microscope at 7X to 20X magnification. All classes of items, particularly seeds, bones, charcoal, and various vegetative structures, were separated, weighed, and recorded. Items were identified by comparison with modern reference materials in the collections of the Ethnobotanical Laboratory.

Each of the potential plant foods isolated in this manner, and its possible role in the diet, is discussed below.

Cultivated Plants

Corn (Zea mays L.). Corn was the essence of life for the historic Pueblo Indians. It was prominent in myths and ritual, and appeared at virtually all meals in a nearly endless variety of dishes. One of the simplest was prepared by roasting and shucking the ears, and boiling the kernels in water (Cushing 1920:292). Other ingredients were thrown in to make a stew such as one from Cochiti that included "corn, beans, onions, potatoes, and other vegetables. Very little meat is used, though bones are cooked with the stew for additional flavor. Chili, generally red but also green, is the standard flavoring and certain wild plants are also used for this purpose" (Lange 1959:120). Before the Conquest, corn, beans, wild seeds, and greens were probably the main stew ingredients, with wild onions, ground cherry, and juniper berries serving as seasonings.

A meal made of parched corn kernels was a very useful staple. Mixed with water, it was a beverage (Cushing 1920:266); added to boiling water, it made a "stiff, rather dry, crumbling porridge" (Robbins, Harrington, and Freire-Marreco 1916:91). Before the Tewa Pueblos had tea and coffee, their usual morning drink was a thin gruel of corn meal cooked in boiling water (Robbins, Harrington, and Freire-Marreco 1916:90–91). Sometimes maize gruels were spiked with wild seeds such as chenopod *(Chenopodium* sp.) (Bailey 1940:287) and purslane *(Portulaca* sp.) (Cushing 1920:257–58). Maize meal mixed with a little water and shaped into balls can be boiled to form dumplings (Robbins, Harrington, and Freire-Marreco 1916:90), and bread can be made from a similar mixture pressed into loaves and baked in ashes (Bailey 1940:280).

Corn appears to have been the main food for the people of Arroyo Hondo Pueblo just as it was for their descendants. It was by far the most abundant and widely distributed plant recovered from the site: nearly every excavation unit yielded maize in some form, and three burned storerooms produced stacks of corncobs along with relatively small amounts of other plant foods.

For perspective, it should be noted here that some varieties of corn have a very high probability of being represented at archaeological sites. Chapolote-derived maize, the variety found at Arroyo Hondo, has a tough cob that survives long after the kernels have been stripped off. Not only is the cob slow to decompose, but it has a good chance of being charred because it makes excellent kindling and fuel. In the light of this preservation bias, it is clear that corn cannot be compared with other foods strictly on the basis of grams of macrofloral remains. However, the hypothesis that maize was a very important food seems to be supported by the pollen record. Corn pollen grains were found in slightly over half of the samples in which at least 100 grains could be counted (Bohrer, this volume).

Chapolote-derived maize, with its yellow to brown ears, is different from the distinct varieties of red, blue, white, and yellow corn that the Pueblos cultivated in the nineteenth and twentieth centuries (Ford 1968a:166–67), but the ancient maize recipes probably had similarities to modern ones. In particular, the basic cooking techniques of roasting and boiling must surely date to prehistoric times. Stews, gruels, and breads probably have great antiquity as well.

The basic ingredient of most of Arroyo Hondo's corn dishes would have been mature, dry kernels. The pueblo's inhabitants undoubtedly also enjoyed the green ears that are ready in August, which they may have roasted, boiled, or served as stews. The latter may have been like a dish Cushing (1920:264) called an "ancient" Zuni stew, a "mixture of milky kernels, little round beans and bits of fresh meat, the whole being seasoned with salt, thickened with sunflower seeds or pinyon meal and boiled until reduced to an almost homogenous stew." Mature corn was apparently husked and stored on the cob at Arroyo Hondo. Tidy stacks of carbonized ears were found on the floor of a storage room ravaged by fire, and husked ears were in a pile of rubble apparently cleared from another gutted storeroom.

Common Bean (Phaseolus vulgaris L.). Like the modern Pueblo Indians, the people of Arroyo Hondo raised beans. Traces of them were far less abundant than those of maize (appendix D), but beans were probably more important than the figures indicate, since neither the pods nor their contents would seem to preserve readily. The pods would decompose after shelling, and if the beans were boiled—the manner in which all Pueblos (for example, Cochiti: Lange 1959:120; Tewa: Ford 1968a:168; Zuni: Cushing 1920:561) cook them today—they too would decompose if they were not eaten. In that case, only the stray beans that fell into a hearth or those that happened to burn in a storeroom conflagration might be charred and preserved. If beans were prepared by parching and grinding, a cooking technique sometimes used in Mexico today (Kaplan 1956:214), they might have had a slightly better chance of preservation.

Over half of the Arroyo Hondo beans were found amongst the rubble of storeroom fires. Since these totalled over 360 specimens, one might surmise that beans were of some importance at Arroyo Hondo. The relatively few examples found elsewhere at the site could reflect their tendency to decompose.

On the basis of the Pueblo diet in recent times, one would tend to assume that beans were a major food of any prehistoric pueblo as well. But Gasser (1978:6) cautions that the corn-beans-squash triad may be a post-Conquest development. He found little evidence of this combination in the flotation samples he examined from archaeological sites in Arizona dating from A.D. 650 to 1300. The most abundant plants after maize were weedy annuals, with squash and beans ranking very low. Prehistoric Pueblo coprolites also show scant evidence of beans and squash, though it should be cautioned that beans are among the plants that are so thoroughly digested as to leave few identifiable traces in the feces (Stiger 1977:14–15). Stiger (1977:24) found that in coprolites from Anasazi sites dating from A.D. 600 to 1250, corn was the plant most frequently found, often followed by weedy wild species.

These findings clearly call for a reevaluation of present notions about the prehistoric Pueblo diet, but one should not be too quick to discount beans and squash. Gasser's data need to be examined after the effects of differential preservation have been determined more accurately. This same caution applies to coprolite evidence, as noted above.

Squash, pumpkin (Cucurbita pepo L.). For Pueblo communities along the Rio Grande, squashes and pumpkins have been an important food in historic times. However, their wide usage may be only a recent pattern. Evidence of squash at the Arroyo Hondo site included only a few charred seeds, rinds, and strips of flesh. Like beans, squashes are likely to be underrepresented because of their low probability of being preserved, but they probably were never very abundant at the pueblo. They do not grow well at high elevations, for reasons to be discussed later.

Wild Plants

All of the plants described in the following sections grow without direct human intervention and are considered part of the Arroyo Hondo area's indigenous flora. However, the term "wild" may be misleading. The weedy annuals described below invade disturbed soils, and as a result their lives are often closely linked with human habitation. They flourish around settlements where cultivated fields, trash middens, and other disturbed sites provide choice habitats. When the plants are useful to humans, the relationship may be even more intimate, since people may tolerate, encourage, or actively cultivate them. The relation of these plants to the Anasazi is an intriguing issue that deserves more study.

The following group of weedy annuals may represent a wide spectrum of ecological relationships, ranging from plants that grow more or less independently of humans to those that are purposefully and systematically cultivated. This section considers the evidence for these plants as foods.

Weedy Annuals

Goosefoot, lamb's-quarters (Chenopodium sp.) and Amaranth, pigweed (Amaranthus sp.). These very common weeds spring up in cultivated fields, gardens, and other disturbed areas wherever there is enough moisture. Within about two months, the plants begin shedding huge quantities of tiny, black, lenticular seeds that are similar but can be distinguished by genera-specific features. However, after charring and aging for several hundred years, the seeds often lose their diagnostic traits, and attempting to distinguish between the two genera can be a most trying task. Because of these difficulties and because the uses of the two are so similar, they are combined here into a single category.

Although chenopod and amaranth are often considered no more than weeds, in recent times most peoples in the Southwest have valued them as potherbs (e.g. Hopi: Fewkes 1896:18; Cochiti: Lange 1959:149). The greens were gathered while still young and tender and boiled, fried, or added to stews, or they were air-dried and stored for the winter. The seeds are also edible and make a good flour or porridge. The Zunis (Stevenson 1915:65–66) harvested them regularly in August and September and formed the ground meal into loaves that were baked or pats that were steamed. Goosefoot and amaranth flour could also be mixed with cornmeal for mushes and breads.

The prehistoric peoples of the Southwest also undoubtedly used cheno-am seeds. Specimens have been found at numerous prehistoric sites, and at Arroyo Hondo Pueblo they were among the most abundant and widely distributed of the wild plants. Some of these seeds may have been incidentals deposited by the wind, but it is likely that many of them represent the traces of ancient meals. Ninety-nine percent of the specimens were found in flotation samples containing other edible seeds, and of the specimens, about 10 percent occurred in hearths. A burned storeroom containing stacks of corn yielded a few cheno-am seeds as well.

The pollen record offers additional evidence of cheno-ams at the pueblo. High percentages of cheno-am pollen were found in soil samples from a basin in plaza A and in those collected just outside the basin (Bohrer, this volume). Bohrer suggests that the basin was used for winnowing.

Purslane (Portulaca retusa Engelm.). Purslane, a semisucculent that grows in sunny, open areas (Kearney and Peebles 1960:290), has minute, black, edible seeds and fleshy leaves that are good in salads. In recent times in the Southwest, the purslane plant has been valued mainly for its leaves, which can be boiled or fried and are sometimes combined with meat, beans, or gravy (Robbins, Harrington, and Freire-Marreco 1916:60; Ford 1968a:169). Some people, such as the Zunis, also gathered the seeds. Just before these were ripe, they pulled up and dried the entire plant, then shook or pounded it to free the seeds, which were ground and mixed with cornmeal for use in mushes, breads, and cakes (Cushing 1920:244, 257–58). When Cushing recorded these preparation techniques in the 1880s, the Zunis were collecting and storing large quantities of purslane seeds, but apparently none of the other Pueblo groups was using them.

In prehistoric times, these seeds seem to have been more important. They are not among the most common plant remains from archaeological sites in the Southwest, but there is enough evidence to suggest that they were harvested and stored. Phelps (1968:1, 4) found a vessel partially filled with seeds that Jones (1965) identified as *Portulaca retusa* at an El Paso Mogollon site. Other examples of purslane seeds have only been found where excavators have used a flotation technique, as at the Salmon Ruin (Bohrer and Adams 1977:13), presumably because they are minute and would be very difficult to recover without flotation. Given that purslane seeds were much used by prehistoric peoples of the Southwest, one wonders why they were of so little significance in recent times except among a few groups. It may be that they were replaced by new foods that the Spaniards introduced.

The indigenous American species of purslane, *Portulaca retusa*, which has become rather scarce in recent times, was among the wild plants found in greatest abundance at the Arroyo Hondo site. These specimens could have been incidentals that came from plants growing around the village, but it seems more likely that purslane was used by the inhabitants. An incidental would not have been so widely dispersed through the site as these specimens, which were recovered from more than one-third of the flotation samples examined, nor would it appear in such large quantities. (One midden sample, for example, produced over twelve hundred purslane seeds.) It is possible that the plant was used for something other than food, but improbable, since ethnographic accounts from the Southwest give no other functions for it except use as a medicinal tea (Swank 1932:63). In addition, the Arroyo Hondo specimens were all found in contexts where foods would be expected: in trash middens and in association with other foods. If the leaves were used to make tea, some stray seeds might end up in a fire hearth, but probably not in large quantities. However, if the seeds were parched for storage some might char, or seeds that spilled while being ground might fall into a hearth.

The people of Arroyo Hondo may have used both the seeds and the leaves of purslane but there is no record of the latter. Of course, the fleshy leaves probably would not leave any archaeological traces, although mature plants gathered as potherbs might shed some seeds at the pueblo.

Winged-pigweed (Cycloloma atriplicifolia Spreng.). The winged-pigweed, a close relative of the common pigweed, is an invader that crops up in waste places (Bohrer 1973:429). Its small, lenticular black seeds were not among the most popular wild foods in the Southwest, but in the recent past both the Hopis and Zunis harvested them. After winnowing the fruits, the Hopis ground the seeds and prepared a mush (Vestal 1940:161), while the Zunis mixed the flour with cornmeal and water to form pats which they steamed (Stevenson 1915:67).

Cycloloma was known and used in prehistoric times, too. At Broken K Pueblo in Arizona, its seeds were found in six different mealing bins (Hevly 1964:87). Evidence from Point of Pines, Arizona, also clearly indicates that the seeds were gathered as a food: 30 milliliters of them turned up in a pot there, as well as in room fill (Bohrer 1973:429).

The contexts in which winged-pigweed seeds appeared at Arroyo Hondo Pueblo do not indicate so definitely that it was a food. Like the other weedy plants, *Cycloloma* may have grown in the disturbed ground around the settlement and shed some of its seeds in archaeological contexts. There is a good possibility, though, that some of the archaeological specimens had originally been collected as foods. Two of the seeds were found in a burned storage room and 59 in a hearth, while most of the others occurred in trash middens. It is interesting to note that all of the *Cycloloma* specimens were found with cheno-am seeds, indicating that they may have been harvested at the same time or used together. It may also be that *Chenopodium* and *Cycloloma* were placed in the same category in the Arroyo Hondo native taxonomy since the plants resemble each other and the seeds are approximately the same size, shape, and color. The food classification systems of the prehistoric peoples of the Southwest is an area that deserves greater attention.

Rocky Mountain Bee Plant (Cleome serrulata Pursh.). A member of the caper family, the Rocky Mountain bee plant (also known as bee-weed or skunkweed) grows along roadsides, in fields, and in other disturbed areas. Its pink flowers bloom in the summer, later giving way to small green pods that yield edible seeds.

The Keresan Pueblos (Lange 1959:147), the Navajos (Harrington

1967:72), and the people of Acoma and Laguna all used *Cleome* seeds in historic times. The prehistoric peoples of the southwest may have eaten *Cleome* seeds too. Specimens have been found at the Salmon Ruin (Bohrer 1980:321) and at Pueblo Bonito in Chaco Canyon (Judd 1954:61). While the seeds were not particularly abundant at Arroyo Hondo Pueblo, it seems likely that they were used as a food there. One or possibly two beeweed seeds appeared in hearths, but the majority were associated with other plant foods in trash middens.

Although its seeds offer a potential food source, *Cleome* is more highly regarded for its greens, used by the Rio Grande Pueblos in recent times (Robbins, Harrington, and Freire-Marreco 1916:58; Krenetsky 1964:45). The young leaves could be eaten either fresh or cooked (Vestal 1952:29), or dried for winter storage (Curtin 1965:95).

One would not expect to find archaeological traces of *Cleome* greens. The young, tender stems would be poor candidates for charring if they happened to find their way into a fire, nor would the plants leave any seeds behind, since they were gathered before fruiting. One soil sample from a plaza did contain *Cleome* pollen grains (Bohrer, this volume), which may indicate that the people of Arroyo Hondo gathered the greens for cooking. However, *Cleome* plants serve a variety of nonnutritive functions (Robbins, Harrington, and Freire-Marreco 1916:59; Vestal 1952:20; Ford 1968a:281) and may have been collected at the pueblo for these purposes as well.

Sunflower (Helianthus sp.). Bright yellow sunflowers waving in the wind are a common sight along roads and in fields throughout New Mexico. Like its domestic counterpart, the wild sunflower *(Helianthus annuus, H. anomalous,* and *H. petiolaris)* produces a delicious seed, rich in oil. Curiously, the modern Pueblos of the Rio Grande take little interest in the sunflower seed despite the fact that they value the plant for its stalk, from which the people of San Juan fashion bird snares, arrows, firebrands, and flutes (Ford 1968a:264). Sunflower seeds have been appreciated, however, by the Navajos (Steggerda and Eckardt 1941:223), Zunis (Cushing 1920:152), and Hopis (Whiting 1939:97).

Prehistoric Southwesterners also recognized the value of sunflower seeds, but probably did not count them among their main foods. Small numbers of achenes have turned up at a variety of sites, including Bat Cave (Dick 1965:89) and a Cochiti Dam salvage site (Ford 1968b:259). Evidence from coprolites also seems to indicate that sunflower seeds were a minor food: traces of the achenes appeared in only seven of 176 coprolites that Stiger (1977:42) tabulated from various Anasazi sites.

Helianthus achenes were scarce in the Arroyo Hondo remains, and none were found in definitively food-related contexts. The few that were discovered might be explained away as mere incidentals: a person making snares or firebrands from a sunflower stalk scattered a few seeds. This seems unlikely, though, because the flower's head would not be needed in any functions that required the stalk; indeed, a dry, mature plant that had already flowered and fruited would probably be most suitable for flutes and firebrands. It seems more plausible that these specimens had been intentionally harvested as food; all of them were associated with other edible plants.

The pollen record provides additional evidence, with *Helianthus* pollen appearing in eight of the 39 prehistoric soil samples (Bohrer, this volume). During threshing and winnowing, pollen could readily have been scattered in the pueblo, since the achenes are often coated with it (Bohrer, this volume). In fact, as mentioned earlier, Bohrer suggests that a shallow basin in Plaza A was a threshing ground and that the pollen found just outside the depression and in a midden nearby were scattered during winnowing.

Although sunflower achenes are a likely source of the pollen, some of it may have come from young flowers as well. Bohrer (this volume) points out that the blossoms are used in myriad ways: in rituals (Zuni: Stevenson 1915:93), in decoration and in making plaster (Jemez: Cook 1930:23), and as a face powder for ritual use (Hopi: Whiting 1939:97).

Ground Cherry (Physalis sp.). The ground cherry is a stout, bushy weed that appears along roadsides, in ditches, and in cultivated fields. Its "cherry," enveloped in a papery pod, vaguely resembles a green tomato and is a prized delicacy in the Rio Grande area. It may be boiled or eaten fresh. The Zunis made a relish from cooked ground cherries (Stevenson 1915:70), and from the dried fruits they made a flour that they used in bread (Hough 1898:143). The Navajos prepared a "Life Medicine" from the dried leaves and roots of the ground cherry and used it in Lifeway ceremonials to treat injuries (Vestal 1952:43).

The prehistoric peoples of the Southwest apparently used ground cherry fruits, too. Specimens have been found at various archaeological sites, such as Jemez Cave (Jones 1935). It seems reasonable to surmise that the people of Arroyo Hondo Pueblo gathered and ate ground cherries as well. It would be difficult to account for the specimens occurring there in any other way, since I have found no other functions for the plant reported in the ethnographic literature. As a weed, *Physalis* may have cropped up around the pueblo, but it seems unlikely that this could have been responsible for all the archaeological specimens. One flotation sample from a trash midden yielded 43 *Physalis* seeds, while more than a third of the remaining specimens came from hearths, where foods would be expected to turn up. The Arroyo Hondoans probably cooked or dried the fruits, which would give them the greatest chances of being preserved, since a careless cook might scatter some of the seeds and meal while grinding them. Dried seeds or fruits that made their way into a fire would have a greater chance of being carbonized than fresh or cooked ones, which have a high moisture content.

The people of Arroyo Hondo may have valued the ground cherry as a seasoning for stews. The modern Pueblo favorite, the chili pepper, did not enter Indian cuisine until after the Spanish Conquest (Robbins, Harrington, and Freire-Marreco 1916:111).

Wild Grasses

Indian Rice Grass (Oryzopsis hymenoides Roem. S. Schult.). Indian rice grass thrives on sandy soils in the spring, and by late June or early July it produces a large, starchy grain. Frail bunches of the grass are scattered through the Southwest now, but before cattle and sheep damaged the grazing lands, it probably grew in abundance. These grass stands may have been dense enough, in fact, to provide the peoples of the Southwest with an important source of food (Bohrer 1975a:206). Bohrer (1975a) suggests that Indian rice grass and other early-maturing species, the so-called "cool-season grasses," helped see people through the spring, when food supplies were low and crops just barely in the ground. Specimens of Indian rice grass caryopses, panicles, and stems have turned up at prehistoric sites throughout the Southwest (Bohrer 1975a:202), including Chetro Ketl in Chaco Canyon (Jones 1938:45), Paiute Cave in Nevada (Jones 1938:45), and the Salmon Ruin (Adams 1980:42).

In more recent times, the Paiutes harvested large crops of Indian rice grass each year (Steward 1933:244); the Hopis turned to the plant during famines (Whiting 1939:65). The Navajos parched and ground the seeds and used the flour in mushes or breads (Vestal 1952:17), while the Zunis mixed Indian rice grass flour with meal and water and shaped the mixture into pats, which they steamed (Stevenson 1915:67).

At Arroyo Hondo Pueblo, *Oryzopsis* caryopses were abundant in a few locations. One household, for example, yielded a total of 502 charred grains from its two hearths. The remaining specimens were found scattered across the site, mainly in midden contexts. The people of Arroyo Hondo undoubtedly collected the grains for their food value, and they may have used the stems as well for kindling or insulation.

Wild Fruits

Hedgehog cactus (Echinocereus triglochidiatus Engelm.). These low, barrel-shaped cacti with formidable spines are scattered in clumps on rocky hillsides and in grassy areas among pinyons and junipers. In midsummer, they are covered with a profusion of bright red, cup-shaped flowers which mature into a fruit that some people consider the best cactus fruit in the Southwest. The fruits are delicious fresh, and they may also be baked or cooked as a conserve (Isleta: Jones 1931:27–28). The Hopis (Whiting 1939:85) dried the fruits of another species, *E. fendleri*, and stored them for the winter to be used as a sweetener for other foods.

No doubt the people of Arroyo Hondo also relished these cactus fruits. Some of the archaeological seed specimens were found in contexts that would suggest use as food: a few came from hearths, and one was found in a burned storeroom. Other possible evidence of hedgehog cactus at the pueblo comes from two pollen samples (Bohrer, this volume) of the *Mammilaria* type, which includes hedgehog and several other genera of cactus. Hedgehog cactus buds and stems, which are also edible, have been recovered from Jemez (Jones 1935:64) and Tularosa (Cutler 1952:479) caves, and Stubbs and Stallings (1953:141) found a charred portion of the cactus's tough outer rind (Jones 1936) at Pindi Pueblo near Santa Fe.

Pincushion cactus (Mammilaria sp.). These small, globular "pincushions" are sparsely scattered throughout the Southwest. Their tiny fruits are edible, but they could never have been an important food because of their low numbers, though the Navajos (Vestal 1952:37) and Apaches (Castetter and Opler 1936:41) occasionally gathered the fruits and stems. The two seeds found at Arroyo Hondo Pueblo may have come from fruits that were a rare treat.

Prickly-pear cactus (Opuntia sp.). The prickly-pear cactus with its flat, jointed stems or pads is common throughout the Southwest and is much appreciated as a food source. The pear-shaped fruit, the "tuna," is spiny but sweet and juicy. Many of the peoples of the Southwest, including the inhabitants of Acoma and Laguna (Swank 1932:56–57), Isleta (Jones 1931:35), and Tewa pueblos (Robbins, Harrington, and Freire-Marreco 1916:62), gathered and stored them.

Prickly-pear pads were apparently regarded as a food in prehistoric times as well: desiccated specimens were found at Cordova Cave, New Mexico (Kaplan 1963:354), and at Tonto National Monument, Arizona (Bohrer 1962:97), and carbonized prickly-pear pads turned up in a jar recovered from a burned room at Point of Pine Ruins (Bohrer 1973:431).

It is reasonable to suppose that the people of Arroyo Hondo also harvested prickly-pear fruits and possibly the pads, but the archaeological record of these is thin, consisting of only three seeds. However, the seeds would not have been preserved if the fruits were seeded in the field in preparation for storage or if they were cooked. The pollen record is richer, with small numbers of the grains occurring in five samples (Bohrer, this volume). Some of this pollen may have been carried in with flowers that were eaten in salads, but Bohrer (this volume) feels that it probably came from pads or joints since the counts were so much lower than that which flowers would leave.

Cholla cactus (Cylindropuntia sp.). The fact that fleshy vegetative structures do not lend themselves to being preserved in the archaeological record may be the reason why the macroflora from Arroyo Hondo shows no traces of the cholla cactus, a familiar part of the Southwestern landscape whose young buds and joints make quite a decent dish. The historic Hopis (Nequatewa 1943:19), Pimas, and Papagos (Castetter and Underhill 1935:15) all ate cholla buds, and the prehistoric peoples of the Southwest apparently fancied them too. Desiccated specimens were found at Tonto National Monument (Bohrer 1962:97), and carbonized buds and stems were recovered from three burned rooms at Point of Pines Ruin (Bohrer 1973:431–32). Although there are no comparable cholla remains at Arroyo Hondo Pueblo, Bohrer (this volume) found traces of cholla pollen in 16 soil samples there, which suggested to her that the pollen was scattered in the village when it came in with buds and joints.

Banana yucca (Yucca baccata Torr.). In the late spring, enormous white blossoms sprout from spikes of the banana yuccas dotting the rocky hillsides of the Arroyo Hondo area, and by fall the spikes are heavy with large, sweet, banana-like fruits that were much esteemed by peoples of the Southwest. The Tewa Pueblos (Robbins, Harrington, and Freire-Marreco 1916:50), the Hopis (Whiting 1939:71), and the Navajos (Franciscan Fathers 1910:194, 210) all harvested the fruits. These are tasty when fresh, but they were usually air-dried for winter storage in the form of strips (Hopi: Nequatewa 1943:18), or they were preserved as a cooked jelly, paste, syrup, or cake. Yucca syrup must have been highly prized as a sweetening agent since there were so few sweets in the Pueblo diet until refined sugar came to the trading posts in historic times.

Few yucca seeds were found at Arroyo Hondo Pueblo, but the inhabitants could hardly have ignored such a potentially rich and tasty food. Since the large, fleshy fruits could not have made their way into the pueblo by chance, the five seeds collected are a good indication that the fruits were harvested. They may well have been seeded and dried in the hills where they were gathered, so that seeds did not normally reach the pueblo at all; or some of the seeds might have been ground to a meal, as the Papagos prepared yucca (Castetter and Underhill 1935:23), or eaten with the fruit, as at Zuni (Stevenson 1915:72; Bohrer 1980:248).

Arroyo Hondo's inhabitants may have valued the yucca plant for its flowers, leaves, and "heads" (the base of the leaves) in addition to the fruits. The leaves are not particularly palatable because of their fibers, but they could have been eaten as a famine food.

Tree Fruits and Nuts

Pinyon pine (Pinus edulis Engelm.). The scrubby little pines that dominate the pinyon-juniper forests of the Santa Fe area bear a delicious, much-prized nut. Even today, people hope for a good crop wherever the pinyon grows. The nuts are usually roasted before being eaten or stored away (Hopi: Nequatewa 1943:18; Cochiti: Lange 1959:145). Today pinyons are primarily a snack, but in the past the Hopis and other peoples put pine nuts or pine nut meal into soups, stews, and breads, and they sometimes pounded them into a pinyon nut butter to spread on corn cakes (Vestal 1952:13).

Archaeological specimens of pinyon nuts have turned up at a wide variety of prehistoric sites, such as Pecos (Bohrer 1962:97) and the Cochiti Dam salvage sites (Ford 1968b:289) in the Rio Grande area. At Arroyo Hondo, charred nuts, shell fragments, and bracts were found, evidence that the villagers harvested and enjoyed pinyon nuts.

One-seeded juniper (Juniperus monosperma Engelm.). The one-seeded juniper, one of the most common trees in the Arroyo Hondo area, has a pungent blue berry that is now sold as an exotic seasoning. The Pueblo Indians valued the berry as a spice and also enjoyed it as fruit. According to Cushing (1920:243), juniper berries were an "ancient" food that the Zunis once harvested in large quantities. At one time the people of Acoma and Laguna also gathered the ripe berries, particularly when food was scarce (Swank 1932:50), and ate them raw or boiled.

Archaeological specimens of juniper seeds have come from Tonto (Bohrer 1962:98) and Jemez caves (Jones 1935). Only a single berry was found at Arroyo Hondo Pueblo, but the juniper was probably more important than this evidence would seem to suggest. The archaeological traces of these berries may be scanty because they were prepared in a way that afforded them very little chance of being preserved. It is hard to imagine that the pueblo's inhabitants would have ignored such an abundant resource, particularly since all the historic peoples of the Rio Grande, including the villagers of Cochiti (Lange 1959:146), Jemez (Cook 1930:24), and Isleta (Jones 1931:33), valued juniper berries.

Chokecherry (Prunus virginiana L. var. melanocarpa [A. Nels.]). The chokecherry is a rare but welcome tree in the northern Rio Grande area. Its fruit, a treat when fresh but also good after cooking, was used by the Cochitis (Lange 1959:150) and Navajos (Vestal 1952:31). The people of Arroyo Hondo probably prized chokecherries, and a few dried cherry stone fragments, which most likely came from someone's snack, were encountered in the excavations. Since the trees are not very abundant, the fruit could never have been an important food.

Acorns (Quercus sp.). Scrub oaks are scattered on the hillsides of the Santa Fe region. Their acorns are now harvested only by animals, but in the past they were probably collected by the Pueblo people of the area too. The villagers of Acoma and Laguna (Swank 1932:64) used ground acorn nutmeats in mushes or in cornmeal breads, and the Zunis also added acorn meal to cornbread as a "seasoning or shortening" (Cushing 1920:252).

Archaeological examples of acorns are rare, and nearly all that I know of come from dry cave sites such as Tonto National Monument (Bohrer 1962:96). Considering that acorn shells are very thin and delicate, it is not surprising that they fail to appear at open archaeological sites. This may be the reason that no traces of acorns were found at Arroyo Hondo, since it is quite plausible that the Pueblo's inhabitants harvested them in small quantities.

Other Potential Plant Foods

Several other possible plant foods not documented in the archaeological record deserve mention here. The squaw bush *(Rhus Trilobata)*, a common shrub in Arroyo Hondo today, bears a small, tart berry that the ancient pueblo inhabitants may have nibbled. They may have also snacked on the bland little currants *(Ribes* sp.) that grow in the arroyo and on wolf berries *(Lycium pallidum)*, found on shrubs around the pueblo mound. All of these berries were eaten by historic Pueblos such as the people of San Juan (Ford 1968a:271, 276, 284).

In the spring, the Arroyo Hondoans may have gathered cottonwood buds *(Populus* sp.) and such roots and tubers as chimaha *(Cymopterus purpureus)*, as some of the Pueblo people do today (Ford 1968a:286, 266). The women almost surely gathered the wild onion *(Allium cernum)* as a seasoning for their stews. The bulbs are not particularly abundant in the area, but their flavor is rich.

In addition, the Arroyo Hondo region offered other edible plants that the pueblo's inhabitants may occasionally have gathered, such as the seeds of the tansy mustard *(Descurania pinnata)*, the stickleaf *(Mentzelia albicaulis)*, and the roots and shoots of the cattail *(Typha latifolia)*. None of the above-mentioned plants is particularly abundant (see Kelley 1980:81–94), and it is unlikely that any of them could have been major foods, if they were used at all.

ANIMAL FOODS

Direct information about Arroyo Hondo's animal resources comes from the faunal remains found at the site. Like plant materials, they offer a wealth of information but must be interpreted with caution because of biases in the archaeological record. Both differential preservation and bone disposal practices favor certain types of animals, such as large mammals, while selecting against small, fragile-boned animals like birds and against those processed in the field such as the antelope (Wing and Brown 1979:6, 121). Both of these biases must be considered in evaluating the types and quantities of animals recovered.

Faunal remains were systematically collected at Arroyo Hondo Pueblo between 1970 and 1974. Bone was hand-picked during excavation and also retrieved by sieving the fill through 1/4-inch mesh window screen. A total of 24,589 animal bones was collected, representing a minimum of 4,448 individuals of at least 91 species (Lang and Harris 1984:5). A chronologically well-documented sample of about 92 percent of the collection was selected for study by Lang and Harris (1984), whose list of identifications is presented in their table 15. Arroyo Hondo Pueblo's animal foods and hunting patterns for the entire occupation are described briefly below in general terms. However, the relative importance of various meat sources and hunting strategies apparently varied as the climate changed during the pueblo's life, issues that will be considered in chapter 4.

Mammals

Mammals provided most of the meat in the Arroyo Hondo diet, and the greatest share of it came from the mule deer *(Odocoileus hemionus)*, a large animal that spends part of the year in the pinyon-juniper zone. Bones of the hoofed mammals (artiodactyls), primarily mule deer, represented 9 percent of the faunal collection, but because of their size, this class contributed 83 percent of the usable meat represented by the remains. Individuals that could be specifically identified as mule deer accounted for 28 percent of the meat (Lang and Harris 1984:47), but their contribution was significantly more than this, since many of the unidentifiable artiodactyl bones were almost certainly those of deer. In addition, it is very likely that deer were underrepresented at the site since the hunters most likely butchered their kill in the field and cut the meat into strips to carry it home, just as historic Pueblo hunters did (Goldfrank 1954:418). As a result, little of the deer bone would have ended up at the village, and the few items that were brought in may not have been very diagnostic.

The pronghorn antelope *(Antilocapra americana)* was a distant second in the artiodactyl group. A quick, wary animal that ranges widely across the grasslands of New Mexico in herds (Russell 1964:8, 9), the antelope could have been hunted on the short-grass plain west of the pueblo.

The most abundant animals in the Arroyo Hondo faunal collection were hares and rabbits (lagomorphs), which represented 28 percent of the economic fauna (Lang and Harris 1984:46). Both the jackrabbit *(Lepus* sp.) and cottontail *(Sylvilagus* sp.) are common in the area and could easily have been taken in drives or possibly with snares or traps. They were important in the Arroyo Hondo economy for two reasons: they were readily available and easy to kill. However, their caloric contribution was small compared to that of the large mammals because each individual offers so little food. They represent 5.7 percent of the meat in the faunal collection (Lang and Harris 1984:47), but this figure may be inflated since the lagomorphs are probably overrepresented compared with the other mammals. Unlike the deer and antelope, rabbits were probably butchered not in the field but in the village, ensuring that some traces of the animals were preserved in the archaeological record. The faunal remains suggest that this was indeed the case, since far more bone items per individual were recovered for hares and rabbits than for most other mammals.

Squirrels and prairie dogs were nearly as numerous as rabbits in the faunal collection and contributed 1.7 percent of the meat represented (Lang and Harris 1984:47), but they were probably not a very important food source. Like the rabbits and hares, they are undoubtedly overrepresented at the site since the whole carcass would have been carried home. In addition, many of the specimens found at Arroyo Hondo may have come from prairie dogs that occupied the pueblo after it was abandoned.

Rats and mice, also abundant in the faunal collection, were almost certainly residents of the pueblo and probably died natural deaths there. However, the people of Arroyo Hondo may have eaten them occasionally, particularly during lean periods.

A variety of other mammals, such as the gopher and bear, were found at Arroyo Hondo, but it appears that none was hunted systematically or contributed much to the diet. Small quantities of bone representing only one or a few individuals of these species were recovered. Some of these animals, moreover, may never have been used for food, serving other functions instead: for example, foxes and coyotes were trapped by the Hopis for their pelts (Beaglehole 1936:18).

Birds

Bird remains were abundant at the Arroyo Hondo site, and more than 20 species have been identified (Lang and Harris 1984:table 15). Some of these may have died natural deaths at the pueblo, but most were probably snared or trapped. Arroyo Hondo hunters would have sought them for their feathers, used for ceremonial or utilitarian functions. Cuts on some of the bones indicate that the carcasses were skinned and robbed of their quills (Lang and Harris 1984:72–74). Some of these specimens may have wound up in stew pots, but they would have offered very little meat.

The one exception to these generalizations is the turkey, which probably was a main food item at Arroyo Hondo. This large bird left abundant bone remains, representing at least 384 individuals, and some of the bones bear marks of butchering. Most of the turkey bones probably come from wild birds, which would have been easy to kill and were most likely abundant and close at hand, as discussed in the next chapter. But the people of Arroyo Hondo tended turkeys too; traces of pens, turkey dung, and eggshells were found throughout the excavations (Lang and Harris 1984:101–5). These penned birds probably supplied far more feathers than meat, an issue that will be considered later.

2

Making a Living in a Marginal Environment

The inhabitants of Arroyo Hondo Pueblo must have faced a serious challenge in trying to make a living. This chapter examines their possible food resources, both cultivated and wild, and attempts to estimate how much food the pueblo was able to produce and collect. Since the archaeological evidence is scanty at best, such estimates are of necessity based on analogy and conjecture. However, we do possess sufficient knowledge about the ecology of the region and the agricultural, gathering, and hunting practices of its modern-day Pueblo inhabitants to enable us to establish well-informed hypotheses.

A brief sketch of the pueblo's setting, based on Kelley's (1980) detailed study of the contemporary ecology of the Arroyo Hondo region, will help clarify the limitations its early inhabitants faced. The pueblo ruins sprawl over a level plain overlooking the deep Arroyo Hondo canyon. The foothills of the Sangre de Cristo Mountains rise abruptly just east of the site, and 14.5 kilometers (9 miles) to the northeast the mountain peaks reach over 3,048 meters (10,000 feet). South and west of the ruins, the alluvial plain tilts gently westward.

Along the north side of the pueblo, the Arroyo Hondo stream cuts a deep canyon that runs in a southwesterly direction, eventually feeding into the Santa Fe River about 32 kilometers (20 miles) from the site. Charged by the runoff from its headwaters about 13 kilometers (8 miles) northeast of the pueblo and by two springs, the stream flows only intermittently. These springs, the single permanent source of water in the area, must have been one of the major attractions that prompted Anasazi people to settle here. The Arroyo Hondo pueblo overlooks one spring, while a second, smaller site, Upper Arroyo Hondo, is located adjacent to the other, less than 2 kilometers upstream.

About 0.8 kilometer west of the pueblo, the canyon soil is relatively fertile, and it can be cultivated during wet years; during the moist period of the 1890s through the 1940s, corn and beans were successfully raised there (Kelley 1980:9).

The site is situated in a woodland area dominated by pinyon pines and one-seeded junipers, among which are scattered cholla cactus, muhly grass, and soapweed yuccas. Before livestock began grazing here, the trees were sparser and grasses, especially cool-season grasses, and perennial shrubs were more common (Bohrer, this volume). The steep slopes of the Arroyo Hondo canyon are sprinkled with pinyons, junipers, and grasses, and it is likely that in prehistoric times its north-facing slopes were dotted with ponderosa pines as well (Kelley 1980:11). Rabbit brush and grama grass dominate the terraces at the bottom of the canyon where the pueblo's fields were probably located, and a riparian community of willows, cottonwoods, grasses, sedges, and bulrushes thrives in waterlogged areas of the canyon.

The Arroyo Hondo region is one of the narrowest segments of the pinyon-juniper zone; to both the east and west of the pueblo, the vegetation quickly changes. Less than 2 kilometers to the east, scattered patches of ponderosa pine signal the beginning of a ponderosa forest, while to the west, about 4.8 kilometers (3 miles) from the pueblo, the pinyons and junipers give way to a short-grass plain. Such proximity to other vegetation zones must have been useful to the pueblo's inhabitants, and may have been a factor in their decision to settle here.

The ponderosa pine forest, a major source of timber and a summer range for mule deer, emerges fully about 4 kilometers (2.5 miles) east of the pueblo at an elevation of 2,300 meters (7,500 feet). The people of Arroyo Hondo could easily have reached these forests by traveling up their canyon, which cuts across the north-northwest–trending ridges of the foothills (Kelley 1980:13).

The elevation continues to increase to the east, with concomitant changes in vegetation. By about 2,400 meters (8,000 feet), the forest is transformed into a mixed conifer association, with white fir, Douglas fir, Englemann spruce, and aspen dominating. Spruce-fir forests emerge approximately 150 meters (500 feet) further up, giving way at 3,700 meters (12,000 feet) to alpine tundra and meadows.

A plain inclines gently away from the pueblo in a westerly direction. At about 2,000 meters (6,500 feet) elevation, the pinyon pines disappear and the junipers become sparse, marking the edge of the short-grass plain dominated by rabbit brush, grasses, and cacti. Pronghorn antelope were common here until the nineteenth century.

With a few changes, this sketch of the contemporary Arroyo Hondo landscape would be a relatively accurate description of conditions during the fourteenth and fifteenth centuries A.D. The area's climate, which will be discussed more fully later, probably has not changed significantly in the last six hundred years; in fact, there is good evidence that the climate of the Southwest has remained stable for twenty-two hundred years (Schoenwetter 1962:191–94). There may have been some erosion along hillsides and canyon walls, but otherwise the topography of the region is most likely very much as it was in the fourteenth century, despite the fact that the canyon floor may have been rising slowly over the last hundred years because of alluvial build-up (Kelley 1980:23–24).

The greatest differences between the modern and the prehistoric landscapes are probably in vegetation. Livestock has so seriously disturbed the ground cover at Arroyo Hondo that the present plant growth can be used only cautiously to draw inferences about prehistoric resources. In addition, the village must have had a significant impact on the landscape during the century and a quarter of its occupation, when several hundred people were clearing and cultivating land, collecting plants and firewood, and hunting.

ARROYO HONDO PUEBLO'S TERRITORY

Vita-Finzi and Higgs's (1970; Higgs 1975; Higgs and Vita-Finzi 1972) technique for "site catchment analysis" offers a useful method for examining Arroyo Hondo Pueblo's territory. Following their procedure, the site was plotted on a topographic map, and around it was drawn a circle with a radius of 5 kilometers (3 miles)—the distance they propose (Higgs and Vita-Finzi 1972:31, 33) as the upper limit of a farmer's range, about a one-hour walk from the village. Higgs and Vita-Finzi concluded on the basis of ethnographic data that farmers would be very unlikely to carry on any subsistence activities beyond this distance since it would be unusual for them to walk any farther than 3 or 4 kilometers to their fields. They also noted that outlying fields would not be used as intensively as those close to the village, with only land within a kilometer used to its full potential. Accordingly, they weighted the land within 1 kilometer for 100 percent use, that within 2 kilometers for 50 percent use, and so forth.

Figure 2 shows the topographic features of the Arroyo Hondo re-

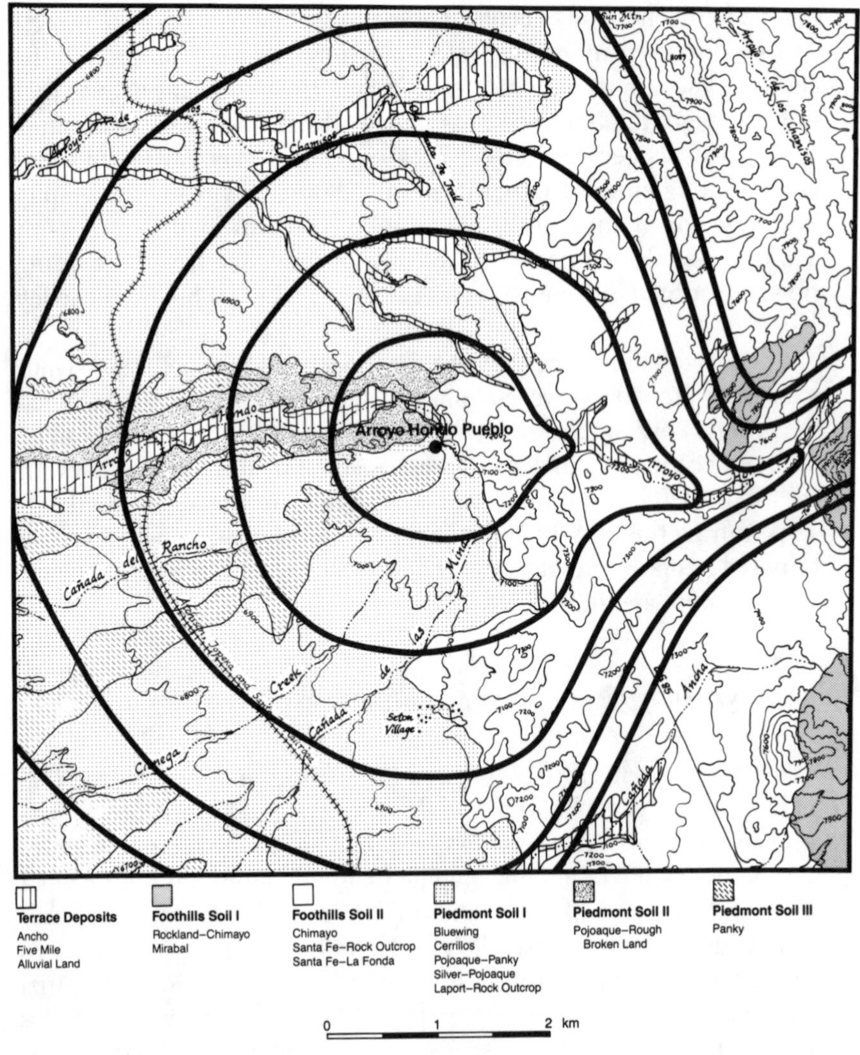

Fig. 2. Site catchment territory for Arroyo Hondo Pueblo.

gion, with the site catchment territory indicated by concentric, irregular "circles" that reflect the way in which the terrain would have influenced travel times. Except through the canyon, walking is slow east of the site because of the north-south–trending ridges. North and northwest of the site the terrain is relatively level, but a hiker departing from the pueblo must first descend the steep canyon walls and then scale them again on the other side. One would cover ground more quickly walking south or southwest, where the alluvial plain inclines gently, and could probably travel faster still by going west through the Arroyo Hondo canyon.

Neighboring villages undoubtedly put another set of constraints on the pueblo's territory. On the basis of site distribution, Dickson (1980:81–85) has proposed a set of "political" boundaries for Arroyo Hondo. He placed the southern boundary roughly 5 kilometers (3 miles) south of the site, about halfway between it and a pair of contemporaneous communities on the dry washes, Canon Ancha and Canada de los Alamos. He could not draw a boundary on the north because most of the archaeological record here lies buried underneath, or has been obliterated by, the modern city of Santa Fe, so that the age and extent of prehistoric settlements are unknown. Nonetheless, it seems a good guess that such a choice location as the Santa Fe River valley saw occupation at the same time as the less desirable Arroyo Hondo, Canon Ancha, and Canada de los Alamos sites. Another political boundary, then, might be envisioned somewhere between Santa Fe and Arroyo Hondo Pueblo, possibly 4 kilometers north of the pueblo.

About 1 kilometer east of the main village, the smaller community of Upper Arroyo Hondo is perched in the canyon overlooking the springs and a tract of arable land. Dickson (1980:83–84) has suggested that the two sites were "complementary parts of a single system" and that the eastern boundary of Arroyo Hondo's "sustaining area" lay "somewhere *beyond* LA76 [Upper Arroyo Hondo] in the ponderosa–pinyon-juniper ecotone or in the ponderosa pine zone itself."

West of Arroyo Hondo Pueblo, Dickson (1980:85) discovered traces of settlement in the canyon, but none of these was helpful in establishing possible political boundaries. One very small site about 0.8 kilometer west of the pueblo could not be dated, but it is possible that it served as a field house for the Arroyo Hondo people. Dickson found evidence of three small sites in the canyon about 8 kilometers (5 miles) west of the main pueblo; two had preceded it, and the third could not be dated. On the basis of this scanty evidence, it appears that the pueblo's inhabitants shared the Arroyo Hondo canyon with few or no neighbors.

Farm Lands

On the basis of soil characteristics and locations, shown in figure 2, Kelley (1980:49–55) identified six major soil formations in the Arroyo Hondo area. Foothills soils I and II, which cover the rolling hills east of the pueblo, are shallow and gravelly. Situated on steep slopes with much exposed bedrock, they offer virtually no potential for agriculture.

Terrace Deposits, well-drained, moderately permeable, mixed alluvial soils, are found in the Arroyo Hondo canyon and in the Arroyo de los Chamisos and other, smaller washes north of the site. The Terrace Deposits outside the canyon were probably ignored since they were for the most part meager and had no dependable water supply. Although arable land in the Arroyo de los Chamisos is fairly extensive, it is more than 3 kilometers (1.9 miles) from the pueblo and also lacks a constant water supply. It is hard to imagine that Arroyo Hondo farmers would have been tempted to hike that far to a wash that was dry much of the time. The Terrace Deposits upstream in the Arroyo Hondo canyon were probably off limits too, but for a different reason: they were undoubtedly farmed by the inhabitants of Upper Arroyo Hondo, who lived adjacent to them. But if this site was in fact part of the Arroyo Hondo community, as Dickson has suggested (1980:83), then some of the food produced on these soils was probably consumed at the main pueblo.

Piedmont Soils I, II, and III blanket most of the remaining area. They range from poor, thin soils along the canyon walls (II) to the moderately fertile, well-drained alluvium (I and III) found on the plain or piedmont above the canyon. The best soil on the piedmont is the Panky Fine Sandy Loam (Kelley's Piedmont Soil III) that covers a swath running west-southwest of the pueblo. As noted earlier, these soils were dry-farmed until the early 1950s.

Table 2 indicates the amount of each type of arable land within 1, 2, 3, and 4 kilometers of the site. According to Higgs and Vita-Finzi (1972:31–32), the soils within 1 kilometer would have been farmed most heavily, with use diminishing beyond this point. But because the canyon was so much better irrigated than the plain, the Terrace Deposits

TABLE 2.
Arable land in hectares within 1, 2, 3, and 4 kilometers of Arroyo Hondo Pueblo.

Km from Pueblo	*Canyon Land*	*Piedmont Land*	*All Arable Land*	*Cumulative Totals*
0–1	20	29	49	49
1–2	33	47	80	129
2–3	24	51	75	204
3–4	34	52	86	290
TOTAL	111	179	290	

were almost certainly farmed more intensively than the Piedmont Soils. During dry periods, the people of Arroyo Hondo probably had to do all their farming in the canyon, and some of the fields may have been several kilometers from the pueblo. However, long excursions to the fields are not unusual in the Southwest. The Hopis, who live in a very arid environment, scatter their gardens in dry washes that may be 10 to 15 kilometers (6.2 to 9.3 miles) from the village (Hack 1942:27), but the daily commuting distance that they tolerate still seems consistent with Higgs and Vita-Finzi's (1972:31) observations, since they move to field houses to be close to their plots. For example, Hack (1942:28) found a Hopi farmer staying in a field house in order to tend gardens about 13 kilometers (8 miles) from his village.

Although the canyon was obviously the Arroyo Hondoans' first choice for cornfields, the piedmont offered several advantages during wet years. It is less vulnerable to the cool air masses that sometimes funnel down the canyon from the mountains and settle on the canyon floor, killing young plants and retarding the growth of older ones, and it is also safer during flash floods. In the canyon, flood waters sometimes scour out fields, carrying away topsoil, crops and all. (The willows and cottonwoods there today may never be more than shrubs because periodic floods sweep away the young trees [Kelley 1980:67].) Flash floods can also dump sands and alluvium, burying crops and fields. In sum, it would have been a good hedge for a Pueblo farmer to plant some crops on the plain in case those in the canyon were destroyed.

Plant Collecting

The most intense plant collecting at the pueblo would have occurred close to home since the largest crops of weedy annuals must have been found in cornfields and along their margins, and possibly on trash middens. Gatherers in search of other types of wild plants would have been forced to go out beyond the cultivated fields. Cactus buds and fruit, yucca fruit, and pinyon nuts were most abundant in the pinyon-juniper woodlands. It is likely that Indian rice grass, which thrives on disturbed sandy soils (Adams 1980:42), was found along the steep sides of the Arroyo Hondo canyon and neighboring washes. The woodlands and foothills closest to the pueblo must have seen the most intense collecting, with the thoroughness of harvesting diminishing as the distance from the village increased. But where did the harvesters stop?

Vita-Finzi and Higgs (1970:7) turned to Richard Lee's (1969) work on the !Kung San for insights into how far gatherers will forage. Lee found that 10 kilometers (6.2 miles) was the limit for !Kung San women because longer trips could not be made within one day. The sedentary villagers of Arroyo Hondo, however, probably covered far less ground than do hunter-gatherers, since for them gathered plants were primarily supplements to crops, not the sole source of food. The demands of agricultural life also limit mobility; and custom may have discouraged women from wandering far. Richard Ford (1968a:141) found that the women of San Juan Pueblo rarely ventured far from home and only went with men or other women into the hills beyond their cultivated fields, a distance of a few kilometers.

Higgs and Vita-Finzi's (1972:33) observation that agricultural people rarely go 5 kilometers beyond home for farming and gathering may be essentially correct for the Arroyo Hondo people. Nevertheless, certain circumstances, specifically family harvesting expeditions, could have carried them beyond the 5-kilometer mark. Until recently, whole families at San Juan Pueblo would pack up, travel into the hills, and camp for about a week to harvest pinyon nuts (Ford 1968a:35). The families of Arroyo Hondo Pueblo may also have set up temporary camps out in the pinyon-juniper woodlands to harvest and process pinyon nuts, Indian rice grass, and prickly pear and yucca fruit. Such jaunts would have fitted into their agricultural schedule since Indian rice grass is ready in late June or early July, about a month after planting and a couple of months before any crops can be harvested, and other wild plant foods ripen some time after the crop is in.

These collecting expeditions, if they were carried on by the pueblo's inhabitants, did not involve great distances. In deciding how far to travel, the people probably weighed a number of factors: the potential size of the wild harvest, the pueblo's needs, the conditions of the field crops. In drought years they must have ranged some distance for wild foods that could make up the deficits left by a poor corn crop, but a family carrying a harvest of nuts, seeds, or fruits on its back surely did not travel very far. In addition, the borders of the pinyon-juniper ecotone, which are close to the site, bounded their search for pinyon nuts and yuccas to both the east and west and for Indian rice grass and cactus fruit to the east.

Traveling north and south, the Arroyo Hondo people would have been restricted by the presence of other communities, as noted earlier. But what did such restrictions entail? Richard Ford's (1968a:43) work at San Juan Pueblo offers some insights into how prehistoric Pueblos may have defined and used their territories. The people of San Juan considered their cultivated fields and the lands immediately adjacent to the pueblo as their own, for their exclusive use, but they shared the resources of the hills beyond with neighboring communities. A similar situation probably prevailed in the Arroyo Hondo region: some of the area lying between a pueblo and its neighbors may have been used jointly, while the territory immediately surrounding each village was its exclusive domain. Thus, some of the land north and south of Arroyo Hondo would have been off limits to the people of that pueblo, but they may have ranged freely to the west and southwest since there appears to have been no one living there.

Upper Arroyo Hondo probably had exclusive rights to the arable land adjacent to it in the canyon but shared the ponderosa forests with the inhabitants of the main Arroyo Hondo pueblo. These latter may not have gathered many plant foods in the forest, but they certainly prized the area for its construction timber and firewood.

Hunting Territories

Arroyo Hondo hunters probably appreciated the proximity of the adjacent ecotones. Within an hour or two of home, they had access to the pronghorn antelope of the grasslands or the deer and other game of the mountains. How far they ranged must have depended on the movements of game, the pueblo's needs, and the abilities and energy of the hunting party. For the historic Pueblos, rabbit drives were sometimes a community outing involving women and children as well as men (for example, Cochiti: Lange 1959:125–26; Acoma: White 1932:102). These were held near home, but when men set off alone to hunt, they might travel for several days in pursuit of the wide-ranging pronghorn. Attempting to specify borders for Arroyo Hondo's hunting territory is thus a futile task. The antelope remains found at the village indicate that some hunters ventured at least as far as the short-grass plains, and they probably hunted in the mountains as well. There are no traces of hunting camps east of the Arroyo Hondo site, but such camps dating to the Pueblo period have been found elsewhere in the Sangre de Cristo Mountains (Dickson 1980:84). In addition, it seems likely that Arroyo Hondo's hunting territories overlapped with those of other communities and that game was equally available to all hunters.

ARROYO HONDO'S POPULATION: HOW MANY MOUTHS DID THE TERRITORY FEED?

If the inferences made in the last section are correct, the people of Arroyo Hondo had access to farmlands extending several kilometers west and southwest of the pueblo as well as to the plant resources lying within a radius of a few kilometers. How much of these lands and resources they chose to use would have depended on several factors, the most important of which was probably population. For lack of any definitive information on numbers of residents, it is necessary to rely on inference and guesswork in making an estimate. Two lines of evidence come into play here. The first, the remains of the pueblo, offers insights into the minimum number of inhabitants; while the second, the carrying capacity of the region, enables us to determine an upper limit. In this section we focus on what the archaeological remains reveal about population.

The ruins of the pueblo are impressive, some 1,200 rooms or more, the majority of which, about 1,000, were built and occupied during the first 30 years after A.D. 1300. Over the course of the next 30 or 40 years much of the pueblo was abandoned, with only a small remnant population remaining. Starting in the 1370s the pueblo saw renewed growth and eventually attained the modest proportions of about 200 rooms.

To translate the Arroyo Hondo room figures into population estimates requires information on a number of variables: the number of rooms per family, average family size, and the number of rooms not in use at any given time. Architectural evidence from the site offers some clues to the first variable. Most of the rooms formed sets of interconnected chambers or suites that were thought to be residence units, each housing a family. These units consisted of two, three, or sometimes more adjacent rooms sharing common walls or a common ceiling-floor, along with a connecting doorway or an opening through the ceiling-floor. One of each set of rooms had a hearth and other features such as milling bins which suggested they were living quarters, while the adjoining rooms appeared to be for storage (Beal and Creamer 1986). Among the excavated residence units, twelve had two rooms, four had three rooms, and one each consisted of four, six, seven, eight, and ten rooms (Beal and Creamer 1986). This gives an average of 3.38 rooms per family at Arroyo Hondo Pueblo.

Family size can be estimated using demographic data from the historic Pueblo Indians. In 1776 Fray Francisco Atanasio Dominguez reported figures for family size at Tesuque, Santa Clara, Taos, Picuris, and Zuni which averaged 3.93 persons per family (Kidder 1958). In 1890 Donaldson (1893) in an "Extra Census Bulletin" reported that New Mexico Pueblo families ranged from 3.43 persons at Nambe to 6.90 at Acoma, with a mean of 4.62. In the early twentieth century Kroeber (1917) found an average of five people per household in a sample of 14 pueblos. Census data for San Juan indicates a mean family size of 4.2 individuals in 1790, 3.5 in 1863, and 4.1 in 1890 (Ford 1968a:86). From the spotty records kept at Cochiti, it appears that family size ranged from 2.8 to 5.0 during the period from 1707 to 1952, with an average of four (Lange 1972:426).

With these data on family size and residence units, we would be in a good position to estimate Arroyo Hondo's population were it not for the third variable. The number of rooms unused at any given time is impossible to determine with precision. While we know that the pueblo had achieved its maximum of 1,000 rooms by about 1330, we have little information on the chronology of construction and use. Undoubtedly all rooms were not used simultaneously; by 1330 some of the earlier ones had probably been abandoned. Those from the initial settlement were almost certainly deserted, for by this time the children of the first settlers would have grown up and most likely established their own households, the common pattern among modern Tewa Pueblos. At San Juan, for example, Ford (1968a:86) found that 80 percent of the families were nuclear, and only 20 percent extended. Once the Arroyo Hondo children set up their own homes, the first residence units would have been left vacant on the death of the elderly parents.

Changes in the family were probably not the only factors that prompted people to abandon rooms and residence units. After some years adobe walls and ceilings probably deteriorated beyond repair. The architectural remains clearly indicate that many rooms underwent remodeling and were ultimately sealed up or given over to trash. Unfortunately, the chronological controls are not tight enough to determine precisely when rooms were used and when they were abandoned.

Nor can we pinpoint when new immigrants set up households at Arroyo Hondo. If most of them were early arrivals, we might speculate that the 1,000 rooms represented initial construction and much subsequent turnover of residence units, resulting in a large proportion of vacant units by 1330. On the other hand, far fewer rooms would have been empty at this time had many households been constructed by migrants arriving in the 1320s.

Unfortunately, there is no way to unravel this knotty problem. As an alternative, we can consider population figures using a range of values for each of the three variables. These estimates are presented in table 3, where population is calculated as occupied rooms divided by rooms per family times persons per family. The four values used for number of rooms per family seem to best bracket the range seen among the architectural remains. The figures for family size, 4, 4.5, and 5 are consistent with the ethnographic data. The values for number of rooms in use, 50 to 80 percent, cover the range of most reasonable figures. It seems unlikely that fewer than half the rooms were used around 1330, since this would presuppose that much of the pueblo was constructed by the first settlers and had already been abandoned. This is not supported by the scant evidence we have for the construction sequence. It also seems unlikely that more than 80 percent of the rooms were occupied simultaneously, given the extensive evidence for sealed and abandoned rooms. All of the initial residence units would probably have been deserted by this point, or portions of them may have been sealed off. Rooms lying in the core of the roomblocks were apparently abandoned or given over to storage as rooms were added to the exterior (Beal and Creamer 1986).

TABLE 3.
Population estimates for Arroyo Hondo Pueblo.

Percentage of Rooms in Use	*Number of Rooms Per Family*	*Average Family Size*	*Population*
80 (800 rooms)	3 (266 res. units)	4.0	1,067
		4.5	1,200
		5.0	1,333
	4 (200 res. units)	4.0	800
		4.5	900
		5.0	1,000
	5 (160 res. units)	4.0	640
		4.5	720
		5.0	800
70 (700 rooms)	3 (233 res. units)	4.0	933
		4.5	1,050
		5.0	1,167
	4 (175 res. units)	4.0	700
		4.5	788
		5.0	875
	5 (140 res. units)	4.0	560
		4.5	630
		5.0	700
60 (600 rooms)	3 (200 res. units)	4.0	800
		4.5	900
		5.0	1,000
	4 (150 res. units)	4.0	600
		4.5	657
		5.0	750
	5 (120 res. units)	4.0	480
		4.5	540
		5.0	600
50 (500 rooms)	3 (167 res. units)	4.0	667
		4.5	750
		5.0	833
	4 (125 res. units)	4.0	500
		4.5	563
		5.0	625
	5 (100 res. units)	4.0	400
		4.5	450
		5.0	500

The population estimates in the table range from 400 to 1,333. These two extremes can probably be ruled out. The maximum figure requires 80 percent of the rooms to be occupied, with an average family of five and a residence unit of only 3 rooms. The minimum figure is achieved only if a mere 50 percent of the pueblo is in use, the average family is four, and the residence unit consists of five rooms. While these combinations of conditions seem unlikely, the values they yield offer us some insights into the Component I population—it was almost certainly greater than 400 and less than 1,300. In order to narrow this range we must consider other lines of evidence, the task of the next section.

ARROYO HONDO'S BOUNTY: ESTIMATING THE RESOURCES OF THE PUEBLO'S TERRITORY

It is clearly impossible to calculate the food resources of the Arroyo Hondo area with precision: there are far too many variables that cannot be specified. But some rough estimates will suggest the problems and potentials confronting Arroyo Hondo's inhabitants in their effort to make a living.

Maize

Table 4 offers estimates of Arroyo Hondo Pueblo's maize crops. The first part of the table indicates yields for the canyon lands, within 1 kilometer of the pueblo, within 2 kilometers, and so forth, assuming that all of the Terrace Deposits in each of these areas were under cultivation.

The figures for maize yields—500, 600, or 700 kilograms per hectare (446, 536, or 625 pounds per acre)—are educated guesses based on modern field and experimental data. The last comes from Human Systems Research (1973:445), which planted a 15-by-20-foot experimental plot of Chapalote corn at an elevation of 1,469 meters (4,820 feet) in the Tularosa Basin of New Mexico.

At the end of the season, the group harvested 360.5 kilograms of kernels, which can be extrapolated to about 890 kilograms per hectare (Human Systems Research 1973:450). In another experiment, a very small, irrigated patch of Chapalote corn grown at 1585 meters (5,200

TABLE 4.
Potential harvest of maize in kilograms and calories.

		Yield per Hectare					
		500 kg/ha		*600 kg/ha*		*700 kg/ha*	
Km from pueblo	*Arable land (ha)*	*kg*	*cal (millions)*	*kg*	*cal (millions)*	*kg*	*cal (millions)*
A. *Canyon lands only (periods of average precipitation)*							
0–1	20	10,000	36.0	12,000	43.2	14,000	50.4
0–2	53	26,500	95.4	31,800	114.5	37,100	133.6
0–3	77	38,500	138.6	46,200	166.3	53,900	194.0
0–4	111	55,500	199.8	66,600	239.8	77,700	279.7
B. *Piedmont lands only (periods of above-average precipitation)*							
0–1	29	14,500	52.2	17,400	62.6	20,300	73.1
0–2	76	38,000	136.8	45,600	164.2	53,200	191.5
0–3	127	63,500	228.6	76,200	274.3	88,900	320.1
0–4	179	89,500	322.2	107,400	386.6	125,300	451.1
C. *Combined canyon and piedmont lands (above-average precipitation)*							
0–1	49	42,500	88.2	29,400	105.8	34,300	123.5
0–2	129	64,500	232.2	77,400	278.7	90,300	325.1
0–3	204	102,000	367.2	122,400	440.6	142,800	514.1
0–4	290	145,000	522.0	174,000	626.4	203,000	730.8

NOTE: Caloric value of maize estimated at 3,600 calories per kilogram (see appendix C.).

feet) along the Rio Grande produced a healthy yield that was the equivalent of 750 kilograms per hectare (Michael P. Marshall, written communication). These experiments suggest the potential of Chapalote corn, but their yields are probably higher than those that would be found under ordinary conditions. Because of the plots' small size, the harvests are vulnerable to sampling error; these studies also fail to account for the range of variability found in a real field.

Actual fields of native corn are not as productive as these tiny gardens. For example, in 1900 San Juan Pueblo raised only 667 kilograms of Indian corn per hectare in an irrigated field along the Rio Grande at a 1700-meter (5,600-foot) elevation (Ford 1968a:156).

It is hard to believe that Arroyo Hondo farmers could have achieved even these yields. Living more than 450 meters higher than San Juan, they had to contend with a shorter growing season and cooler temperatures as well as poorer soils. (The Soil Conservation Service has rated Arroyo Hondo's Terrace Deposits at VI on a scale of I to VIII in which VIII is the lowest value for contemporary agricultural capability [Kelley 1980:49, 51].) In addition, the Arroyo Hondo farmers had a smaller, less reliable stream with which to water their crops. Today most of Arroyo Hondo's water is submerged in the alluvium and flows on the surface only when there is a heavy runoff; in the past there may have been more surface flow because of a thinner alluvium (Kelley 1980:23–24). Indeed, a Bureau of Land Management field worker reported in 1880, after two dry years, that the Arroyo Hondo stream was one foot wide and one inch deep at a point about 5.6 kilometers (3.5 miles) west of the place where it now dives below the surface (Kelley 1980:23–24). The situation in prehistoric times must have been more similar to that in the nineteenth century than to present conditions if Arroyo Hondo farmers raised crops on the Terrace Deposits. The modern stream is too erratic for crops to rely on, and its underflow, averaging 3 to 6 meters (10 to 20 feet) below the surface (Kelley 1980:24), is too deep for crop roots to tap. Even with a more regular surface flow, the waters of the Arroyo Hondo would have been no match for those of the Rio Grande. It would appear, given these factors, that Arroyo Hondo crop yields were not particularly large. Accordingly, potential harvests were estimated for yields of 500, 600, and 700 kilograms per hectare to suggest the possible range of maize production.

The second part of table 4 shows yields estimated for maize cultivated on the soils of the piedmont. If crops planted here received enough water through rainfall and moisture stored in the soil, piedmont harvests would probably have been comparable to those in the canyon. The Soil Conservation Service also rated the piedmont soils at VI or VII (Kelley 1980:49, 51), and modern farmers raised crops on them until the drought of the 1950s. Hence the values of 500, 600, and 700 kilograms per hectare were used in these calculations also. It should be noted, however, that these figures represent better-than-normal conditions, since above-average precipitation is a prerequisite for dry-farming here (Kelley 1980:9).

The figures from the first two parts of table 4 have been combined in the third part which gives total potential crop harvests from piedmont and canyon lands. Again, above-average precipitation is assumed, but there must at times have been conditions intermediate between moist and dry, not shown on the table, under which the piedmont produced partial harvests: at the beginning of a drought, for example, the soil might have held enough moisture from previous wet years to nourish a small crop (N. Edmund Kelley personal communication).

The yield figures in table 4, expressed in kilograms of kernels, give some notion of Arroyo Hondo's potential for food production, but they are more meaningful when related to human needs. Accordingly, the table also indicates the estimated caloric values of the harvests. These values can be compared with the figures in table 5, which gives a rough estimate of the total annual energy needs of four populations—200, 400, 600, and 800 people—based on an average of 2,000 calories per person per day (an estimate discussed in appendix A).

As a staple crop, maize should have provided a large share of the calories consumed at Arroyo Hondo. People in traditional societies today usually derive 70 to 80 percent of their calories from starchy staples (Gaulin and Konner 1977:48–51); at the turn of the century, the inhabitants of San Juan Pueblo depended on wheat and barley for over 70 percent of theirs (Ford 1968a:158). The Pueblo Indians may have relied less on cultivars in prehistoric times, when they presumably derived a portion of their calories from wild products, but it seems safe to say that maize was a major food of the Arroyo Hondoans and supplied a substantial portion of their calories.

The graph in figure 3, based on tables 4 and 5, compares these people's estimated energy needs with the calories that they could have produced by cultivating various portions of their territory. The histogram suggests that a small group of people could have produced a substantial

TABLE 5.
Annual caloric requirements for populations of different sizes.

	Population Size			
	200	*400*	*600*	*800*
Total annual caloric requirement (in millions)	146	292	438	584
75% of annual caloric requirement (in millions)	110	219	329	438

NOTE: Figures based on an average requirement of 2,000 calories per person per day. See appendix A for discussion of this estimate.

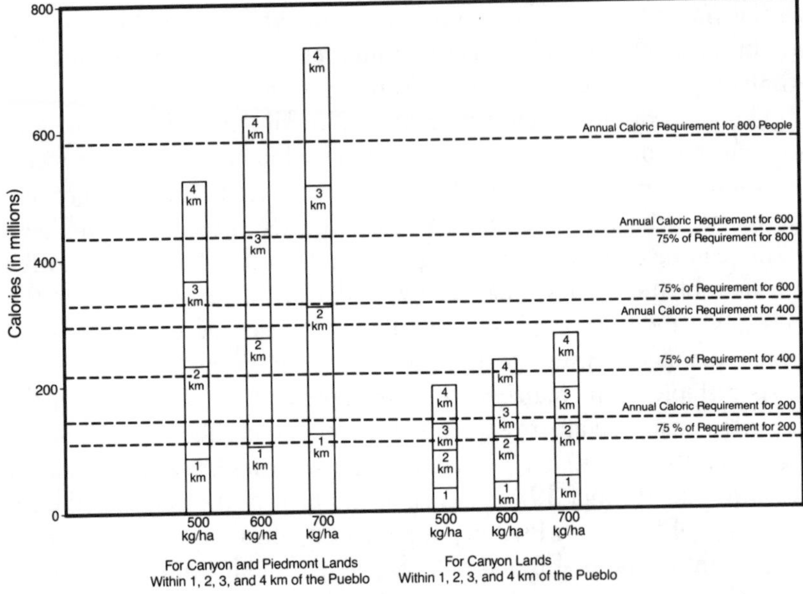

Fig. 3. The food needs of Arroyo Hondo Pueblo compared with estimated maize yields for the area.

share of its food within 1 or 2 kilometers of the pueblo if it farmed both the canyon and piedmont lands. A population of 200 could have supplied 50 to 80 percent of the calories it needed, depending on yields, by planting all arable lands within a 1-kilometer radius; 400 people could have done the same by extending their fields beyond the 1-kilometer mark. In fact, if they had cultivated all the soils within 2 kilometers, their harvests could have produced more than 75 percent of their diet and might even have exceeded their total energy needs. With 600 mouths to feed, the Arroyo Hondoans could have supplied about 50 percent of the necessary calories by farming these same tracts of canyon and piedmont land. Even a population of 800 might have derived 40 percent or more of its requirements from farmlands within 2 kilometers of the pueblo.

When the piedmont lands could not be cultivated and farming was restricted to the canyon, however, the situation changed dramatically. The Arroyo Hondo canyon is so narrow that only a very small pueblo—100 people or fewer—could have raised a substantial portion of its diet within 2 kilometers of the village. A community of 400 would have had to cultivate all of the canyon lands up to 3 kilometers from the village in order to produce 50 to 70 percent of its requirements, since within 2 kilometers it would have reaped less than half of the necessary calories. All of the canyon within 3 kilometers of the pueblo could have yielded only one-quarter to one-third of the food 600 people needed; extending their fields another kilometer in each direction would have enabled the Arroyo Hondoans to satisfy half their requirements. Eight hundred people probably could not have obtained more than 40 percent of their calories from lands within a 4-kilometer radius.

Although these estimates are rough and the figures range widely, there clearly is an overwhelming disparity between moist and dry periods. During wet years, Arroyo Hondo farmers would have been relatively secure, since on their large tracts of arable land in the canyon and on the mesa they could have grown enough corn for as many as 600 people. But when the rains diminished and the piedmont dried up, their fields would have been confined to the narrow strip of land within the canyon, and they would have found themselves pushing farther away from the village in search of farmland. The larger the community, the more vulnerable and precarious it would have been during dry periods. The lack of moist land suitable for fields would have been only part of the problem. Wild plant and animal resources, an important source of food at any time and a potential backup supply in case of crop failure, would have become scarcer with the onset of drought, and might already have been depleted if the population were large.

Other Crops

Beans and squash, the only other crops, probably contributed no more than a small share of the Arroyo Hondo diet, as suggested in chapter 2. The squash, a warm-weather plant, would not have found the area's cool, dry mountain air particularly congenial and would not have produced good yields. Its seeds germinate only in warm soils, preferring a ground temperature of 95 degrees F (Harrington and Minges 1954:146). Squashes grow best in warm weather, perishing if they are exposed to any frost (Whitaker and Davis 1962:144), and need ample water in order to produce good growth and abundant fruit (Whitaker and Davis

1962:149). Given these exacting requirements, it seems unlikely that squashes were a big crop at Arroyo Hondo.

Beans are less particular and could have grown well at Arroyo Hondo. Because there is so little archaeological evidence for them in the prehistoric Southwest, chapter 2 suggested that they were a minor crop; however, since this kind of evidence is not especially conclusive, we will consider the possibility that beans were as important to the fourteenth-century Pueblos as they were in later times.

Modern crop studies offer some insights into the quantities of beans that might have been raised at Arroyo Hondo. The University of California Agricultural Experiment Station tested the common bean *(Phaseolus vulgaris)* under different planting schemes and produced harvests ranging from about 28 to 255 kilograms per hectare (Hendry 1921). The Arroyo Hondo farmers' yields were almost certainly greater than the University of California's lowest value, which was the product of very crowded conditions. Although their field conditions were doubtless not optimum, the Arroyo Hondoans probably did raise beans in separate patches—a practice followed by the modern Pueblos, such as the Hopis (Whiting 1939:13) and the Keresans of Cochiti (Lange 1959:95). Under such conditions, the plants presumably would have had adequate space to develop and bear a good crop.

If the Arroyo Hondo farmers did maintain separate bean fields, they would have had to put more land into cultivation in addition to their cornfields. During moist years they could have had extensive plantings on the piedmont, but when dry periods drove them down into the canyon, arable land would not have been so abundant and the bean patches might accordingly have been smaller. Table 6 estimates the potential bean crop for various tracts of land and for different yields.

Even at the highest yields that the University of California Agricultural Experiment Station achieved, bean harvests fall far short of maize crops on a per-hectare basis. Nonetheless, if the Arroyo Hondoans planted large tracts in beans, they could have had a substantial crop that would have contributed considerably to their diet. For example, if they had cultivated all of the lands lying within 3 kilometers of the pueblo and required about 130 hectares for maize, as suggested earlier, then approximately 75 hectares could have been planted in beans. Under very good conditions, the harvest might have totalled more than 19,000 kilograms of beans.

Of course, we have no way of knowing exactly how much land the

TABLE 6.
Potential harvest of beans in kilograms, calories, and percent of annual caloric requirement.

		Yield = 200 kg/ha				*Yield = 255 kg/ha*			
Km from Pueblo	*Arable land (ha)*	*kg*	*calories (millions)*	*% requirement for population of* 400	500	*kg*	*calories (millions)*	*% requirement for population of* 400	500
Moist periods: canyon lands only[a]									
2–3	24	4,800	16.2	5.5	4.4	6,120	20.6	7.1	5.6
3–4	34	6,800	22.9	7.8	6.3	8,670	29.2	10.0	8.0
2–4	58	11,600	39.1	13.4	10.7	14,790	49.8	17.1	13.6
Moist periods: canyon and piedmont lands combined									
2–3	75	15,000	50.6	17.3	13.9	19,125	64.4	22.1	17.6
3–4	86	17,200	58.0	19.9	15.9	21,930	73.9	25.3	20.2
2–4	161	32,200	108.5	37.2	29.7	41,055	138.4	47.4	37.9
Average or dry years[b]									
4–5	34	6,800	22.9	7.8	6.3	8,670	29.2	10.0	8.0

NOTE: The bean harvest is expressed as a percentage of the annual energy requirement for human populations of 400 (292 million calories) and 500 (365 million calories); see appendix A. The caloric value of beans is estimated at 3,370 calories per kilogram; see appendix C.

[a]For moist periods it was assumed that maize fields required all land up to 2 or 3 kilometers from the pueblo in the canyon and on the piedmont. Bean fields were planted in addition.

[b]For average or dry years it was assumed that maize fields required all canyon lands up to 4 kilometers from the pueblo. Bean fields were planted in addition. Kelley (1980), the source for all the land estimates used here, had no figures for land lying more than 4 kilometers from the pueblo because it did not lie within his study area. For these calculations, it was assumed that this segment of the canyon encompassed roughly the same acreage of arable land as the adjacent segment 3–4 kilometers from the pueblo. These two sections are very similar in topography, width, and vegetation.

pueblo farmed, but ethnographic accounts offer some insights into the acreage that Pueblo farmers can cultivate: the men of Cochiti, a population of 353 people, farmed 243 hectares in 1945, an average of 0.7 hectare per capita (Lange 1959:11, 438). The people of San Juan Pueblo tilled somewhat less land at the turn of the century—205 hectares for 400 people (Ford 1968a:156)—while still less was cultivated at Zia, where in 1936 the figure was 0.44 hectare per person. For the prehistoric Pueblos, the ratio may have been even lower.

The Pueblos of San Juan and Cochiti probably invested more time and energy in farming than did their predecessors. First, they cultivated a larger number of crops, including many that the Spaniards had introduced, and some of these probably replaced wild foods in the diet. For example, wheat, a Spanish introduction, ripens in June, a time when the prehistoric Pueblos may have turned to such wild foods as Indian rice grass. In addition, modern-day Pueblos hunt far less than their predecessors of even a century ago, and so presumably spend more time farming and raising animals. Lange (1959:125) believes that "A century or more ago there might have been a hunting complex that was a strong competitor of agriculture for man-hours and efforts expended."

In light of these factors, it seems unlikely that the people of Arroyo Hondo cultivated more than 0.5 hectare per capita; indeed, a smaller figure seems more reasonable. If this were the case, then it would have been possible for them to cultivate all the lands lying within 3 kilometers of the pueblo (about 200 hectares) if the population were between 400 and 500 people.

Under these circumstances, large plantings of beans would have been feasible and could have made a large contribution to the diet, supplying over 20 percent of the annual caloric requirement for a population of 400. But the ethnographic record suggests that there were no such large bean patches. The historic Pueblos, who regarded beans as a major food, harvested quantities considerably smaller than these estimates. For example, the people of Cochiti harvested 66 bushels (estimated at 2,249 kilograms) in 1945 (Lange 1959:438), which was less than 5 percent of their maize crop by weight. At San Juan and Zia, the harvests were even smaller. San Juan's total bean crop in 1900 was 818 kilograms (Ford 1968a:158), which was a mere 1.55 percent of the maize crop; and only 70 bushels, estimated at about 2,385 kilograms, were harvested in 1936 at Zia. In 1949, the Zia harvest rose to 140 bushels, still only 4,760 kilograms (White 1962:106). In addition, Lange (1959:95) notes that, at Cochiti, "bean patches in a few cases amount to as much as two-acre fields; most are much smaller . . . ." If each Arroyo Hondo family had planted an approximately 0.8-hectare (2-acre) patch, the total area devoted to beans would have been 80 hectares, a value slightly higher than the maximum of 75 hectares estimated above. But if most patches were much smaller, as at Cochiti, bean harvests would have been a great deal less.

In light of this evidence, then, Arroyo Hondo Pueblo probably did not raise large bean crops, perhaps two to five percent of the maize crop, as in the ethnographic examples. Nonetheless, any beans they did grow would have been an important part of the diet because of their high protein content.

Wild Plants: Weedy Annuals

The yields for wild plants are even more difficult to estimate than those for crops because of the many unknown factors, but some attempts at an estimate may shed light on the possibilities for and limitations to making a living in the Arroyo Hondo area.

Perhaps the greatest unknown in estimating weedy annual yields is the human factor. By disturbing the soil, people create habitats in which weeds thrive. It is difficult, however, to estimate how large an area the people of Arroyo Hondo opened to weed invasion. Their corn and bean fields would obviously have been choice sites for weeds, but even if the extent of the fields could be determined, there is still no way to reliably calculate the size of the wild crop. Some weeds might have been torn out once they sprouted; others, such as chenopod, amaranth, and beeweed, may have been tolerated. When the Arroyo Hondoans left some of their fields fallow, they opened another ideal habitat for weeds—but one not readily amenable to estimates. Likewise, the areas in which they dumped trash, trampled the ground surface, and collected firewood would have been congenial to weeds; again, the extent of such areas would not be easy to calculate.

Although this information is inaccessible, it is still possible to gain some insights into potential weed harvests through less direct means. Consider first the cultivated fields where most of the weedy annuals would have been found. Wild greens may have been picked throughout the summer, and in late August or September the seeds could have been harvested. These seeds and shoots would have added variety to the diet, but it is hard to imagine that the yields were anything but modest; it would not have been in the best interests of Arroyo Hondo farmers to give over their fields to weeds.

At San Juan Pueblo today, farmers balance their interest in crops and wild plants by permitting a few desirable weeds to flourish in their fields, while pulling out all others (Ford 1968a:190). Richard Ford (unpublished data) measured some of these weed crops in 1973; for instance, in an irrigated chili field he harvested 295 grams (10 ounces) of chenopod (*Chenopodium* sp.) seeds and 185 grams (6.5 ounces) of amaranth (*Amaranthus* sp.) seeds in 500 square meters. Projected onto a hectare, the yields were 5.9 kilograms and 3.7 kilograms respectively, for a modest total seed yield of not quite 10 kilograms per hectare. Since the size of wild crops must be restricted wherever they grow in a cultivated field, a small weed harvest is probably the rule under such conditions. For example, Whiting (1939:16) notes that "it is a general practice to allow certain weeds to grow unmolested in the otherwise carefully hoed Hopi fields."

If all the Arroyo Hondo fields had yielded small growths of weedy annuals, how much wild grain could the prehistoric inhabitants have reaped? Table 7 shows estimated harvests for various tracts of land, assuming a yield of 10 kilograms per hectare. If the pueblo cultivated roughly 200 hectares for a population of 400, as suggested earlier, the total yield would have been about 2,000 kilograms or 6.8 million calories. Since this is only about 2 percent of the estimated annual energy requirement for a population of 400, the caloric contribution is rather small.

However, this calculation probably underestimates the potential of weedy annuals, since given adequate moisture, any fields left fallow would have been covered with them. It is possible only to speculate on how much such a field could have offered, but we know that under exceptional conditions wild plants can produce sizable harvests. Zohary (1969:56) estimated that during rainy years wild emmer wheat yields 500 to 800 kilograms of grain per hectare in the Upper Jordan Valley of Israel, where the plants grow in dense stands nearly comparable to those in fields of cultivated wheat. In the lower Illinois River valley, Asch and Asch (1978:313–14) found even higher yields for a wild plant: in two one-meter-square plots with pure stands of *Chenopodium bushianum*,

TABLE 7.
Potential harvest of field weed seeds in kilograms and calories.

Kilometers from Pueblo	*Hectares*	*Kilograms*	*Calories (millions)*
Combined canyon and piedmont lands (moist periods)			
0–1	49	490	1.7
0–2	129	1,290	4.4
0–3	204	2,040	6.9
0–4	290	2,900	9.9
Canyon lands only (below-average precipitation)			
0–1	20	200	0.7
0–2	53	530	1.8
0–3	77	770	2.6
0–4	111	1,110	3.8

NOTE: Yield is estimated at 10 kilograms per hectare. Caloric value is estimated at 3,400 calories per kilogram; see appendix C.

they gathered a crop of chenopod seeds that would have been comparable to a harvest of between 1,330 and 1,740 kilograms per hectare. Since their estimate is based on small, open plots in which the plants had maximum opportunities for growth, the Asches cautioned that such yields probably would not be achieved in larger stands, where the plants would have to compete with one another as well as with other species. Nonetheless, this indicates that weedy annuals can be extremely productive under special circumstances. However, wild plant yields usually fall far short of those of cultivated grains, which have been selected and bred for large returns. For example, Asch and Asch (1978:311) harvested only an average of 295 kilograms per hectare of sumpweed *(Iva annua)* seeds at various locations in the Mississippi River valley, again in one-meter plots where conditions were optimum. This is a substantial yield, but no match for a cornfield. By contrast, only 12.2 grams (less than 0.5 ounce, or the equivalent of 122 kilograms per hectare) of purslane (*Portulaca oleracea*, an introduced species) seeds were harvested from a 1-meter-square area at Arroyo Hondo in 1973, although the purslane plants covered the entire plot with a dense mass of procumbent stems. Again, one would have to caution that over a larger area yields would be lower still.

In light of the fact that all of these estimates are based on exceptionally rich little patches, what can be said of weed seed production in the Arroyo Hondo fields, where useful weeds were not uniformly distributed and where they competed with useless ones as well? It is difficult to spell out a figure for any one plant, but to estimate the collective yield for all useful weed seeds is reasonable. The total for chenopod, amaranth, purslane, sunflower, and beeweed was probably not less than 50 kilograms over a hectare. The individual yield for each of these plants was surely much smaller than the estimates derived from test plots, but it seems unlikely that it would have fallen to the level of Ford's harvest in the weeded fields of San Juan Pueblo. Ten kilograms per hectare might have been an average value, with a collective total of 50 kilograms, but larger harvests seems quite possible in light of *Chenopodium*'s ability to be prolific under good conditions. Over a large area with diverse vegetation, the collective yield might have been as high as 200 or more kilograms per hectare. It is hard to believe that it would have consistently exceeded 200 or at most 300 kilograms per hectare, since the individual harvests for these plants rarely match such figures even under exceptional circumstances. For purposes of this discussion, then, imagine that the Arroyo Hondoans could have harvested between 50 and 300 kilograms of weed seeds per hectare of fallow land.

How extensive were the fallow fields? Of course this is not obvious from the archaeological record, nor can it be estimated with great confidence, but several factors may be considered. First, during dry years, most if not all of the piedmont fields were abandoned. In really dry periods, they could have supported neither crops nor weeds, since weedy annuals are opportunists that require moisture to sprout and grow, but there were probably intermediate years during which the crops were all but ruined by late frosts or dry spells during the critical period of pollination (Aldrich 1970:27). At such times, farmers might give up on the corn crop and abandon the fields to weeds, which, being less vulnerable than the cultivars, might survive and produce a seed crop. Any seeds harvested on these fields would have been not a supplement to the diet but a poor substitute for the crops that farmers had hoped to harvest.

During those dry years when the Arroyo Hondo farms were confined to the canyon, most of the fields were probably under a crop of corn. Fallow acreage would have been sparse if the pueblo required as much crop land as estimated here. In better times, when the piedmont saw farming, fallow fields may have been numerous. At San Juan Pueblo around the turn of the century, about half the arable land lay fallow at any given time, for each field was used only every other year (Ford 1968a:157). Such a scheme may have been followed at Arroyo Hondo, but this seems unlikely, since the fallow fields at San Juan Pueblo probably reflected Spanish influence. Specific crop rotation schemes may have been introduced with wheat and other foreign plants, and fallow fields, one of the few good places to pasture livestock in this dry area, may have become particularly important with the advent of ranching. Before European agriculture was introduced, the Pueblos may not have been as systematic in rotating their land and may not have rested such a large portion of it.

Imagine for the sake of discussion that Arroyo Hondo farmers allowed one-quarter of their fields to lie fallow. If the estimates made earlier are accurate, 200 hectares of land would have been under cultivation for a population of between 400 and 500. Then approximately 50 hectares would have lain fallow, producing a harvest of weed seeds ranging from 2,500 to 15,000 kilograms. Assuming 3,400 calories per kilogram, these would have yielded 8,500,000 to 51,000,000 calories, as indicated in table 7, or between 2.5 and 15 percent of the community's annual caloric needs. If these figures are at all correct, weed seed crops from fallow fields might have been substantial.

Arroyo Hondo farmers could have boosted these harvests through special practices. For example, at San Juan Pueblo, farmers set aside a strip of land 12 feet wide or less at the edge of their fields for useful wild plants such as sunflowers, purslane, and beeweed (Ford 1968a:138). If the Arroyo Hondoans had done likewise, the total acreage given over to weeds would not have been especially large, and the crop would accordingly have been modest, but it could have been a good supplement.

One other source of weed seeds needs to be considered—the trash middens and open areas around the pueblo. These were surely home to many weeds, but their yield was probably small because the total area is no more than a few hectares.

The modern Pueblos, such as the people of San Juan, value the weedy annuals more for their young shoots than for their seeds, and undoubtedly the Arroyo Hondo people harvested the greens as well. With careful picking, they could have had both greens and grains. How much was available is extremely difficult to estimate. These wild spinaches are best when small and tender, and if they are picked regularly, young shoots may continue sprouting through the summer. Thus the harvesters' habits as well as acreage, plant density, and moisture levels would determine how many sprigs of chenopod shoots or amaranth greens were gathered in a summer. In any case, for the purposes of this discussion the total harvest is probably not significant because in general greens are not a particularly rich source of energy. With their high moisture content (usually exceeding 85 percent), they offer few calories on a per-weight basis. For example, mustard greens *(Brassica juncea* var. *foliosa)* are 90.6 percent moisture by weight; turnip greens *(Brassica rapa)*, 89.8 percent; curly dock *(Rumex crispus)*, 92.6 percent; and *quelite (Chenopodium album)*, 88.0 percent (Leung and Flores 1961:33, 35, 37). To satisfy 10 percent of one's daily energy needs, estimated at 2,000 calories, one would have to eat 625 grams (almost a pound and a half) of quelite, which averages 32 calories per 100 grams (Leung and Flores 1961:37). One would need enormous quantities of leaves in order to make a significant dent in one's appetite with greens such as these.

In sum, weedy annuals could have helped balance the diet at Arroyo Hondo with greens rich in vitamins and trace elements but low in calories, and their seeds could have been a valuable supplement, possibly contributing a substantial share of calories under certain conditions. The best crops would have been available during moist years when the maize harvest was also good; and when that crop was poor because of untimely frosts or a dry spell during pollination, weed seeds could have been a helpful backup. During very dry years, the weed crops probably fared better than maize, but it is unlikely that they could have remedied the pueblo's food shortages since their productivity per unit area was most likely too low to compensate for any serious failures of the maize crop. Though weed seeds could not totally replace a lost crop, they were probably a most valuable supplement because their protein content is higher than that of maize, as indicated in appendix C.

Other Wild Plants

Trying to estimate wild plant resources lying beyond the cultivated field is even more challenging than calculating the weedy annual crop. This task is further complicated by two problems in addition to all those noted above: there is neither enough information about the nature and extent of the prehistoric woodland nor sufficient ecological data about useful plant resources. Nonetheless, the scant information available can shed some light on the potential and problems of collecting wild crops.

First, it is unlikely that these resources were stable and abundant throughout the entire occupation of the pueblo: by collecting firewood and cutting timber, the inhabitants almost certainly affected plant distribution and abundance. One clue to the community's impact on the forest, for example, is the age of the timbers used for construction. In the earliest phases of building, 60 percent of the timbers that could be dated were from trees older than 50 years, but by the last phase of occupation, this class represented only 16.5 percent of the datable timbers (Bohrer 1979:34). By this time, mature trees must have been scarce and scrub growth abundant.

The prickly pear cactus may have been the only wild plant that could easily tolerate the transformation of the forest and persist unchanged through the entire lifespan of the pueblo. At the present time, these hardy cacti thrive in overgrazed and badly disturbed areas. Therefore, the Arroyo Hondo people may have been able to harvest cactus fruit in all the areas that were not tilled throughout the whole occupation. Table 8 estimates how much fruit they might have found in different areas. In all these calculations, the Panky Loam Soils were excluded, even though all such deposits may not have been farmed. The yield estimates are based on Richard Ford's harvesting trials of 1973. In a 500-square-meter area of pinyon-juniper woodland near San Juan, New Mexico, he collected about 98 grams (after drying) of edible cactus, the equivalent of about 2 kilograms per hectare. Because the trials occurred in an exceptionally wet year, yields under normal conditions would most likely be somewhat lower than Ford's. In earlier times, they were probably lower still, since Ford's figures are based on prickly pears growing in overgrazed areas. It is unlikely that conditions were comparable to this in the prehistoric Arroyo Hondo region even after many years of human disturbance.

Using Ford's "inflated" figures, the table indicates that over 2,000 kilograms (dried weight) of prickly pear fruit might have been collected within a 2-kilometer radius of the pueblo; within a 3-kilometer radius, the Arroyo Hondo people might have gathered more than twice this quantity. Going out farther and scouring the entire area within 4 kilometers of the village, they might have harvested nearly 9,000 kilograms. This quantity of fruit could yield roughly 19 million calories, which

TABLE 8.
Potential harvest of prickly pear fruit in the Arroyo Hondo area, in kilograms, calories, and percent of annual caloric requirement.

Km from Pueblo	*Estimated Hectares of Uncultivated Land*[a]	*Kilograms*	*Calories (millions)*	*Percent Requirement for Population of* 400	500
0–1	307	614	1.3	0.4	0.4
0–2	1,065	2,130	4.6	1.6	1.3
0–3	2,324	4,648	10.1	3.5	2.8
0–4	4,426	8,852	19.3	6.6	5.3

NOTE: Yield is estimated at 2 kilograms per hectare. The caloric value of prickly pear fruit is estimated at 2,175 calories per kilogram; see appendix C. The annual caloric requirement for 400 people is estimated at 292 million calories; for 500 people, 365 million; see appendix A.

[a]These figures include all land within the specified radius from the pueblo that presumably was not cultivated, that is, all soils except terrace deposits and Panky loams.

TABLE 9.
Potential harvest of banana yucca fruit in the Arroyo Hondo area, in kilograms, calories, and percent of annual caloric requirement.

Km from Pueblo	*Estimated Hectares of Uncultivated Land*[a]	*Kilograms*	*Calories (millions)*	*Percent Requirement for Population of* 400	500
0–1	307	706	2.8	1.0	0.8
0–2	1,065	2,450	9.6	3.3	2.7
0–3	2,324	5,345	20.8	7.1	5.6
0–4	4,426	10,180	39.7	13.6	10.9

NOTE: Yield is estimated at 2.3 kilograms per hectare. Caloric value is estimated at 3,900 calories per kilogram; see appendix C. The annual caloric requirement for a population of 400 is estimated at 292 million calories, and for 500, 365 million; see appendix A.

[a]These figures include all land within the specified radius from the pueblo that presumably was not cultivated, that is, all soils except terrace deposits and Panky loams.

would represent about 7 percent of the annual caloric requirement for a community of 400. Since this yield figure probably represents the upper limit of prickly pear harvest, it seems unlikely that these fruits were an important source of energy.

The Arroyo Hondo people could have found additional prickly pears in the grasslands west of the pueblo, where as suggested earlier, they might have camped for several days in family groups, collecting and drying the fruits. However, it is hard to imagine that they could have gathered enough fruit in this way to add substantially to the harvests estimated above.

The banana yucca, another source of wild fruit, is now sparsely scattered over Arroyo Hondo's rocky hillsides. It is very difficult to determine whether this pattern was typical of prehistoric times as well, but assume for the moment that it was. Table 9 shows some very rough estimates for yucca crops using a yield value derived from Richard Ford's 1973 productivity studies (unpublished data). Within a 500-meter-square area where yuccas were particularly abundant, he collected 232 grams of fruit (dry weight, seeded). A value of half this figure was used in the table to calculate yucca harvests since the plants would not have been as abundant over large areas and the yield would accordingly have been lower than Ford's. On the basis of this adjusted value, it appears that the Arroyo Hondo yucca harvest would have been modest but potentially significant. If the fruits were collected intensively over the entire area within a 4-kilometer radius of the pueblo, the harvest could have contributed a little over 13 percent of the annual energy needs of a community of 400. But it is unlikely that the Arroyo Hondoans combed all of this region, since the inhabitants of the upper village probably claimed part of the crop. In addition, the yucca harvests per unit area were probably smaller than those estimated here, particularly if the spotty distribution of yuccas today reflects conditions in the past. Moreover, yields would not have been consistent over time because the formation of yucca fruits depends on stored food reserves, and therefore a plant does not produce fruit in consecutive years under normal growth conditions (Wallen and Ludwig 1978:419, quoted in Bohrer 1980:247).

Pinyon nuts, unlike the wild fruits, could have made a significant contribution to the Arroyo Hondo diet. The nuts are rich in calories, and the crops are sometimes enormous. However, it is very difficult to estimate the pinyon nut crops of the area without knowing the density of the prehistoric pinyon-juniper forest and how it changed through time, and estimates are also problematic because nut yields vary widely from year to year. Nonetheless, some insights into the prehistoric pinyon crops can be gained by looking at modern pinyon forests. A yield of 73 kilograms of pinyon nuts per hectare was reported in 1909 for one New Mexico pinyon-juniper forest (Philips 1909:220), but in prehistoric times, the forests were probably less dense (Lang and Harris 1984:26) and the nut yields proportionately lower. Accordingly, a value of about half the 1909 figure was used to estimate the potential prehistoric nut crops of the Arroyo Hondo area, as shown in table 10. The estimates include only untilled land and areas located 1 kilometer or more beyond the pueblo, since most of the pinyon pines within a kilometer of the site were probably soon cut for construction and firewood by its inhabitants.

The table suggests that Arroyo Hondo Pueblo was surrounded by an extremely rich source of food. The pinyon crop from trees within a radius of 4 kilometers could have provided more than the community's annual caloric requirement, according to these estimates. However, the figures in fact far exceed what would have been available to the pueblo. Good pinyon crops such as those used in formulating the table would have appeared only once every five (Philips 1909:221) or six years (Ford

TABLE 10.
Potential harvest of pinyon nuts in the Arroyo Hondo area, in kilograms and calories, estimated at two different yield levels.

		37 kg/ha		*55 kg/ha*	
Radius from Pueblo (km)	*Estimated Hectares of Uncultivated Land*[a]	*Kilograms*	*Calories (millions)*[b]	*Kilograms*	*Calories (millions)*[b]
1–2	1,065	19,702	125	29,554	188
2–3	2,324	42,994	273	64,491	409
3–4	4,426	81,881	520	122,822	780

NOTE: The estimates for yield in kilograms per hectare are based on Phillips's (1909: 220) figure of 73 kg/ha. Since the contemporary pinyon-juniper forest is denser than the prehistoric one, figures of one-half and three-fourths of Phillips's estimate were used here. The yield figure in kilograms was then divided by two to derive the edible portion; approximately half the pinyon nut is waste because of the shell.
[a]These figures include all land within the specified radius from the pueblo that presumably was not cultivated, that is, all soils except terrace deposits and Panky loams.
[b]The caloric value of the pinyon nut is estimated at 6,350 calories per kilogram; see appendix C.

1968a:160); the intervening seasons would have seen meager crops or none at all. The harvests of a good season may well have been stored and rationed over several years. Furthermore, the residents of Arroyo Hondo would not have succeeded in harvesting the entire nut crop since they would have been competing with animals and other people, and they would not have had exclusive rights to the crop.

If we assume that these people harvested all of the potential crop estimated in the table but had to ration it over six years, then the annual caloric yield was 86 million, or about 30 percent of the annual energy needs of 400 people. If we assume they harvested only half of the estimated crop, their annual nut supply would have represented about 15 percent of the diet, which would have been a significant contribution to the food storerooms. However, evidence based on the harvests of modern Pueblos suggests that the Arroyo Hondoans might not have been able to collect such a large quantity of nuts. Ford (1968a:160) found that the people of San Juan Pueblo around the turn of the century tried to collect a total of 3,600 kilograms of nuts in good years, which they then rationed over a six-year period, consuming on the average about 4 percent of their diet or 12 million calories per year in nuts. The prehistoric Pueblos may have tried to collect larger quantities than their descendants since they relied more heavily on wild products. On the other hand, before the Conquest the Pueblos may not have been able to bring in such large harvests because they lacked horses and wagons in which to travel and carry pinyon nuts.

In sum, it is very difficult to estimate the pinyon nut harvests of Arroyo Hondo, but it seems likely that they were highly variable. A very good crop might have represented more than a year's diet for the whole pueblo but would probably have been rationed over five or six years, contributing perhaps 5 to 15 percent of the diet annually. The nut stock could have been an important emergency ration after a season of poor crops, but the supply would not have been replenishable until the next good pinyon crop, and during drought periods, the intervals between these crops probably extended well beyond five or six years. In addition, the harvest probably dwindled through time as the Arroyo Hondo people cleared the woodland.

One additional wild plant which may occasionally have been important to the people of Arroyo Hondo was Indian rice grass. Growing primarily in grasslands and in scattered patches in the pinyon-juniper forest, the grass would have been found in untilled soils beyond the range of cultivated fields. We have few data on the extent and distribution of the plant in the past, but present-day yields offer some insights into the quantities that prehistoric people might have harvested. The modern yields, like those of other wild plants, seem very low compared with cultivated crops. In my 1973 productivity studies at Arroyo Hondo, Indian rice grass averaged 2.48 grams of edible portion per square meter in the scattered patches where the plants were dense and vigorous. Extrapolated to larger areas, this equals 24.8 kilograms or 101,680 calories per hectare, based on an average of 4,100 calories per kilogram (see appendix C). In order to harvest only 1 percent of their annual food needs, a population of 400 Arroyo Hondoans would have had to scour at least 287 hectares, an area nearly twice that of the cultivated fields, where Indian rice grass grew in dense stands—an effort that seems improbable.

Even if these modern figures underestimate the prehistoric yields of Indian rice grass, the Arroyo Hondo people would still have had to collect over a very large area in order to make a significant contribution to their larders. If Indian rice grass yields were twice as high as estimated above, an area equal in size to that cultivated would still have produced only 1 percent of the annual caloric requirement.

It seems unlikely, then, that Indian rice grass was an important source of calories at Arroyo Hondo. However, the plant may have served another very important role. Because it ripens in June, Indian rice grass offered protein- and carbohydrate-rich grains long before the crops would have been ready. During particularly lean years, this early crop, albeit small compared with the annual food budget, might have ensured survival.

Animal Resources of the Arroyo Hondo Area

The faunal remains from the Arroyo Hondo site only hint at the numbers of animals that could have been found in the area during the fourteenth century. Modern wildlife studies offer insights into the population dynamics and behavior of these animals, and from this information, educated guesses can be made about the densities and distribution of animal populations in the prehistoric period. Unfortunately, such conjecture cannot tell us how much game the Arroyo Hondo people may have eaten. Hunting, as Richard Lee (1968:37) has pointed out, is a risky, uncertain business: days of patient stalking may be rewarded with a large kill or no more than tired feet. Luck and skill in the chase are too elusive to be plugged in to any formula for estimating hunting success. Nevertheless, contemporary game ecology research does give us some grasp, albeit tenuous, of the potential and problems of hunting in the Arroyo Hondo region.

Animal Populations. Arroyo Hondo hunters had to contend with ever-changing populations of game since animal numbers vary with the seasons, climatic fluctuations, and other factors. In temperate climates, animal populations usually are highest in late spring or summer, decline slightly through summer and autumn, and drop sharply during the winter, reaching their lowest point in early spring just before the survivors, the breeding population, begin to produce the next generation of young.

Density-dependent factors are responsible for most of the pruning of herds that goes on through the fall and winter. For example, when numbers are high immediately after the breeding season, some species fall easy prey to carnivores because escape cover is inadequate. For others, internal regulatory mechanisms are more important controls than predators: these animals will not tolerate crowding and drive away young animals or curtail breeding when the density surpasses their limits (Wynne-Edwards 1962:503–5, 528). Food may also be an important limiting factor, particularly in arid environments, and predatory animals are especially sensitive to fluctuations in their prey (Dasmann 1964:99).

In addition to these seasonal swings, animal populations can vary over the years as the presence of resources and predators changes. Some species are remarkably stable and maintain a close balance with their environment, while for others the equilibrium comes at the cost of wild fluctuations—population explosions followed by cataclysmic crashes (Dasmann 1964:165–79).

Rabbits and Hares. Jackrabbits or hares (*Lepus californicus texianus*) and cottontail rabbits *(Sylvilagus audubonii)* are abundant today in the pinyon-juniper woodlands and the grasslands of the Santa Fe area. Both are prolific breeders, producing several litters in a season (Bailey 1931:50, 58), and they tolerate inordinate crowding, so that their populations sometimes reach very high densities before natural mechanisms cut them back (Bailey 1931:49). Their normal pattern, however, is a relatively stable population (Hendrickson 1943).

As low successional animals, which feed on young vegetation, cottontails and jackrabbits flourish in habitats disturbed by clearing or fire, where new growth is abundant (Vorhies and Taylor 1933). Hence there may have been an increase in rabbit populations over the course of Arroyo Hondo Pueblo's occupation, which could have been both a boon to hunters and a problem to farmers. Rabbits and hares are voracious feeders and can inflict severe damage to crops (Bronson and Tiemeier 1959:194), especially in regions where the surrounding territory offers little forage.

Modern wildlife studies from several areas suggest possible ranges for Arroyo Hondo's prehistoric hare and rabbit populations. Data collected in New Mexico in the 1920s indicate 1.24 jackrabbits per hectare on a stock range (Bailey 1931:51), while on Kansas grasslands, this animal averaged 0.63 to 0.42 per hectare in the 1950s (Bronson and Tiemeier 1959:197). The pinyon-juniper woodland does not offer as much forage as grassland; consequently its hare population would probably be lower. Indeed, jackrabbit densities were only about 0.25 animals per hectare in the most favorable areas of a pinyon-juniper woodland on the Kaibab Plateau of northern Arizona in the 1930s, with the per-hectare mean for the entire area only 0.10 (Rasmussen 1941:249). The Kaibab Plateau is not strictly comparable to the Arroyo Hondo region since the elevation of its pinyon-juniper woodland is slightly lower and the dominant vegetation includes Utah juniper (*Juniperus osteosperma*), which does not grow in Santa Fe County. Still, the contrast between these figures and the grassland densities suggests a possible range for hares in the Arroyo Hondo area. It seems unlikely that jackrabbit densities ever reached 0.50 animals per hectare, nor is it likely that they ever dropped to less than 0.10, the average hare density for the pinyon-juniper woodland of the Kaibab Plateau; the Arroyo Hondo area, with its cultivated fields, would presumably have had a higher density. During better periods, the average may have been close to 0.25 per hectare, the figure for the best areas of the Kaibab Plateau. This value is one of three used in table 11 to estimate jackrabbit populations within 5 kilometers of Arroyo Hondo Pueblo. High and low populations were estimated at 0.40 and 0.10 hares per hectare, respectively. If these values represent the population peak of June or July and the low of February or March, then the summer and fall values would have ranged

TABLE 11.
Estimated hare populations in the Arroyo Hondo area, at different densities of hares per hectare.

Area	*Hectares*	*0.10 Hares/ha*	*0.25 Hares/ha*	*0.40 Hares/ha*
Circle of 5-km radius	7,850	785	1,963	3,140
Semicircle of 5-km radius	3,925	393	982	1,570

between them; that is, between 785 and 3,140 jackrabbits might have been found within a 5-kilometer radius of the pueblo.

Populations of cottontail rabbits are harder to estimate than those of hares since there are very few data available on their density. Rasmussen (1941:249) noted that on the Kaibab Plateau, "the cottontail is found throughout the association in small numbers but is not so abundant as the jackrabbit." On the other hand, Bailey (1931:58) estimated "1 to every 2 acres" (1.23 rabbits per hectare) in a favored area in New Mexico. This is the same value as his figure (1931:51) for jackrabbits where they are locally abundant. In general, the proportion of hares to cottontails varies with the environment: in open parklands with well-developed grass-forb strata, the former predominate, but in open disturbed areas with abundant shrub growth to provide shelter, the latter are more common (Lang and Harris 1984:29). In the Arroyo Hondo area, the pinyon-juniper forest would probably have been more favorable to hares, but the faunal remains from the site suggest that during drought periods in the mid-fourteenth and early fifteenth centuries, rabbits were slightly more numerous than hares. The dry, open areas and abandoned agricultural fields apparently favored them (Lang and Harris 1983:25–26). In order to estimate Arroyo Hondo's hare and rabbit populations, it was simply assumed that for the most part hares were somewhat more common. In this case, the cottontail population within a five-kilometer radius of the site would have been less than 3,000 animals and possibly less than 2,000, the figure calculated for the jackrabbit population based on a density of 0.25 animals per hectare.

In prehistoric times, both cottontails and jackrabbits were probably taken in communal drives similar to those held by historic Pueblo hunters. The participants formed a very large circle that gradually converged, forcing the animals within the original circle into an enclosure of human bodies. Once trapped, the rabbits and hares were clubbed to death (Lange 1959:128). Sometimes women and children helped trap the animals; at other times only men participated. If Arroyo Hondo Pueblo hunted hares and rabbits in this fashion, the drives involving the whole community were probably held close to home, certainly no more than 5 kilometers away and probably much less. The total number of animals that could have been taken would have been far below the estimated population because many animals would have evaded the hunters. A pool of breeders usually manages to survive from one year to the next to reproduce, and after the excess individuals have been pruned, cover and shelter become abundant, making it very difficult to trap those that remain. These usually represent one-sixth to one-fourth of the population, depending on the number and size of the litters. If the Arroyo Hondo people could have taken about a third of the excess animals or a quarter of the population, then their jackrabbit kill within 5 kilometers of the pueblo would have been between 196 and 785 animals, as shown in table 12, while their cottontail take might have been slightly lower except during drought periods, as noted above. In addition, cottontails were probably more difficult to capture in drives than hares because when threatened, cottontails dart into their burrows or into crevices in rocky slopes where they are relatively safe (Bailey 1931:58). The total cottontail kill, therefore, was probably under 785 animals most of the time.

The figures in the table almost certainly err on the high side. The total area within a 5 kilometer radius would not have been available for the exclusive use of Arroyo Hondo's inhabitants, as noted earlier, nor would all of this territory have been suitable for communal drives, due to the rough terrain of the foothills section. A better estimate of hunting potential would be based on the rabbit populations found west of the foothills within a radius of 5 kilometers of the pueblo. This area is roughly half of the territory within a 5-kilometer radius and its estimated population would be between 390 and 1,570 jackrabbits, with a smaller number of cottontails. Culling one-quarter of this population would net between 98 and 393 jackrabbits, a caloric contribution of 200,000 to 800,000. The cottontail yield might have been similar in numbers but smaller in caloric value: the total number of rabbits might have been more than 98 but less than 393, for a contribution of between 70,000 and 290,000 calories. Hares and rabbits together would

TABLE 12.
Potential harvest of hares and rabbits in the Arroyo Hondo area, at different density levels for hares, minimum and maximum for rabbits.

	0.10 Hares/ha; Minimum for Rabbits			*0.25 Hares/ha*			*0.40 Hares/ha; Maximum for Rabbits*		
Area	*No. of Animals*	*Kg. of Meat*	*Calories (millions)*	*No. of Animals*	*Kg. of Meat*	*Calories (millions)*	*No. of Animals*	*Kg. of Meat*	*Calories (millions)*
Hares									
Circle of 5-km radius	196	296	0.40	491	741	1.00	785	1,185	1.60
Semicircle of 5-km radius	98	148	0.20	246	371	0.50	393	593	0.80
Rabbits									
Circle of 5-km radius	196	109	0.15				785	432	0.58
Semicircle of 5-km radius	98	54	0.07				393	216	0.29

NOTE: Culling rate for hares is estimated at one-fourth of the population. Meat weight for hares is estimated at 1.51 kilograms, and for cottontail rabbits, at 0.55 kilograms; see appendix C. The caloric value of hares and rabbits is estimated at 1,350 calories per kilogram; see appendix C.

have made a modest addition to the Arroyo Hondo diet, representing between 0.1 percent and 0.4 percent of the annual energy requirement for a population of 400.

More rabbits might have been taken in the territory lying west of the pueblo's domain. The men could have made one-day excursions to the short-grass plain, where rabbits were probably more abundant. It is futile to try to calculate how many animals they might have taken, but we can turn to ethnographic sources to see how many rabbits could have been trapped in a drive. Rabbit hunting is relatively unimportant to contemporary Pueblos, yet a fair number of rabbits were caught at Cochiti in the 1940s. During one drive, "some fifteen or twenty men went out and got four or five animals apiece" (Lange 1959:127) for a total of 60 to 100 animals. Usually the hunts for the *cacique* or governor netted 25 or 30 cottontails and jackrabbits. If Arroyo Hondo hunters had similar luck on the grasslands and if they held one drive each month from May through December, they might have taken an additional 150 to 180 animals, representing roughly 200,000 to 250,000 calories. Adding these to the kill from the hypothesized communal drives gives us a total caloric contribution of at most about 0.5 percent of the annual energy requirement for a population of 400.

Additional rabbit hunts may have been held between December and May, but they probably would not have been very worthwhile because the rabbit population would have been at or near its lowest level. In summary, it appears that rabbits were not a major source of calories, although they may have been an important supplement as a source of high quality protein.

Mule Deer. In Santa Fe County today, the mule deer (*Odocoileus hemionus*) is rare, but it is still seen occasionally in areas above 6,500 feet (Stacy 1969:34). In the summer, the deer herds range through the cool, moist conifer forest, and with snowfall, they begin to descend to the pinyon-juniper zone, returning year after year to the same home ranges. They gradually move to lower elevations through the winter, reaching the Arroyo Hondo area around late February. By the end of April, they begin to move to higher elevations again, although a few animals now seem to remain in the area year-round (Lang and Harris 1984:51).

Barring drought and other calamities, the size of a deer herd remains relatively constant through the year. The population is at its peak in the summer just after each doe gives birth to a single fawn. The herd suffers its greatest losses through the fall and early winter, and by spring it is reduced to its lowest point. Within a single year, these fluctuations are rarely large, but over time wild swings in the population are not unusual. Deer thrive on the vegetation of disturbed habitats, which is transitory, but have few regulatory mechanisms to keep their populations in check as the environment changes. They proliferate after fires, floods, or logging, when secondary vegetation is abundant. But a dense herd cannot be sustained for long; as the vegetation changes and good forage becomes scarce, the population begins to dwindle. This response, however, is late and does little to check rapid growth while forage is still good, and as a result, deer herds sometimes eat themselves out of their habitats and starve to death (Dasmann 1964:183–84).

During the fourteenth century, deer herds in Santa Fe County probably never exceeded the carrying capacity of the environment, since both human and nonhuman hunters regularly pruned the herds. Nonetheless, the numbers of deer must have varied with climatic fluctuations. Through clearing and cutting, the Arroyo Hondo inhabitants and their neighbors would have encouraged the secondary vegetation that deer prefer. During wet periods, this forage would have been abundant, and the deer may have responded with a population boom, but droughts and harsh winters probably cut back deer herds at other times.

The studies mentioned earlier from the Kaibab Plateau offer insights into the possible range in the size of the deer herds. In the early 1920s, the Kaibab herd, which had been protected from predators for 18 years, reached a precarious 100,000 and promptly crashed (Rasmussen 1941:237). By 1940, the herd had stabilized at about 10,000, with densities ranging from 8.50 to 10.65 animals per square kilometer in the pinyon-juniper winter range (Dasmann 1964:166). The Kaibab Plateau, as noted earlier, is far from identical to the Arroyo Hondo area, but this study nonetheless suggests the potential herd size in a pinyon-juniper forest. The maximum densities that the protected Kaibab deer achieved are clearly far above the level of the regularly pruned Arroyo Hondo herd, but the stabilized herd of 10,000 may be less dense than that of prehistoric Santa Fe County. Because of constant human activity, the Arroyo Hondo area probably supported more secondary vegetation than the Kaibab Plateau and consequently could have maintained a denser deer herd. This may have been more similar to the Kaibab herd of the late 1920s, which was about 20,000, with a density of 17.00 to 21.30

animals per square kilometer in the pinyon-juniper forest, than to the stabilized herd of 10,000. The deer herd in the Arroyo Hondo area might, then, have varied between 8 and 21 animals per square kilometer. Since we know little about the prehistoric Arroyo Hondo woodland, these numbers are no more than guesswork, but they are useful in trying to understand how people may have supported themselves here. In table 13, these figures have been used to estimate the size of the mule deer herd in the pinyon-juniper belt within 5 and 10 kilometers of the pueblo.

Only some of these animals would have been available to hunters. Normally, a herd loses members over the course of a year until it reaches a security threshold, the level at which cover is adequate for all individuals. Thereafter, it is difficult to kill any additional animals, even with modern rifles. The survivors not only find plentiful cover, they also adapt to hunting by becoming extremely cautious, changing their feeding times to avoid hunters, and traveling in small scattered groups (Dasmann 1964:168). If the population remains relatively stable, the unlucky excess deer probably represent about as many as are born each year. Assuming that each adult doe has one fawn, these excess animals would represent less than one-third of the population, and prehistoric hunters would have competed for this fraction with natural predators and other decimating factors.

Arroyo Hondo hunters may have used efficient techniques, but most likely they did not take a large share of deer from other predators. They probably hunted in communal drives such as the ones Goldfrank (1927:87–88) observed at Cochiti:

> The hunters, men and boys, left early in the morning and toward nightfall they set up their camp in the mountains . . . . In the morning . . . two boys are chosen as leaders and these starting in opposite directions followed by the rest of the camp encircle the mountain while the war captain and his assistant bring up the rear remaining nearest the camp. This formation is similar to that used in rabbit hunts. When the animal is caught, it is divided among the hunters . . . The animals were hung on trees, the hunters returning at nightfall to collect their kills and take them back to camp . . . The following day the hunt is carried on in the same way, but in a new canyon.

TABLE 13.
Estimated mule deer population in the Arroyo Hondo area, at two different densities of deer per square kilometer.

Area	*Square Kilometers*	*Deer Population*		*Excess Deer Available*	
		8 Deer/km²	*21 Deer/km²*	*8 Deer/km²*	*21 Deer/km²*
Within a 5-km radius	78.5	628	1,649	209	550
Within a 10-km radius	314.0	2,512	6,594	837	2,198

NOTE: Excess deer are estimated at one-third of the population.

These communal drives were clearly time-consuming affairs that required planning and organization. They may not have been held very often, and probably were no serious match for the other decimating factors that claimed excess deer. It is hard to imagine that the prehistoric hunters took even 50 percent of the excess individuals, although the faunal remains suggest that during Component I, the Arroyo Hondoans hunted very intensively and may have taken a substantial number of deer each year (Lang and Harris 1984:47–49).

Table 14 shows estimated deer kills for Arroyo Hondo hunters. It is assumed that the excess animals represent about one-third of the herd, as explained above, and that the hunters took 25 to 50 percent of these individuals. The table shows that within a radius of 5 kilometers, the deer kill may have ranged from 52 to 275 animals, and within 10 kilometers, from 209 to 1,099 deer. These figures are estimated on the basis of densities in the pinyon-juniper zone, which deer inhabit in the fall and winter when most hunts probably occurred. This is when the Pueblo men would have had more time for hunting, since their farming tasks would have been completed for the season. In addition, the deer would have been more accessible in the woodlands than in the coniferous forest. Some hunters may have trekked to the high forest in the summer or early fall to hunt deer, but even if this were the case, it would change the calculations in the table very little, because the hunters would have been stalking the same deer that they would have tried to hunt closer to home in the winter. By getting an earlier chance at the deer, they could perhaps have taken a slightly larger share of the excess animals.

Whether they hunted in the pinyon-juniper woodland or the conif-

TABLE 14.
Potential harvest of mule deer in the Arroyo Hondo area, at two different densities of animals per square kilometer.

Area	*Density = 8 Deer per* km^2			*Density = 21 Deer per* km^2		
	Number of Deer	*Kilograms of Meat*	*Calories (millions)*	*Number of Deer*	*Kilograms of Meat*	*Calories (millions)*
Culling rate = 25% of excess animals						
Within a 5-km radius	52	2,366	3.45	138	6,279	9.17
Within a 10-km radius	209	9,510	13.88	550	25,025	36.54
Culling rate = 50% of excess animals						
Within a 5-km radius	105	4,778	6.98	275	12,513	18.27
Within a 10-km radius	419	19,065	27.83	1,099	50,005	73.01

NOTE: Meat weight of deer is estimated at 45.5 kilograms. Caloric value is estimated at 1,460 calories per kilogram. See appendix C.

erous forests, the people of Arroyo Hondo would have shared some of the game with people of neighboring pueblos. Thus their total kill for a year was probably below the estimates presented in the table. Within 10 kilometers of Arroyo Hondo Pueblo, the hunters probably took fewer than 1,000 deer. If the density of deer had been closer to the low estimate of eight per square kilometer, the hunters probably could not have taken more than 300 animals, whose caloric contribution would have been about 19.8 million calories, or about 6.9 percent of the energy needs of a community of 400. Five hundred animals would have represented about 11 percent of the caloric needs.

The Arroyo Hondoans might have taken additional deer if they hunted beyond 10 kilometers north and south of the pueblo. Between 10 and 20 kilometers away, they would have found roughly the same number of deer as within 10 kilometers. Assuming a kill rate of 25 percent of the excess animals, approximately 500 of these deer could have been taken by human hunters, but only a portion of them could have been claimed by Arroyo Hondoans. The largest share would have been killed by inhabitants of the communities in these areas, such as the Tesuque By-Pass Site, 8 kilometers north of Santa Fe, and Pecos Pueblo, 32 kilometers southeast of Arroyo Hondo Pueblo. Both of these villages, and probably the one lying unexcavated under modern Santa Fe, were occupied for at least part of Arroyo Hondo's lifespan. Given this situation, the hunters of Arroyo Hondo probably took most of their game within 10 kilometers of their home. If the guesses and estimates made above are realistic, they would have found between several hundred and 1,000 deer available for the taking in this area.

But how many of these animals could they actually have killed, considering the manpower and time available? The number of hunters, or adult men, may have been between 85 and 105 if the population were 400 to 500 people and had a structure similar to that of most modern nonindustrialized societies. (See appendix A for details of the population estimate.) A total annual kill of 500 deer would mean that each hunter would have had to kill between 4.8 and 6.0 animals. This was probably possible, but historic Pueblo hunters were never so successful. Around the turn of the century, San Juan Pueblo took a total of 75 deer per winter, an average of 0.9 deer per adult male (Ford 1968a:159); however, the men of San Juan raised stock and probably had less incentive to hunt than did their prehistoric predecessors. Groups in the Southwest that have no livestock do indeed hunt more: for example, the Paiute on the Kaibab Plateau averaged three deer each fall in the 1930s (Rasmussen 1941:25). It is difficult to say whether a prehistoric Pueblo relying entirely on hunting for meat could have killed as many as six deer in a year, but the examples above make it clear that he could have taken several in a winter.

From these rough estimates, we can conclude that Arroyo Hondo hunters might have killed as many as 500 deer a year, and possibly even more with intensive hunting. The contribution of deer meat to the diet could have been 10 percent of the community's annual caloric needs or even more.

Turkeys. The people of Arroyo Hondo kept turkeys but probably ate few of their own birds. In historic times, the Pueblo Indians raised domestic turkeys for their feathers, which were used in ceremonials, and Henderson and Harrington (1914:35) suggested that the prehistoric Pueblos did likewise, not using domesticated birds as food because of their ceremonial significance.

The people of Arroyo Hondo most likely hunted the wild Merriam turkey *(Meleagris gallopavo merriami)*, which still ranges over Santa Fe County (Lang and Harris 1984:91–92). The bird probably migrated seasonally between 6,000- and 10,000-foot elevations, as it now does elsewhere in New Mexico. In the summer, turkeys congregate in pine forests above 7,000 feet, feeding on fruits, seeds, succulent greens, and insects. With the onset of winter, they descend to the pinyon-juniper woodlands, where they subsist primarily on acorns and pinyon nuts. If these foods are scarce, they may travel to lower elevations in search of such alternatives as sumac berries (Ligon 1946:59).

Turkeys usually congregate in flocks of a dozen up to several hundred, but they disperse briefly in the early summer for breeding. The hens lay an average of 9 to 12 eggs apiece in April, of which some 25 to 50 percent hatch by May. Half of the hatchlings are then lost within five months, as their survival rate is poor (Schorger 1966:288). Thus, seasonal fluctuations in the population are not great, and the peak population of May is only 100 to 300 percent above the population low.

Schorger (1966:60) estimates that New Mexico's pre-Columbian turkey population averaged 0.6 birds per square kilometer. The figure for pinyon-juniper forests was undoubtedly higher, since Schorger's value is an average for summer and winter ranges and also includes grasslands, where the density is especially low. In a modern pinyon-juniper forest in Arizona, turkeys averaged 2.4 to 2.8 birds per square kilometer, a figure that Ligon (1946:30) believes is close to levels for average years during the prehistoric period. For exceptional years, Ligon (1946:55) estimates the density rose to six birds per square kilometer in forested areas.

The Arroyo Hondo region was almost certainly a winter range for turkey flocks, and in light of the figures above, the density for the area was probably at least three and perhaps sometimes as high as six birds per square kilometer. Table 15 estimates the turkey populations in the pinyon-juniper forests of the Arroyo Hondo area, using a range of values for density. Within 5 kilometers of the pueblo, the population could have ranged between about 236 and 473 birds, and within 10 kilometers, between 942 and 1,892.

Arroyo Hondo hunters may well have taken a substantial share of these birds, as they are easy prey. They travel in large flocks that return night after night to roost in the same grove of trees. Roosting turkeys are not easily disturbed; if besieged by hunters, they often do little more than fly to the next tree. In fact, they are so vulnerable at night that roost-shooting is prohibited in New Mexico (Ligon 1946:13). Turkeys are easy prey even when they are active, for they fly only short distances and tire so quickly that hunters can run them down (Schorger 1966:185).

Apache hunters in the 1930s took advantage of the turkey's vulnerability. One group of men would flush a flock from the area where it was feeding, and a second group, positioned where the birds were expected to land, shot or clubbed them as they descended (Opler 1941:328). Arroyo Hondo hunters may have used similar techniques, with which they might have been able to take as many as 75 percent of the excess birds. The excess would represent about half of the population, which increases by 100 to 300 percent after breeding, but because of high mortality among the young declines over the summer by half the increase. The density figures proposed above, an average for the year, are about 50 percent greater than the breeding population. If they are correct, hunters would have killed about 350 turkeys within 10 kilometers of the pueblo when populations were low or as many as 710 when they were high. Since turkeys are so vulnerable, hunters could have taken far more than the excess birds, but would have done so at the price of poorer kills in the following years. Once reduced, the breeding popula-

TABLE 15.
Potential harvest of wild turkeys in the Arroyo Hondo area.

Area	*Square Kilometers*	*Turkey Population*	*Number of Excess Turkeys*	*Number of Excess Killed*	*Meat Weight (kg)*	*Calories (millions)*
Density = 3 turkeys per square kilometer						
Within a 5-km radius	78.5	236	118	88	203	0.35
Within a 10-km radius	314.0	942	471	353	812	1.38
Density = 6 turkeys per square kilometer						
Within a 5-km radius	78.5	473	237	178	409	0.70
Within a 10-km radius	314.0	1,892	946	710	1,633	2.78

NOTE: The number of excess birds is estimated at 50 percent of the population, and the culling rate is estimated at 75 percent of the excess individuals. Meat weight of turkeys is estimated at 2.3 kilograms per bird. Caloric value is estimated at 1,700 calories per kilogram. See appendix C.

tion could not produce large enough broods to match the former level of turkeys.

Even if 50 percent or more of the turkey population was supernumerary, Arroyo Hondo hunters probably did not kill the entire 75 percent share estimated here, since a portion of these flocks surely would have been taken by neighboring communities and nonhuman predators. Thus the Arroyo Hondo kill was probably greater than 350 birds but no more than 710, as shown in table 15. The caloric contribution of the latter crop would have been 2.8 million calories, so the potential contribution of turkeys to the Arroyo Hondo diet was at most 1 percent of the annual needs for 400 to 500 people.

Pronghorn Antelope. Until the early twentieth century, bands of pronghorn antelope *(Antilocapra americana americana)* ranged over the grasslands of New Mexico (Bailey 1931:22). Unlike deer, antelope have no specific home territories, moving frequently to new ranges. They may graze for several days or weeks within an area of a few square kilometers, but they inevitably move on as the food supply dwindles. During a drought they move often, sometimes traveling great distances in search of the forbs that are their major foods (Buechner 1950a:319). In the cooler portions of their range, antelope also migrate in the fall from the windswept plains to lower, more sheltered valleys for the winter. However, these movements are local, irregular, and quite different from year to year, depending on climatic conditions (Bailey 1931:26).

As a result, the local population density of pronghorns is highly variable, linked primarily to rainfall. During droughts, the bands must forage widely for forbs, whereas in moist years, they can concentrate in larger groups. Buechner (1950a:343, 345) estimated a density under average conditions of four antelope per square kilometer on Texas rangeland where cattle also grazed. On prehistoric grasslands, the average density probably would have been a little higher, since fewer other animals would have competed with the antelope for vegetation.

The size of antelope bands varies seasonally, reaching its lowest point in the spring. With fawning in May, the total population nearly doubles as each doe bears twins, but the bands remain extremely small and widely scattered. The does hide in secluded places, while the males roam alone or in small groups. In July, the does and their young begin to join the males, and larger groups gradually coalesce. By winter the herds consist of several hundred animals, but with the onset of spring, the bands dwindle and the animals scatter once more (Buechner 1950a:294–95; Buechner 1950b:637–39).

During prehistoric times, pronghorn antelope may have come within 8 to 10 kilometers of Arroyo Hondo Pueblo, but hunters probably traveled much farther to locate these far-ranging animals. Although they would have found the largest herds in the late fall, it is more likely that the Arroyo Hondoans hunted in the summer. During the autumn, their time would have been taken up with harvests and later with deer hunting; and winter was an unlikely time for antelope hunts as well, since the men would have had to travel even farther to locate the animals in their lower-altitude winter ranges. But in July and August, the hunters would have been relatively free to leave the fields, and they would have found moderate-sized antelope herds in their summer ranges.

It is difficult to estimate the size of these herds or the number of animals taken by the Arroyo Hondo hunters, but recent accounts of pronghorn hunting offer some clues. In the nineteenth century, Pueblo hunters mounted on horses sometimes killed 100 (Bailey 1931:23) or more animals (White 1943:336) in a hunt. Prehistoric hunters, traveling on foot and armed only with spears and arrows, were probably not as successful. They would have had little chance in an open attack on these quick, alert animals; driving them into enclosures would probably have been the only method that worked. However, the process of locating a herd, positioning it for driving, and trapping individuals would have been a challenging task. The New Mexico Game and Fish Department discovered in its first attempt to transplant antelope that the animals were difficult to drive into traps even with cars, high woven-wire fences, and a team of cowboys (Russell 1964:25). Just as an antelope was driven into the pen, it would turn around and make a frantic dash for freedom, darting between cars and men. On later attempts, the Game and Fish people discovered that the older members of the band remembered the event and led the group away before it was in the drive lane. As a result, the game managers succeeded in capturing antelope only after they located a new band, unfamiliar with traps.

Hence it is hard to imagine that the men of Arroyo Hondo could very often have outwitted a pronghorn herd and maneuvered it into a box canyon or other natural trap. However, on occasions when they did succeed, they probably killed a large share of the confined animals. Antelope are small, rarely exceeding 50 kilograms, so they could easily be speared to death, particularly since the hunters probably could have entered the traps and speared from very close range. The New Mexico Game and Fish Department found that "it was practical for a man to go cautiously into the loading-chute section of the trap, or into the crowding pen, with antelope confined there; catch one with hands; and unassisted carry it out through the chute, then put it into a waiting crate or vehicle with a minimum of assistance" (Russell 1964:26).

The prehistoric Arroyo Hondo hunters may have found it equally easy to handle trapped antelope, but it is unlikely that they had the chance very often. Success would have depended on a series of improbable events: First, the hunters would have had to locate a herd, a task that might have required days of walking across the grasslands. Once they found one, they somehow had to avoid frightening the shy, quick animals. Then, moving about quickly on foot, the men had to drive the animals into an enclosure. On rare occasions, they might have found themselves near a box canyon, but more likely they would have had to construct a brush corral, requiring that they carry and stack branches of juniper and other grassland trees without frightening the herd. Given all these difficulties, it is hard to imagine that the Arroyo Hondo hunters even succeeded once in a summer. The sparse remains of antelope found at the pueblo support the premise that antelope hunting was a rare event.

Even if these hunts were held once a year, they would not have made a significant contribution to the diet. Consider, for example, a successful hunt in which each of the adult males took one antelope. The kill might have been between 85 and 105 animals, assuming 85 to 105 adult males in a population of 400 to 500 people, and assuming the hunters were out for some days and stalked several herds. The energy value of these animals, as indicated in table 16, would have been between 3 and 4.5 million calories, which represents no more than 1 percent of the annual requirement for 400 or 500 people. In order to raise the caloric contribution to 5 percent, Arroyo Hondo men would have needed to kill over 350 animals. Assuming that the prehistoric pronghorn herds were a little larger than the bands that were being reestablished in the 1940s, which consisted of 4 to 23 animals (Buechner 1950a:294), the prehistoric herds may have varied between 20 and 40 animals in the summer. If this were the case, the hunters would have had to trap and slaughter between 9 and 18 bands, which, given the difficulties of antelope hunting, seems highly unlikely. We must conclude, therefore, that antelope contributed less than 5 percent of the diet and probably less than 1 percent.

TABLE 16.
Potential harvest of pronghorn antelope, in kilograms of meat, calories, and percent of annual caloric requirement.

Number of Pronghorn	*Meat Weight (kg)*	*Calories (millions)*	*Percent Requirement for Population of* 400	500
80	2,176	3.18	1.1	0.9
90	2,448	3.57	1.2	1.0
100	2,720	3.97	1.4	1.1
110	2,992	4.37	1.5	1.2

NOTE: Meat weight for pronghorn is estimated at 27.2 kilograms, and caloric value is estimated at 1,460 calories per kilogram; see appendix C. The annual caloric requirement for 400 people is estimated at 292 million calories, and for 500 people, at 365 million; see appendix A.

THE SUM OF ARROYO HONDO PUEBLO'S FOODS

Table 17 brings together all of the estimates for Arroyo Hondo's food resources presented in previous sections. Some of the figures suggest possible ranges for productivity; others are estimated maximum values. The totals, like all of the individual estimates, are educated guesses, and can do no more than suggest the potential and problems of making a living in the Arroyo Hondo area. Specifically, the estimates point to two problems:

First, the total yield of the wild resources must have been modest except under unusual circumstances. As shown earlier, some of these potential foods, such as turkeys and rabbits, could have contributed no more than 1 percent of the diet each, and collectively they could fulfill only a small percent of the population's annual energy needs. Weed seeds, yucca fruits, and prickly pears together might have supplied over 30 percent of the diet under exceptional conditions, but they were probably this heavily exploited only when the cultivated crops were poor. However, when crops failed as a result of drought or other natural calamity, the wild plant yields were probably meager as well. One potentially rich source of food, the pinyon nut, is such an erratic crop that most of the time it probably was not especially important.

Table 17 also suggests that the maize crops at Arroyo Hondo were relatively modest, normally providing perhaps 75 percent of annual ca-

TABLE 17.
Summary of the estimated harvests of Arroyo Hondo Pueblo's food resources, expressed as a percentage of the total annual caloric requirement for a population of 400 people.

Food	*Percentage*
Maize	50–70 (average years)
	75–100 (wet years)
Beans	0.9–3.3 (average years)
	1.4–4.7 (wet years)
Weed seeds	2.5–15.0
Pinyon nuts	5.0–15.0
Prickly pear fruits	0.4–6.6
Yucca fruits	1.0–13.6
Deer	10.0
Turkey	1.0
Rabbits	0.5
Pronghorn	1.1–1.5
TOTAL	71.8
	(average year with lowest yields)
	137.9
	(wet year with highest yields)

loric needs. Even under the best of conditions, with a large tract of land planted in corn, the farmers probably never raised much surplus. For example, if they cultivated 0.5 hectare per person, at a yield of 700 kilograms per hectare, the total crop for a population of 400 would have been 140,000 kilograms of corn, or 173 percent of the annual caloric requirement. This was almost certainly at the upper limit of maize production for prehistoric Arroyo Hondo Pueblo for reasons suggested earlier: first, the yield of 700 kilograms per hectare would have been high for prehistoric maize fields at this elevation; second, that 0.5 hectare per person is probably an overestimate of the amount of land cultivated at Arroyo Hondo. Historic Pueblo Indians such as the Tewas tilled no more land, and in some cases less. Yet since they relied on domestic animals and a wide range of crops, including wheat and barley as well as corn, they almost certainly farmed more extensively than their prehistoric predecessors, who had to supplement their diet through gathering and hunting.

Even if the maximum maize yields were achieved, the surplus would not have been impressive, especially after seed corn was set aside and the crop had suffered storage losses. If the harvests had been smaller, as was almost certainly the case, any surplus would have been negligible indeed. For example, using the more realistic estimates of 0.4 hectare per person and 600 kilograms per hectare, the maize crop would have been 96,000 kilograms, or 118 percent of the annual caloric requirement. After the subtraction of seed corn and storage losses, the total would probably amount to less than the annual calorie requirement of the population.

In summary, these estimates suggest that the Arroyo Hondoans had little fat in their annual supply even when conditions were good. As a result, drought and other natural calamities must have condemned them to hard times.

3

Lean Times In a Marginal Environment

Located where agriculture was barely possible, Arroyo Hondo Pueblo was anything but an agrarian paradise. As previously discussed, its inhabitants could have dry-farmed the mesa top and the canyon bottom during moist periods, producing an adequate harvest that they supplemented with wild products. However, such periods were probably the exception rather than the rule, and both drought and frost were common threats that must have made agriculture a risky business. We turn now to a consideration of the effects such climatic vagaries had on the community's food supply and in turn on its diet and health.

RECONSTRUCTING THE PREHISTORIC CLIMATE

As noted in chapter 2, there is good evidence that the climate of the Southwest has remained essentially the same over the last twenty-two hundred years (Mehringer 1967; Hansen 1947; Harris, Schoenwetter, and Warren 1967). Archaeological evidence from Arroyo Hondo suggests specifically that the fourteenth- through fifteenth-century environment was a pinyon-juniper forest similar to that of the recent past. Nearly all of the flora found at the site by archaeologists—the plant remains described earlier, the pollen, and construction timbers and firewood—are characteristic of pinyon-juniper woodlands. The few exceptions, such as the ponderosa pine used as house beams, grow in adjacent ecological zones.

The archaeological floral remains not only point to a pinyon-juniper woodland, but also indicate that the region's temperature and rainfall four to six hundred years ago must have been similar to today's. This has recently been verified by a dendroclimatological study conducted at the Laboratory of Tree-Ring Research of the University of Arizona. Using new statistical techniques to correlate archaeological tree-ring sequences with climatic factors that influence tree growth, Rose, Dean, and Robinson (1981) constructed a detailed, quantitative record of annual and spring rainfall in the Arroyo Hondo area for the last thousand years. It is possible with these data to identify the droughts and the moist phases that occurred during the lifespan of Arroyo Hondo Pueblo. But before the dendroclimatological record is examined, it will be useful to consider some of the salient features of the rainfall regime in this area.

Contemporary Rainfall

One of the most striking aspects of rainfall in the Arroyo Hondo area is the wide variation in nearly all parameters, a feature that would have had important implications for prehistoric agriculture. Between 1890 and 1960, annual rainfall has averaged 356.9 millimeters (14.05 inches), with a standard deviation of 42.9 millimeters (1.69 inches) for winter and 69.6 millimeters (2.74 inches) for summer (Tuan et al. 1973:52), a small variation in absolute terms but a critical one because the average rainfall is so low that a difference of literally a few inches stands between dry-farming and barren fields. Annual rainfall varies widely, and within a few years conditions may range from drought to deluge. These fluctuations are also seen in the dendroclimatological record from Arroyo Hondo, which means that ancient farmers would have had to adjust to a broad range of conditions.

Seasonal patterns of precipitation would also have had important consequences for agriculture. Rainfall is unevenly distributed through the year, with the lightest and most consistent precipitation falling during the winter months. Spring rainfall is slightly heavier, but June is usually a dry month, though its rainfall can vary greatly. The rainy season, July and August, typically sees over 30 percent of the annual precipitation, but it also shows the widest fluctuations (Tuan et al. 1973:21,

28). As a result, prehistoric farmers had to plant their corn and watch it develop while rainfall was light. Some years they might even have seen no rain in the planting season: several times over the last 100 years, a reading of 0.00 has been recorded for precipitation in May. If enough moisture is stored in the soil, however, seeds may sprout without additional rain. By July and August, rainfall could have supported the rapid growth of the crop; but because it is so variable at this time, there were probably years when precipitation was meager, with serious consequences. If midsummer conditions are too dry, tasseling fails to occur and the maize embryos abort, reducing crop yield (Aldrich 1970:27).

Yet even when monthly rainfall averages were good, the crops may have been drought-stricken because of the northern Rio Grande area's erratic pattern of summer precipitation, which often comes in short, heavy cloudbursts that sometimes deliver an entire month's allotment of rain in a few hours (Tuan et al. 1973:39). The effective moisture from such a cloudburst is likely to be nil because so much of it is lost as runoff. Other hazards of summer thunderstorms are flashflooding, which tears away topsoil, uproots crops, and sometimes buries fields under silt, and hail, which can demolish crops by shredding the leaves.

Dendroclimatology and Prehistoric Rainfall

Rose, Dean, and Robinson (1981) conducted the dendroclimatological analysis for Arroyo Hondo, reconstructing spring and annual precipitation for the Arroyo Hondo area from A.D. 1290 through 1450 (see their tables 21 and 22). Rose and his colleagues found that for their entire study period, A.D. 985 through 1970, the estimated mean annual rainfall was 338.8 millimeters (13.34 inches), with a standard deviation of 54.9 millimeters (2.16 inches), while spring rainfall had an estimated mean of 106.9 millimeters (4.21 inches) and a standard deviation of 46.0 millimeters (1.81 inches). Their tables clearly show that precipitation in the Arroyo Hondo region varied widely during prehistoric times, as it does now, with both exceptionally moist and unusually dry years or springs seen in the sequence. The isolated dry years may have posed some problems, but they were not nearly so threatening as a series of such years. In order to segregate climate trends of several years' duration, Rose and his colleagues (1981:92) converted the yearly spring and annual precipitation estimates into departure values that reflect time intervals of 10 years, as shown in figures 4 and 5.

Several significant trends are apparent from the figures. The early years of the pueblo, A.D. 1295 to 1335, were a moist phase, with both spring and annual precipitation consistently above the average (Rose, Dean, and Robinson 1981:106). These favorable conditions might well explain why such an inhospitable area was colonized at all and why the pueblo grew so extensively at this time (Schwartz 1980:xi). In contrast, the period between 1335 and 1400 saw much variability in rainfall and several dry phases, including 1335–1345, 1360–1370, 1375–1380, and 1395–1400. Rainfall shot above the mean between 1400 and 1420, but declined precipitously thereafter until 1425, a drought period which coincides with the abandonment of the pueblo (Schwartz 1980:xv).

Temperature Past and Present

There is no information on prehistoric temperature comparable to the precipitation record reconstructed by Rose and his colleagues, but their work with tree rings and climate suggests that the temperatures of the past were similar to modern ones. Specifically, the pueblo's inhabitants must have seen a pleasant but not always benevolent climate. Today, the Arroyo Hondo area enjoys warm summer days that rarely exceed 90 degrees Fahrenheit, but the thermometer often drops into the 50s at night. During the winter, temperatures nearly always rise above freezing in the day, usually reaching the low 40s, but after sunset they fall into the 20s and lower. The same wide variation between day and night temperatures occurs during the spring and fall as well (Kelley 1980:36): in May, daytime temperatures can reach 70 degrees Fahrenheit, but frost and snow are still a threat; likewise, September temperatures range between 60 or 70 degrees Fahrenheit during the day and around 40 degrees at night, but may fall below freezing (Kelley 1973:23–24).

During both the spring and fall, frost is highly erratic, which has important implications for farmers. The date of the last killing frost (measured as temperatures of 32 degrees Fahrenheit or less) varies in the spring by 48 days, with April 7 as the earliest date recorded at the Santa Fe weather station and May 25 as the latest (Tuan et al. 1973:95). The first killing frost in the fall is even more variable, with a recorded range of 66 days—September 3 to November 8 (Tuan et al. 1973:93).

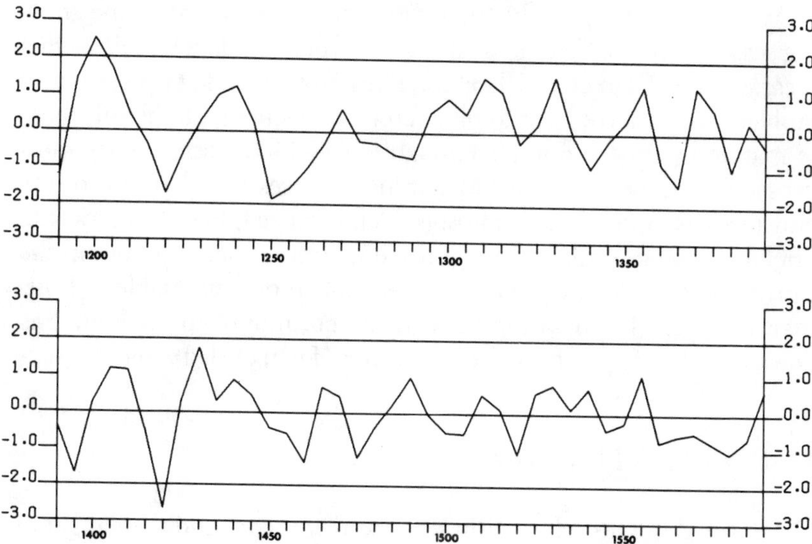

Fig. 4. Reconstruction of spring precipitation for the Arroyo Hondo area, A.D. 1190 to 1590 (reproduced from Rose, Dean, and Robinson 1981).

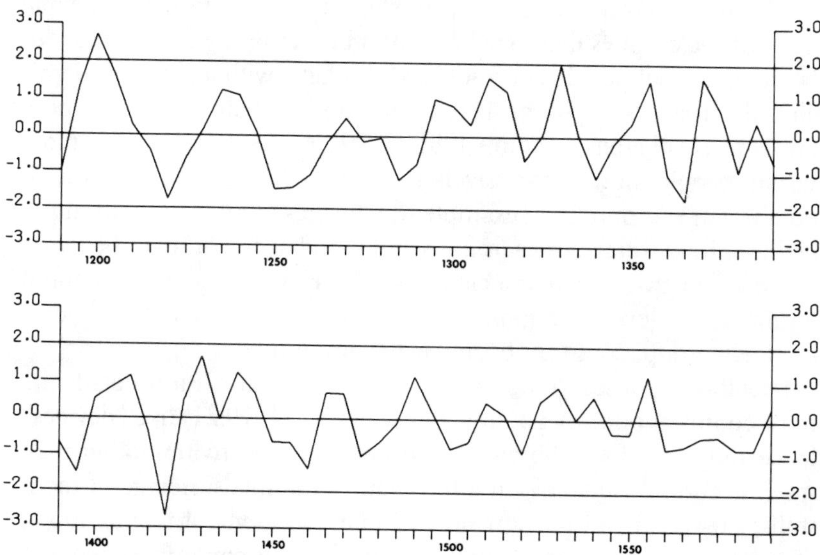

Fig. 5. Reconstruction of twelve-month precipitation for the Arroyo Hondo area, A.D. 1190 to 1590 (reproduced from Rose, Dean, and Robinson 1981).

As a result of the great fluctuations in spring and fall frosts, the growing season at Santa Fe ranges all the way from 113 days to 209, with a mean of 164 (Tuan et al. 1973:95). The Arroyo Hondo farmers' major problem would have been to plant crops early enough to permit them to mature by the fall but late enough to avoid frost losses. They must occasionally have lost crops to untimely freezes at either end of the growing season, but because frost is often localized, the damage would not have been as uniform as that resulting from drought. Crops in the canyon bottom, for example, were probably more vulnerable to frosts than those on the mesa top because of cool mountain air funneling down into the canyon from the mountains (Tuan et al. 1973:69–70).

LIFE DURING LEAN TIMES

Given the droughts reflected in the tree-ring record and the danger of frosts and flash floods, it is inevitable that the Arroyo Hondoans occasionally suffered through lean periods. Since their resources were clearly limited during the best of times, one wonders how they coped with the worst.

Minnis (1981) has proposed a model for the way in which people deal with lean times that may be helpful in examining Arroyo Hondo. He suggests that people confront food shortages with a series of hierarchically arranged responses, beginning with less inclusive ones—those involving small groups (Minnis 1981:23–29). As the stress becomes more severe, people move progressively to more inclusive responses, which involve larger groups. For example, the first response to drought might be more food storage in each household, and as the drought becomes worse, a kin group such as a clan might begin storing food in a central location. The levels of response included in Minnis's model are household, kin group, community, and extracommunity.

Specific responses to food stress are diverse, but Minnis details the most common ones, beginning with Colson's (1979:21) five "devices" for dealing with food shortages: diversification of activities rather than specialization or reliance on a few plants or animals; storage of foodstuffs; storage of and transmission of information about famine foods; conversion of surplus into durable valuables that could be stored and traded for food in an emergency; and cultivation of social relationships to allow one to tap resources of other regions (Colson 1979:21, cited in

Minnis 1981:41). Minnis (1981:51–52) also catalogues a variety of other responses, including conservation of food supplies; splitting the community into small, temporary foraging groups; placing a disproportionate share of the burden on certain groups within the community, such as the young or very old; regional economic specialization; raiding and warfare; and changes in ritual and ceremonial activity that may help to redistribute food.

Minor Food Shortages at Arroyo Hondo Pueblo

During Arroyo Hondo Pueblo's first 30 years, its inhabitants probably faced only minor food shortages. At this time, the region enjoyed above average precipitation, as shown in figures 4 and 5, permitting them to dry-farm the mesa top as well as the canyon floor. In these two locations, they could have raised a little more than their annual caloric needs, as estimated previously.

Even during this bountiful period, the pueblo people probably had to contend with several types of stress. The region would have been vulnerable to the flash floods and untimely frosts described earlier, and occasionally its annual precipitation fell below 355.6 millimeters (14 inches). The frosts and floods likely were localized phenomena, affecting only a portion of the fields: the frosts, for example, might have struck parts of the canyon, depending on topography and patterns of air movements; and floods might have torn away the topsoil only of those mesa fields most vulnerable to erosion. These sediments, in turn, might have been dumped on some of the canyon lands located near the mouths of erosion gullies. An extraordinarily large flood could have washed out fields and plants throughout the canyon, but since most of these calamities were localized, only a portion of the community would have suffered losses.

One solution to these minor stresses may have been diversification, Colson's (1979:21) first device for dealing with food shortages. If the Arroyo Hondo farmers planted on both the mesa top and the canyon bottom, they would have had a hedge against localized disasters.

Stockpiling was another possible solution. The Tewa Pueblos of San Juan tried to prepare for lean times by growing enough food for two years during one season. However, because the northern Rio Grande is such a marginal area, they never succeeded in raising any more than a one-month surplus (Ford 1968a:161–62) beyond their annual needs. Arroyo Hondo's inhabitants might have amassed a comparable modest reserve. Utilizing both canyon and mesa-top lands, they could have produced a little more than their annual caloric requirement, as estimated in the previous chapter. If they consumed roughly 75 percent of their harvest in one year, they would have had enough corn for several months the next. Such a reserve, although modest, might have been adequate to make up for losses to frost or flash floods. With these extra rations, they might have had enough to see them through the year to the following harvest, particularly if they tried to conserve food.

The Arroyo Hondoans might also have collected more intensively in the late summer and fall following a poor season in order to prepare for the lean winter ahead. If the calamities had been localized, wild resource productivity would probably not have been significantly affected, and the flood or frost victims might have been able to gather more weedy annual seeds or yucca and prickly pear fruits than usual. The estimates made earlier indicate that none of the wild resources was especially bountiful, but more food could be had by collecting over a larger area. For example, within 2 kilometers of the pueblo, the prickly pear harvest might have been a little over 2,000 kilograms, whereas it could have been almost 9,000 kilograms within a 4-kilometer radius. Nevertheless, the additional plant foods picked up through a wider net would have represented a small contribution to the entire pueblo's diet, consisting of no more than a few percent of the annual caloric needs. For a few families, however, the additional food may have compensated for the crop losses.

Another solution would have been increased collecting during the summer following a poor year. Living on a meager harvest, the flood or frost victims may not have had enough food to see them through to the next, and they might have tried to restock their empty storerooms with wild plants such as Indian rice grass that ripen in early or midsummer. They might also have tried to compensate for crop losses through more intensive hunting, for example, by setting up snares and traps for small game more frequently than in good years or by organizing more expeditions to bag deer or antelope.

Finally, hard-hit families might have been assisted by other groups in the community. For instance, they may have received food from kinsmen or through community-wide ceremonials or rituals involving redistribution (Ford 1972:12–14).

The other minor stress that the Arroyo Hondo people faced during their first 30 years was an occasional dry season. When precipitation fell below average, especially if it did so in the spring, the crop yields probably declined. But rainfall is not as localized as flash floods and frosts, so the effects of its absence would have been widespread. However, not all fields would have been equally desiccated: the dry-farmed mesa-top fields would have suffered greater crop losses than the less vulnerable canyon fields watered by the Arroyo Hondo stream.

One mechanism for dealing with these occasional dry years was to diversify the fields as described above, planting both in the canyon and on the mesa. The lower fields, watered by the Arroyo Hondo stream, would probably have continued to yield a good harvest despite the drop in rainfall. But even if each family planted in both locations, the effects of a dry year would still have been more widespread than those of untimely frost or a flash flood.

The stored surpluses discussed above would have been another mechanism for coping with food shortages during dry years. The small cushion afforded by a one- or two-months' supply of food could have been adequate since a single dry year would probably not have meant major crop losses. The amount of moisture stored in the soil would have been relatively high, permitting plant growth even in the face of poor rains. A good example of this is recent farming in the Arroyo Hondo area. During the first half of this century, corn and beans were raised on the mesa top even though annual rainfall occasionally dropped below 355.6 millimeters (14 inches). Dry-farming was not abandoned until the 1950s, when a severe drought struck the area (Kelley 1980:33).

Another tack that the Arroyo Hondoans might have taken was to collect wild foods more intensively during a dry year and the following summer, as described above, but this approach would not have been as satisfactory as it was in the earlier case of localized calamities. Since most if not all of the community was affected by a drought, the wild resources would have had to go farther, so that the per-capita addition to the diet could not have been especially large. In addition, wild plant foods and game animals would also have been affected by a dry season and so would have been less abundant than normal.

Major Food Stresses

Beginning about 1335, the people of Arroyo Hondo faced a series of major droughts that must have created serious food shortages. The periods of three or more dry years noted above were significantly different from the short dry spells of the earlier decades. Over the course of several such years, the entire area would have gradually become desiccated, with all plant and animal resources dwindling. The surpluses of previous years would have been quickly exhausted, and opportunities to replenish food stocks would have lessened with each ensuing dry year. Both the magnitude of the stress and the number of people affected would have been far greater than in the minor calamities of the first three decades of Arroyo Hondo Pueblo's life.

At the onset of a drought such as the one beginning in 1335, the Arroyo Hondoans probably adjusted as they had during the earlier single dry years. Their small surplus, along with additional gathered resources, may have made up for crop losses. By the second or third year, though, they would have found themselves in a downward spiral. Eventually they would have had to abandon dry-farming on the mesa top and concentrate their fields in the canyon. With sufficient water, they could have raised a large share of their food there, as calculated in chapter 3. However, as the drought continued, the water table would have dropped, the discharge from the Arroyo Hondo springs would have dwindled, and the snow that supplied the Arroyo Hondo headwaters would have diminished. It is impossible to calculate the stream's prehistoric water level because of uncertainties about the depth of sediments in the canyon and other factors described in the previous chapter. The canyon carried a sizable stream during droughts in the nineteenth century, as noted earlier, and this may have been the case during the fourteenth century as well. Faunal remains dating from A.D. 1330 to 1345 included three birds that live in aquatic environments: the American coot (cf. *Fulica americana*), a possible loon (?*Gavia* sp.), and two long-billed curlews (cf. *Numenius americanus*) (Lang and Harris 1984:37). However, faunal samples dating from the later part of this sequence, A.D. 1340–45, included no aquatic species, suggesting that the canyon may have been relatively dry in the 1340s (Lang and Harris 1984:37), while those dating between A.D. 1345 and 1370 again produced aquatic birds, including three geese, a coot, and a duck (Lang and Harris 1984:40).

Even if water were relatively ample in the canyon, the Arroyo Hondoans would have been hard pressed during droughts. For example, if the crop yields from canyon lands were as high as those during the wet phase, the population still would barely have satisfied its annual caloric needs, let alone produced a surplus. As shown in table 4, Arroyo

Hondo farmers could have raised between 200 and 280 million calories in corn if they cultivated all arable land in the canyon up to 4 kilometers away from the pueblo. The upper figure, based on a yield of 700 kilograms per hectare, represents 96 percent of the annual caloric requirement for a population of 400; whereas the lower figure, based on a yield of 500 kilograms per hectare, represents about 68 percent of the requirement.

However, these figures almost certainly overestimate Arroyo Hondo's harvests during droughts. Even if water flowed through the canyon consistently through the summer, all the fields may not have received equal or adequate shares of it. With the decline in stored soil moisture and drop in the water table, it seems very likely that some fields were not adequately watered, resulting in lowered crop yields. In addition, Arroyo Hondo farmers probably lost a larger percentage of their crop to frost and the other calamities to which the canyon is prone because they no longer had the hedge of the less vulnerable mesa-top fields. Moreover, with all of the canyon lands in cultivation, soil fertility and crop yields would soon have declined. Fallowing or rotating bean crops with corn would have helped to restore the soil, but would have required the use of even larger tracts of the canyon.

As the corn harvests declined, most of the wild resources would have diminished too. The weedy annuals normally collected along field margins and in fallow fields would probably have been less abundant for several reasons. First, with a scarcity of arable land in the canyon, farmers may have set aside fewer areas for useful wild plants and probably limited fallow, as noted above. Some weedy annuals may have grown on the abandoned mesa-top fields, but with poor rains and dry soils they would have been sparse. Purslane plants (*Portulaca retusa*), for example, "derive moisture from the normally predictable summer or fall rains, but should the rains be either inappropriately timed, or meager in amount, stands of *Portulaca* plants could be much reduced in density" (Bohrer 1980:272–73). Other annuals would likewise have been at the mercy of the rains for successful germination and growth.

However, under certain circumstances weedy plants may have been relatively abundant and provided food even when crops were meager. For example, they could have flourished during years when summer rains were good but the spring had been exceptionally dry. Crops probably perished as seedlings under these conditions, but the weedy annuals could have waited until the rains came. As opportunists, they can grow at any time during the frost-free season (Bohrer 1980:267), and as a result, they could have taken advantage of July precipitation, providing a crop of greens and later seeds.

The other wild plant resources would have been affected by dry soil and meager rains to varying degrees as well. Recent studies in southern New Mexico suggest that a major drought may severely limit plant cover. Herbel, Ares, and Wright (1972:1091) found that on a grassland, the Jornada Experimental Range, the total herbaceous cover during the 1950s' drought declined to only 29 percent of its previous level. In addition, drought discourages flowering and fruiting in many perennial plants, such as Indian rice grass (Bohrer 1980:277; Adams 1980:44).

As the plant cover diminished, animal populations would have declined as well. Fertility probably dropped, while mortality almost certainly rose as forage and water became scarce. Mule deer reproduction, for example, is sensitive to environmental conditions; when food is limited, fertility declines and stillbirths become common (Klein 1970: 32–33). Antelope are also affected by the conditions of their range, and when forage diminishes, the herds disperse into smaller, more widely scattered groups (Buechner 1950a:264). As a result, hunters probably had a more difficult time bringing home meat in dry times than during the moist phase.

Finally, in addition to all of these problems, the people of Arroyo Hondo may have had to contend with the ecological consequences of their 30 years' intensive hunting and collecting in the area. For example, they probably thinned the forest early on by cutting timber for construction and firewood. Consequently, with each succeeding decade, they would have had to walk farther and search harder for firewood and construction materials. In addition, pinyon nuts and juniper berries would have been less abundant as trees were felled. Hunters may also have thinned some of the wildlife populations during the early years of the pueblo. For example, mule deer remains were most abundant in the earliest deposits (ca. 1300–1320) of the ruin; after this they were reduced by early hunters (Lang and Harris 1984:49) and were probably affected by the drought of 1335–1345.

Responses to Major Food Stresses

While calculating how much corn and wild resources were lost to drought is impossible, it is obvious that by the second or third year of a dry spell, the Arroyo Hondoans would have had to turn to new mechanisms in order to get by. As noted above, the surpluses of good years would long since have been exhausted. The canyon would probably have been producing a harvest, but it was almost certainly below predrought levels and surely was not enough to see the pueblo through a full year to the next harvest.

The people of Arroyo Hondo probably tried to solve their food shortages through involving the household, kin group, and community. One solution was to collect more intensively, as they no doubt did during short dry spells. But because of the effects of drought, many wild resources would no longer have been available, and gathering would have been limited to only the most reliable wild plant resources—the ones that demonstrate what Bohrer (1975b:3) calls "true seasonality." Such plants bear fruit at a particular time of year regardless of the vagaries of the weather, in contrast to plants with "qualified" seasonality, which fruit at a specific time of year but only when environmental conditions reach a given threshold, or with "shifting" seasonality, which mature at any time when temperature and moisture conditions can sustain growth (Bohrer 1975b:3).

Probably the most reliable of the true seasonal plants in the Arroyo Hondo area were the cacti. "These plants are so well-adapted to the vicissitudes of desert weather that they are rarely overcome by drought, and often seem to flower and fruit under the most adverse conditions" (Bohrer 1980:284). As a result, the Arroyo Hondoans probably could have harvested a crop of prickly pear fruits every year; and gathering beyond their normal collecting areas, they could have increased their harvests and compensated for some of their crop losses. The most promising areas would have been those west and southwest of the pueblo, where they were unlikely to encounter other people. In addition, they would have found the cactus pads or joints available year-round, with the tender new pads of the spring probably being a welcome relief as stored supplies began to run low.

Like the prickly pear, the cholla cactus would have continued to fruit annually during droughts. Its woody fruits and stems are not very palatable, but its young, fleshy buds could have been collected in the spring. The hedgehog and pincushion cacti may have been equally reliable through droughts, but because these plants are so sparsely scattered, they could not have been a significant source of food.

In contrast to the cacti, pinyon nuts, acorns, and banana yucca fruits are "qualified" seasonal plants and could not be expected to fruit during droughts (Bohrer 1975b:3; 1980:247). For example, Lange (1959:145) observed that in the Cochiti area, "drought in recent years has resulted in poor harvests" of pinyon nuts.

The only other plant foods in the Arroyo Hondo area that could be depended upon during droughts may have been those growing in the canyon. As noted above, weedy annuals probably grew in the fields or along their margins, but it is very difficult to estimate how much food they could have provided. Chokecherries, discussed in the previous chapter, and currants (*Ribes* sp.) probably continued to fruit during poor times, but their contribution to the Arroyo Hondo diet could not have been very large since they are not particularly abundant.

As the Arroyo Hondoans collected more intensively during severe droughts, they probably added famine foods to their diet. A number of wild plants might have been reliable enough to provide additional food at such times. Sedges (*Cyprus esculentus*), bulrushes (*Scirpus olneyi*), and rushes (*Juncus saximontanus*), all sources of seeds and roots, may have been growing in the canyon during this period. The faunal remains from the drought years, described above, suggest that the canyon might have been wet enough to support a riparian community, but the total contribution from these plants must have been relatively small. The wild grasses that continued to fruit even during drought were another potential emergency food. Game not normally eaten, such as rats, mice, small birds, and reptiles, might have served as starvation food as well.

Under extreme conditions, the Arroyo Hondoans might even have turned to unpalatable and seemingly inedible substances such as bark, leaf fibers, and corncobs. The people of the Salmon Ruin, an early pueblo in northwestern New Mexico, apparently did so, since several coprolites from the site contained juniper bark, yucca fibers, and small pieces of maize cob (Bohrer 1980:241). In addition, they apparently chewed on yucca leaves and native grasses, as suggested by quids found at the site (Bohrer 1980:241). Although such unappetizing alternative foods offered additional calories, it is impossible to estimate how many they might have contributed.

Community-Wide Responses to Food Stress. As drought and erratic rainfall became common, Arroyo Hondo Pueblo may have moved to more inclusive responses involving larger groups, as Minnis (1981:23) proposed. However, since we have no information on the pueblo's organization during its first three decades, it is difficult to suggest ways in which it might have changed after 1335. Prior to this time, the pueblo was obviously sufficiently well integrated to allow 400 or more people to live together as a community, and the ruin contains several kivas dating prior to 1335, which bespeaks some kind of religious unification. Later, however, under the stress of repeated dry years, the community may have become more highly integrated. A single body might have begun to make more and more decisions about food production and storage—areas that previously would have been the private affairs of each household. The community might have also acted as a unit to redistribute canyon land when the mesa fields had to be abandoned.

Minnis (1981:257) suggests that such increasing community integration can take one of two forms. First, it may involve hierarchical changes: decision making may become more centralized, as is the case for some of the modern Pueblos. (For example, among many Eastern Pueblos, a small group of individuals controls many of the decisions about ceremonials, land use, and water regulation [Minnis 1981:257].) Alternatively, increased sociopolitical unity can be horizontal, and in the Southwest this takes the form of a "complex interweaving system of sodalities" (Minnis 1981:258). These associations, which cut across the community, perform specific ritual functions and participate in decision making.

If such integration had developed at Arroyo Hondo Pueblo, whether horizontally or hierarchically, it could have had important implications for managing famines. An administrative body or a group of sodalities planning for the whole community's future would probably have prepared the pueblo better than could each individual household making decisions for its own needs. Such an organization might, for instance, have prompted farmers to plant beyond their own requirements in order to fill a communal store room; it could have coordinated check-dam irrigation in the canyon to assure a better distribution of water across the fields; it could also have encouraged more intensive collecting and hunting.

Although better integration would probably have improved Arroyo Hondo's chance of survival, the group could instead have disintegrated if food shortages were severe and extended. Numerous ethnographic examples indicate that people retract and hoard food during major shortages, even though they are most generous during minor ones. Sahlins (1972:214) described the situation in the following terms:

> Probably every primitive organization has its breaking-point, or at least its turning-point. Every one might see the time when cooperation is overwhelmed by the scale of disaster and chicanery becomes the order of the day. The range of assistance contracts progressively to the family level; perhaps even these bonds dissolve and, washed away, reveal an inhuman, yet most human, self-interest. Moreover, by the same measure that the circle of charity is compressed that of "negative reciprocity" is potentially expanded. People who helped each other in normal times and through the first stages of disaster display now indifference to each others' plight, if they do not exacerbate a mutual downfall by guile, haggle, and theft. Put another way, the whole sectoral scheme of reciprocities is altered, compressed: sharing is confined to the innermost sphere of solidarity and all else is devil take the hindmost.

Sahlins (1972:273) also observed that in Melanesia, under the stress of famine, the individual household becomes more tightly integrated, while the larger kin group atomizes. "This atomization tended to be most strong where food was most desperately short." Stevenson (1894:12) observed a similar pattern at Zia Pueblo:

> Each year a period comes, just before the harvest time, when no more pottery is required by their Indian neighbors, and the Sia must deal out their food in such limited portions that the elders go hungry in order to satisfy the children. When starvation threatens there is no thought for the children of the clan, but the head of each household looks to the wants of its own, and there is apparent indifference to the sufferings of neighbors.

In addition, with semi-starvation and starvation, people undergo dramatic psychological changes that make it difficult for them to function socially. In a classic study of human starvation, Keys and his colleagues (1950:835–36) found that volunteer subjects, after several months of a very low-calorie diet, became emotionally unstable, depressed, apathetic, and highly irritable. Outbursts of temper and sulking were common, and a few men had strong urges toward violence.

> Social initiative especially, and sociability in general, underwent a remarkable change. The men became reluctant to plan activities, to make decisions, and to participate in group activities . . . . They spent more and more time alone. It became "too much trouble" or "too tiring" to have to contend with other people . . . . Attempts to keep the interpersonal relationships tolerable, if not gracious, often produced an uncomfortable and emotionally charged atmosphere in which politeness was artificial and social interaction stilted. (Keyes et al. 1950:836–37)

Accounts of natural famines describe the same type of asocial and pathological behavior (Keyes et al. 1950:786–818).

At Arroyo Hondo Pueblo too, social bonds may have broken down if the community had been severely stressed. Families may have withdrawn from the larger social units and kept food to themselves, and at times even family bonds may have disintegrated, leaving each individual to fend for him- or herself. It is more likely, though, that other strategies for dealing with the food shortages were attempted before the pueblo reached such dire straits.

Regional Approaches to Food Stress. Yet another solution might have been for Arroyo Hondo to look to its neighbors for relief. For example, the pueblo's inhabitants might have accumulated imperishables, such as shell pendants and turquoise, during good times, or they might have specialized in some craft item, such as pottery. These items could then be traded for food during crises.

However, such mechanisms are useful only where famines are localized and trading partners are not also devastated by food shortages (Minnis 1981:48–49). Such would not have been the case in the northern Rio Grande area, where the droughts were widespread phenomena, so that Arroyo Hondo Pueblo would have found most of its neighbors with little or no food to trade.

Nevertheless, pueblos located on large, permanent waterways such as the Santa Fe River and the Rio Grande probably fared slightly better than their neighbors on small, potentially ephemeral streams such as the Arroyo Hondo. The Rio Grande pueblos could still have irrigated their fields even during severe drought. In addition, they probably suffered fewer losses to frost because they were located at a lower elevation. It is hard to imagine, however, that they were affluent or even had much surplus during any period. As noted earlier, in the nineteenth century San Juan Pueblo, located at the confluence of the Rio Grande and the Chama River, never managed to produce more than a one-month surplus (Ford 1968a:161). It is unlikely that the fourteenth-century pueblos on permanent streams traded away much food during droughts; furthermore, there is no archaeological evidence of any economic specialization at Arroyo Hondo Pueblo nor any signs of additional trading during the period after 1335 (Lang and Harris 1984:63).

Another regional response might have been to take a neighbor's meager food stores by force (Minnis 1981:52), but this was apparently not attempted either. There is no evidence of raiding or warfare at Arroyo Hondo. The pueblo has no obvious fortifications, and it is not in a strategic location for defense. The grave goods accompanying its burials show no concern with warfare. Of the 111 burials excavated there, only two included weapons: an adult male, who apparently held an important ceremonial post was buried with four projectile points and an axe as well as a raven skin, eagle's claws, and other ritual paraphernalia; and a second adult male was found with a single obsidian point (Palkovich 1980:162). The bodies likewise showed little evidence of warfare or violence (Palkovich 1980:21). Only one male suffered from an embedded point, while another exhibited a healed fracture (Palkovich 1980:168). Both conditions could have resulted from accidents rather than conflict.

Probably only one regional response offered the people of Arroyo Hondo any relief from food shortages: when conditions became unbearable, they apparently abandoned their pueblo and joined friends and relatives at the villages on permanent streams. By cultivating kinship and friendship ties during better times, they may have been able to call upon their social network during severe droughts. Arroyo Hondo's inhabitants may have stayed in these communities for brief periods, or they may have joined them permanently. Archaeological evidence suggests that most of the population did indeed abandon the pueblo during the 1340s (Schwartz 1980:xvi); it appears that from 1340 until about 1370 only a very small portion of the town was occupied. With the advent of somewhat better conditions in 1370, the population began to expand once again, but it never reached its former size (Schwartz 1980:xvi).

Food Resources and a Small Population

As Arroyo Hondo's population declined in the 1340s, the remaining inhabitants would still have faced the problems arising from drought, but shortages might not have been as severe since the per-capita quantity of arable land and wild resources could have increased. This probably was not the case, however. The Arroyo Hondo resource base was almost certainly shrinking through the drought period of 1330–45, and it probably did not return to moist-phase levels until the next century. Since rainfall was erratic and droughts frequent during this period, it is hard to imagine that plant and animal resources were as abundant as they had been earlier. The maize harvests would certainly have been smaller because farming would have been restricted to the canyon for much of this period. Even during wetter years, such as 1370–75, dry-farming may have been considered too big a risk because most of the recent past had been so dry. Planting only in the canyon, the Arroyo Hondo farmers would have had less arable land and probably lower yields than during the moist phase.

Table 18 offers estimates for the potential corn harvests of this period. The crops are calculated for yield values ranging from 200 to 500 kilograms per hectare and for areas of land within the canyon ranging from 1 to 4 kilometers from the pueblo. The harvests are expressed in kilograms and in calories, and as a percent of the community's annual caloric requirement for populations of 100, 200, and 300 people.

The figures suggest that a population of 300 could have produced a large share of its food in the canyon if yields were not dramatically affected by the drought and did not fall below 500 kilograms per hectare which was used earlier as the low yield value for calculating maize crops during the moist phase. As can be seen in the table, 300 people could have raised enough corn to satisfy about 90 percent of their energy needs if they farmed all of the canyon land up to 4 kilometers from the pueblo. After seed corn and storage losses were subtracted from this total, the crop would not have been bountiful, but it probably could have supplied over 75 percent of the caloric needs. In order to plant beans as well and to allow some fields to lie fallow, the Arroyo Hondoans would have had to plant well beyond the 4-kilometer mark, but as they moved farther away from the springs and toward lower elevations, water for the fields may have become scarcer and productivity may accordingly have declined.

TABLE 18.
Potential maize harvest on canyon lands during dry periods.

Km from Pueblo	*Arable Land (ha)*	*Kilograms*	*Calories (millions)*	*Percentage of requirement for Population of:* 100	200	300
Yield = 200 kg/ha						
0–1	20	4,000	14.4	19.7	9.9	6.6
0–2	53	10,600	38.2	52.3	26.2	17.4
0–3	77	15,400	55.4	75.9	37.9	25.3
0–4	111	22,200	79.9	109.5	54.7	36.5
Yield = 300 kg/ha						
0–1	20	6,000	21.6	29.6	14.8	9.9
0–2	53	15,900	57.2	78.4	39.2	26.1
0–3	77	23,100	83.2	114.0	57.0	38.0
0–4	111	33,300	119.9	164.2	82.1	54.7
Yield = 400 kg/ha						
0–1	20	8,000	28.8	39.5	19.7	13.2
0–2	53	21,200	76.3	104.5	52.3	34.8
0–3	77	30,800	110.9	151.9	76.0	50.6
0–4	111	44,400	159.8	218.9	109.5	73.0
Yield = 500 kg/ha						
0–1	20	10,000	36.0	49.3	24.7	16.4
0–2	53	26,500	95.4	130.7	65.3	43.6
0–3	77	38,500	138.5	189.9	94.9	63.3
0–4	111	55,500	199.8	273.7	136.8	91.2

NOTE: The caloric value of maize is estimated at 3,600 calories per kilogram; see appendix C. The annual caloric requirement for 100 people is estimated at 73 million; for 200 people, 146 million; and for 300 people, 219 million; see appendix A.

If the community of 300 produced 75 percent of its diet by raising corn, the remainder would have had to come from beans and wild products. The former probably supplied no more than a small percentage of the diet, as estimated in chapter 2, but wild plants and game might have made up the difference. The most reliable wild plant under drought conditions, the prickly pear, might have been able to supply up to almost 9 percent of the caloric needs, as estimated in table 19.

Weed seeds from fallow fields might have contributed about the same quantity of calories. For example, if one-fourth of the fields, or roughly

TABLE 19.
Potential harvest of prickly pear fruit in the Arroyo Hondo area during drought periods.

Km from Pueblo	*Estimated Hectares of Uncultivated Land*	*Kilograms*	*Calories (millions)*	*Percentage of Annual Caloric Requirement for Population of:* 100	200	300
0–1	307	614	1.3	1.8	0.9	0.6
0–2	1,065	2,130	4.6	6.3	3.2	2.1
0–3	2,324	4,648	10.1	13.8	6.9	4.6
0–4	4,426	8,852	19.3	26.4	13.2	8.8

NOTE: Prickly pear yield is estimated at 2 kg/ha, and its caloric value at 2,175 calories/kg (see appendix C). The annual caloric requirement for 100 people is estimated at 73 million calories; for 200 people, 146 million; and for 300 people, 219 million (see appendix A).

25 hectares, were left fallow, as suggested above and in chapter 2, the Arroyo Hondoans might have collected from these fields between 1,250 and 7,500 kilograms of seeds if the yields ranged from 50 to 300 kilograms per hectare. Under drought conditions, however, yields were probably well below the maximum figure. If they had been 150 kilograms per hectare, 3,750 kilograms or 12.75 million calories could have been gathered, representing about 5.8 percent of the diet. Additional wild seeds could have been collected from weeds growing in the cultivated fields, but these probably produced no more than 10 kilograms per hectare, as suggested earlier, and their contribution to the diet would have been little more than 1 percent. Throughout the summer months, the Arroyo Hondoans could also have gathered wild greens from the fallow fields, but these would not have represented a large share of calories.

Game might have contributed the remainder of the diet; however, it is very difficult to estimate how much was available during poor years. The most reliable game at these times may have been rabbits, hares, and other small mammals. Although each individual offers little meat, these animals breed rapidly, so the populations would quickly recover from the effects of severe droughts and could also sustain a high level of predation. Moreover, during dry years rabbits and hares would have been particularly abundant in the canyon because of its relatively richer vegetation, and by killing the animals the farmers would have served the additional purpose of helping to save their crops from these voracious feeders. Hares and rabbits are easy to catch and demand only limited hunting skill. If the Arroyo Hondoans hunted them intensively, increasing the culling rate from one-fourth to one-half of the excess individuals, their kill might have been higher than those during the earlier, moist phase. The number of hares and rabbits available to the pueblo may have remained constant, or it could even have increased if animals from a large area were attracted to the canyon. If as many as 800 hares—the maximum estimate for moist conditions—were trapped, they could have contributed about 1 percent of the diet, and with very intensive hunting this might have increased to 2 percent. By also hunting cottontail rabbits and other small mammals, such as gophers and prairie dogs, the Arroyo Hondoans might have obtained 5 percent or more of their diet in this form.

Turkeys were another food source that might have been hunted more intensively with profitable results. Because the birds are easy to kill, even for unskilled hunters, the pueblo people may have hunted them rigorously during poor years. However, the flocks are vulnerable and probably declined after several years of intense predation. In addition, their numbers probably fell dramatically during poor years, when their major foods became scarce. The turkeys' contribution to the diet may therefore not have been any more than 1 or 2 percent.

As a large animal, the mule deer would have been an excellent source of meat if its numbers were not dramatically affected by the drought. If the deer population maintained a density of eight animals per square kilometer, for example, the estimated minimum value for the moist phase as shown in table 13, Arroyo Hondo hunters might have taken more than 1,000 of them by hunting intensively. This would have represented 5 to 6 percent of the diet. But as noted earlier, the deer herds may have been decimated in the early part of the fourteenth century and never fully recovered (Lang and Harris 1984:141).

These very rough estimates suggest that the Arroyo Hondoans might have been able to survive under drought conditions, but that resources would have been just barely adequate during the less severe years of the dry phase. There would have been no margin to cover crop losses to flash floods, frosts, or pests, nor would there have been an adequate surplus to see the community through a very dry summer.

If maize harvests were consistently less than 500 kilograms per hectare for very long, some of the population would probably have had to abandon the village. At a yield of 400 kilograms per hectare, the crop in the canyon covering all of the fields up to 4 kilometers from the pueblo would have totaled no more than 73 percent of the annual caloric requirement for 300 people. After corrections for seed corn and storage losses, it may have been only around 60 percent of the diet, leaving the pueblo's inhabitants to find the remaining 40 percent elsewhere. In light of the above calculations on wild-product availability, it seems that this might have been impossible to do every year.

If maize yields were only 400 kilograms per hectare consistently, the Arroyo Hondo population probably could not have exceeded 200 people. The figures in table 18 suggest that a community of this size could have cultivated enough corn on 4 kilometers of the canyon to satisfy over a year's caloric requirement. To allow land for fallowing and for a bean crop, maize might have been planted in the fields up to 3.5 kilometers from the pueblo. This area would probably have provided over three quarters of the diet, with the remaining 25 percent or so contributed by the bean crop and wild products. With fewer mouths to feed, a community of 200 would have had an easier time accomplishing this than one of 300. Prickly pears, for example, could have provided as much as 13 percent of the diet, as shown in table 19—but food still would not have been ample. During the poorer periods, the community would have been hard pressed, and almost certainly had to resort to even more intensive collecting and to emergency foods.

A population of only 100 people would obviously have found it easier to satisfy all its needs. For example, if maize yields were 400 kilograms per hectare, such a community would have had to cultivate only the lands lying up to 2 kilometers from the pueblo in order to raise enough corn to provide a year's calories. After adjustments for losses and seed corn, this probably amounted to a little less than the annual requirement, but such a harvest could nevertheless have supplied a comfortable cushion for the poorer years because supplementing the diet with wild products would have been easier than for larger groups. The prickly pear crop within a 4-kilometer radius of the pueblo alone could have provided up to 26 percent of the diet. However, during especially bad years, even this small community may have been forced to eat emergency foods. If the corn yield declined to only 200 kilograms per hectare as a result of frost or drought, for instance, the community could have raised only about half of its annual caloric requirement within 2 kilometers of the pueblo. This would encompass 53 hectares, or 0.53 hectare per person, probably about the largest tract of land the community could have cultivated as discussed earlier. The remaining 50 percent of the diet could have been supplied through very intensive collecting and hunting.

It is obviously impossible to estimate Arroyo Hondo Pueblo's food resources and harvests of the period from 1335 to 1400 with any certainty because of the many unknown variables. However, it seems clear that at this time farming became less certain than during earlier periods, while wild resources grew scarcer. Even with a reduced population, the community would have faced some lean years.

Food Distribution and Individual Diets

Everyone undoubtedly suffered hardships at Arroyo Hondo Pueblo during lean times, but different members of the community may have experienced varying kinds and degrees of changes in their diets. Across households and kin groups and even within a single family, individuals probably differed. Some households undoubtedly were more successful than others in farming, gathering, and hunting as a result of individual initiative, skill, and energy or because they had a higher proportion of food producers. Families with several hunters, for example, would have taken more game than others during periods when the inhabitants had to rely heavily on wild resources, while those with a high proportion of women and children may have satisfied most of their needs through intensively collecting prickly pears, greens, and small rodents. In addition, the quantity and types of foods in household stores would have differed because of the localized effects of most natural calamities. Some of these differences among households may have been equalized as the better-endowed families shared with less fortunate kinsmen; the kin group may in fact have pooled and redistributed foods, as suggested earlier.

All kin groups may not have had the same food resources or equivalent quantities of food for their members: for example, some groups may have enjoyed larger harvests because they had access to the best canyon lands. Such differences might have been partially adjusted through rituals and ceremonials involving the redistribution of food (Ford 1972:12–14) or through other forms of community sharing. On the other hand, the wealthier kin groups may have maintained their advantage during bad periods, as suggested earlier. The poorer groups, in fact, may have been the refugees who fled the pueblo.

It is impossible to determine individual diets at Arroyo Hondo from the archaeological evidence, but it seems likely that they varied in type of food and in the quantity of food proportional to body weight. Even within the households, diets were almost certainly not uniform. Most likely food intake differed according to age and sex, as it does now in many societies. For example, Ford (1968a:171, 173) found that at modern San Juan Pueblo, men eat more types and larger quantities of meat than do women and children because they have meat in hunting camps. Children, in turn, eat a greater variety of the plants found near the village because they snack on them while playing. But young children at San Juan and in most nonindustrialized societies eat fewer foods and receive disproportionately smaller shares than older individuals as a result of the weaning practices that will be discussed below.

Dietary Implications of Lean Times

During poor years, Arroyo Hondo's inhabitants must have seen dramatic changes in their diet for short crisis periods as well as alterations and adjustments that lingered for many months. At the height of an acute food shortage, such as might occur in the spring, everyone almost certainly ate fewer calories than under normal circumstances. People may at times even have endured starvation for several days on end or possibly longer, and lower caloric intakes may have become a pattern for months at a time during extended droughts. Through such conservation measures, the Arroyo Hondoans may have stretched their meager stores until new food sources could be had.

The composition of the diet almost certainly changed as well, since the regular food supplies were no longer available in the same amounts. As people hunted and collected more intensively and used a wider range of wild foods, their fare would have become more varied, and they would have relied less on maize.

The composition of meals would in turn have been affected. Depending on how the Arroyo Hondoans chose to utilize their stored foods, the diet may have reflected poor crops for many months or for shorter periods. If they used up their corn stores in the spring, for example, they would have had three or four months of meals consisting only of wild products and possibly beans; but if they carefully rationed their corn supply, they could have eaten it, probably in combination with a large proportion of wild products, throughout the year.

During severe crisis periods, there was most likely yet another change in diet at the pueblo: meals composed of a variety of foods probably gave way to very simple, one- or two-item suppers. For instance, when stored provisions were exhausted in the spring, the Arroyo Hondoans would have been forced to focus on the few wild foods available at this time. They may have devoured roots and tubers for several days or weeks; as the first edible green sprigs appeared, they may have gathered and cooked them. When these were spent, they perhaps feasted on a lucky catch of a few hares until yet another food source appeared. There is no direct evidence at the Arroyo Hondo site of such eating patterns, but the coprolites described earlier from the Salmon Ruin indicate that during famines the inhabitants of this pueblo did indeed consume meals consisting of no more than a couple of items.

Nutrient Implications of Lean Times. The most obvious and immediate effect of lean periods would have been the decline in caloric intake, already discussed. Undoubtedly the nutrient composition of the diet was altered as well, though in less obvious ways; but without precise dietary information, it is possible only to suggest what these changes might have been.

First, the quantity of vitamins and trace elements probably varied widely through the year even in good times. Winter meals would have offered the poorest sources of these micronutrients, since they consisted primarily of a small number of stored foods, notably maize, beans, wild grains, and dried fruits. Good sources of vitamin C, such as fresh greens and fruits, would have been particularly scarce at this time. The richest supply of trace elements and vitamins would probably have been found in meals during the summer and fall, when the greatest variety of foods was available. In poor years, when the diet was less consistent and reliable, such seasonal fluctuations were probably exaggerated. Meals limited to one or two foods were undoubtedly deficient in many essential nutrients.

The protein composition of the diet, which will be considered in more detail later, probably varied widely during poor years. The quantity of protein in meals consisting primarily of game would have been high, but much of it would have been burned for energy if other sources of calories were lacking. When plant foods constituted the bulk of the menu, protein content could have varied from very low to relatively high depending on the plants eaten: meals made up of little more than prickly pear fruit would have offered scant protein, while those of wild grains or nuts could have been rich in it. During severe food shortages, when only one or two foods were available, the biological value of the dietary protein may have been even lower, since the protein value of each food would have been checked by its own limiting amino acid. In contrast, during better times, when a meal consisted of a variety of foods, the various amino acid patterns of the combined plant proteins would have complemented each other to produce more usable protein than was found in any individual plant.

Effects of Dietary Changes. During severe food shortages, all the inhabitants of Arroyo Hondo Pueblo would have lost weight and slowed down their activities. If the crisis extended for more than a few weeks, they would have lost much of their fat reserves and muscle mass and eventually become emaciated. Such crises were probably most common in the late winter and early spring, but by May new food resources would have begun to appear, helping to alleviate hunger.

These periods of deprivation would have been unpleasant but rarely life threatening for adults. Even after two weeks without any food, the healthy adult body suffers no serious impairment of physiological function nor any permanent ill effects (Davidson and Passmore 1969:361). Moreover, the adult body can lose 25 percent of its weight without immediate danger; some people have even survived weight losses of up to 50 percent (Davidson and Passmore 1969:360). And adults recover quickly from short periods of starvation once food is again available (Davidson and Passmore 1969:365).

However, for more vulnerable members of the community, such as the elderly and the young, short bouts of famine would have caused painful suffering and even death. The elderly could not have tolerated semistarvation for long because of poor health, while the young would have been vulnerable due to their relatively high needs for protein and energy, which will be discussed in detail in the next section of this chapter.

In particularly poor years, famine would have persisted longer, with more devastating effects. The adaptable, healthy adults would have continued losing weight and eventually would have suffered major pathological changes such as the destruction of organ tissue (Davidson and Passmore 1969:359). At the same time, their personalities would probably have undergone the dramatic and unpleasant changes described earlier, which would have severely disrupted the community. Death might have been the outcome for adults as well as the elderly and young. However, famines of such magnitude were probably rare, if they ever occurred at the pueblo. It is more likely that the inhabitants would have fled to other communities in search of food before conditions became this severe.

Especially after 1335, probably the most pervasive problem at Arroyo Hondo was chronic undernutrition, punctuated by occasional acute food shortages. In light of the estimates presented here and in chapter 2, it seems highly likely that during this period the pueblo's inhabitants ate a marginally adequate diet, one that sustained them but did not permit optimum health. Consequently, the adults may have been quite lean and less active than in better times. Their resistance to disease would have been lower, and they may have suffered specific nutrient deficiencies such as anemia (Astrand 1979:76–77). In addition, their capacity for physical work may have diminished, with important consequences for the community's food production.

For the elderly, a meager diet probably meant illness and premature death, as it does today in the United States, where a recent survey found that the underweight elderly have higher rates of morbidity and mortality than heavier individuals (Anders 1977, quoted in Watkins 1979:42). If the elderly did die early in times of starvation at Arroyo Hondo, their deaths would have caused sorrow but probably would not have affected the functioning of the community. They most likely played a minimal economic role—although they might have been important in ceremonial life—and their loss would have had little demographic significance, since they probably represented a small fraction of the population and they had already contributed to the next generation.

Chronic undernutrition would also have meant hardship for pregnant and lactating women. With the additional burden of supplying nourishment to a fetus or an infant, they must have been weakened by their poor diets, and reproduction in turn would have been affected. The effect may have been surprisingly minimal, however, since human reproduction is astonishingly efficient even under adverse conditions. "Moderate chronic malnutrition has only a minor effect on fecundity, and the resulting decrease in fertility is very small" (Bongaarts 1980:568). Significant drops in fertility are seen only with severe famine and starvation (Bongaarts 1980:568). Moreover, the women who live on chronically impoverished diets are surprisingly strong: ". . . far from being obviously malnourished weaklings, such women often take a considerable share of the agricultural or other hard labour of the community, in addition to bearing and feeding a torrent of children. And their ability to breast-feed, a feat even more demanding than pregnancy from a nutritional point of view, is outstanding" (Thomson and Hytten 1979:112–13).

In light of modern human reproductive powers, it seems that the fertility rates of Arroyo Hondo Pueblo's inhabitants would not have been significantly affected by their poor diets. But undernutrition would have had a significant impact on the health and survival of the offspring. Young children are the most vulnerable members of a community, sensitive to protein and calorie deficiencies and highly susceptible to the infectious diseases that exacerbate malnutrition.

The Young Child's Diet

It is impossible to determine exactly how children were fed at Arroyo Hondo Pueblo, but some reasonable guesses can be made on ethnographic sources. Hrdlicka (1908:76) noted that the Indians of the Southwest nursed their children until they were "2, 3 or even 4 or more years old . . . . The infant does not live exclusively, however, on the mother's milk, except during the first 3 to 8 months; after this stage which differs in duration with various tribes and circumstances, it receives in addition more or less of the food forming the diet of the mother." Since this diet was probably rich in maize dishes, it is unlikely that the child ever ate large quantities of protein.

More recently, Ford (1968a:709) found that the mothers of San Juan Pueblo begin weaning their babies after about six months, feeding them *atole*, a cornmeal gruel, and diluted portions of other foods. Children under one year of age are forbidden to eat "cold" foods, which include nearly all forms of animal products; and although older children are not formally restricted, in practice they have little access to meat because men consume the largest share of it (Ford 1968a:130, 134). The only special infant foods recorded at historic pueblos are "formulas" given when there was no one to nurse the child. At Isleta, this consisted of chewed pinyon nuts (Parsons 1932:218), while at Zuni, a pap of sweet corn was used (Cushing 1920:575).

The "hot-cold" classification may be a Spanish introduction, but the other practices described above probably have their roots in antiquity, and it seems probable that the people of Arroyo Hondo cared for their children in a similar manner. Even if prehistoric weaning methods differed from those of historic Pueblos in such details as the age at which the process commenced, the weaning diet was almost certainly like that which Ford described, since maize was the staple food.

Protein Requirements of Young Children. Subsisting on a diet like that described above, young children at Arroyo Hondo would have faced several serious problems in satisfying their nutritional requirements. Maize is high in bulk but low in protein, containing only about 9 to 10 percent of low-quality protein (FAO 1970:38). It is an adequate staple for an adult, whose protein requirements are modest but whose energy needs are relatively high; but is likely to be insufficient for a young child, who requires a relatively large quantity of protein but has a meager appetite. According to the Food and Agriculture Organization (FAO/WHO 1973:56–57), an adult's protein needs are about one-fourth to one-third of the requirement for the preschool child by body weight.

The composition of the young child's protein requirements is quite different from the amino acid pattern found in maize, which is strikingly deficient in tryptophan and lysine (see table 20). As a result, the child must eat large quantities of maize in order to satisfy the need for these two essential amino acids. The nutritive value of maize is improved, however, if it is eaten together with a better quality protein, one that compensates for maize's deficiency of tryptophan and lysine and thus allows its other essential amino acids to be more fully utilized. In this case, one does not have to eat as much food in order to satisfy one's protein requirements.

Beans, which are frequently combined with maize in Latin American as well as in Pueblo communities, are an excellent complement to maize, as they are relatively high in tryptophan and lysine. Feeding trials have demonstrated that the optimum combination is 50 percent bean protein and 50 percent maize protein, which is about 70 percent corn and 30 percent beans by weight (Bressani, Valiente, and Tejeda 1962:399). Although Arroyave (1975:15), working in a hospital in Mexico, found that smaller quantities of bean protein (24 percent, to 76

TABLE 20.
Amino acid requirements of children and adults compared with the amino acid content of maize protein.

Essential Amino Acids	*Composition of Maize Protein (mg per gram)*	*Composition of Ideal Protein for 2-Year-Old Child (mg per gram)*	*Composition of Ideal Protein for Adult (mg per gram)*
Isoleucine	37.0	40.0	18.0
Leucine	125.0	70.0	25.0
Lysine	27.0	55.0	22.0
TSAA[a]	35.0	35.0	24.0
TAAA[b]	87.0	60.0	25.0
Threonine	36.0	40.0	13.0
Tryptophan	6.1	10.0	6.5
Valine	48.0	50.0	18.0

NOTE: The total protein content of maize is estimated at 9.5 grams of protein per 100 grams of edible portion (FAO 1970:38). The total protein requirement for a 2-year-old child is estimated at 0.90 grams of ideal protein per kilogram of body weight per day, and for an adult, at 0.55 grams per kilogram of body weight per day (after Arroyave 1975:4, 6, 9).
[a]Total sulfur amino acids (methionine and cystine).
[b]Total aromatic amino acids (phenylalanine and tyrosine).

percent corn protein) could sustain growth in two-year-olds, such a diet would almost certainly be inadequate in a real Latin American village for several reasons (Scrimshaw 1975:19). In this kind of environment, many young children suffer from infectious diseases, which raises their requirement for protein; they are unlikely to receive the vitamin, mineral, and fat supplements Arroyave gave his subjects; and they probably consume their daily allotment of food in two or three meals, rather than in the many small meals used in the study. Unable to eat much at one sitting, they are likely to be short on calories at the end of the day (Scrimshaw 1975:19).

The children of Arroyo Hondo almost certainly lived under conditions of health and hygiene similar to those in rural Latin America today, and in order to meet their nutritional needs, they probably would have required a diet in which beans or a similar food source provided 50 percent of the protein. However, on the basis of the crop estimates presented in the previous chapter, it seems unlikely that they could have eaten the optimum 50:50 ratio of corn to bean protein.

If, on the other hand, the Arroyo Hondoans supplemented their diet with other protein-rich foods, they might have provided young children with an adequate diet. Meat, a high-quality protein, would of course have improved the protein value of a maize dish significantly, but it seems unlikely that young children ate meat consistently or that they received anything but very small portions. However, even a little meat combined with beans so that the two represented 30 percent of the caloric intake would probably have been adequate.

The wild grains that the Arroyo Hondoans ate might also have improved the protein value of the diet. Unfortunately, there is very little information available on the protein and amino acid content of wild seeds and nuts, but those that have been analyzed appear to be more nutritious than beans, as can be seen in table 21. For example, *Chenopodium quinoa*, which is cultivated in South America (Simmonds 1965:231, 234), surpasses beans in lysine and tryptophan. If the *Che-*

TABLE 21.
Protein, tryptophan, and lysine content of beans and various uncultivated foods.

	Grams of Protein per 100 Grams of Edible Portion	*Milligrams of Tryptophan per Gram of Protein*	*Milligrams of Lysine per Gram of Protein*
Phaseolus vulgaris			
Beans	22.1	10.0	72.0
Amaranthus species			
Leaves	4.6	12.3	50.6
Amaranthus hybridus			
Seeds	16.6	8.2	49.6
Chenopodium quinoa			
Seeds	12.0	10.6	107.5
Cyperus esculentus			
Rhyzomes	3.5	10.0	49.9
Opuntia species			
Fruits	1.0	8.2	40.0
Quercus suber			
Nuts	—	10.2	52.0

SOURCE: FAO 1970:40, 48, 60, 102, 114.

nopodium species of the Arroyo Hondo area had a similar amino acid pattern, they could have added considerable protein value to the pueblo's maize dishes. *Amaranthus hybridus*, a native in the Arroyo Hondo area, would also improve a maize diet, even though it does not contain as much lysine and tryptophan as beans.

On the basis of the scant information available, it appears that Arroyo Hondo children could have received adequate protein. However, the diet was probably marginal at best, and may often have failed to satisfy amino acid requirements. For example, whenever maize was supplemented with such low protein foods as prickly pear fruits, the young child may have been deprived.

Protein-Calorie Malnutrition. Although the protein content of their diet was almost certainly marginal, a shortage of calories may have posed an even more serious problem for the children of Arroyo Hondo. If the diet is deficient in calories, a child begins to use the precious protein in foods wastefully: these "building blocks" are diverted from tissue synthesis and maintenance, and instead are burned for energy. As a result, fewer and fewer new cells are produced, and growth gradually tapers off. Lesser tissues are cannibalized in order to maintain the most important ones. These adjustments to protein depletion eventually cross the threshold of normal physiology and enter the realm of genuine pathology. All of the body is ultimately implicated, and virtually every function is disrupted. Vitamin and mineral deficiencies usually accompany a poor diet, shifting the body's balance even further into the pathological zone (Viteri et al. 1964).

Protein-calorie malnutrition (PCM) begins unobtrusively. In many nonindustrialized societies today, mothers unknowingly create the ideal conditions for its inception and development among their children. The situation in the Mayan village of Santa Maria Cauque, in the Guatemalan highlands, is typical of those in a great many nonwestern communities: Mayan children are breast-fed for several years, receiving meager supplements of high-carbohydrate food that meet only 17 percent of their nutrient and 15 percent of their caloric needs (Mata, Urrutia, and Garcia 1967:116–18). This subadequate diet can eventually lead to protein-calorie malnutrition, which may either linger for months or years as a mild, subclinical malady or quickly become severe. Kwashiorkor, a virulent form of PCM that results from eating a high-carbohydrate, low-protein diet, usually develops in the second year of life after a long period of breast-feeding supplemented by starchy foods, as described above for Santa Maria Cauque (Jelliffe 1968:108–9).

This condition is a major health problem in nonindustrialized societies today and is so pervasive that a number of scholars have concluded that protein-calorie malnutrition is the main dietary problem of young children in such cultures (Keppel 1968:5; Manocha 1972:3). For example, in India, Gopalan (1975:333–39) found that preschool children received adequate protein but that their caloric intakes were badly deficient, ranging from 70 to 75 calories rather than the requisite 100 per kilogram of body weight. Moreover, on the basis of growth records from many countries, which are a practical index of malnutrition because weight is always affected by protein deficiency, Behar (1968:37, 40) estimated that at least 75 percent of preschool children in nonindustrial countries were underweight for their age and thus had suffered from PCM at some time in their lives.

Childhood Malnutrition at Arroyo Hondo. The young children of Arroyo Hondo probably suffered from both protein and calorie deficiencies, since maize, their main food, is bulky, deficient in amino acids, and only moderately high in calories. (Whole maize kernels contain about 360 calories per 100 grams [Leung and Flores 1961:14], in contrast to oil-rich foods such as sunflower seeds, which contain 575 calories per 100 grams edible portion [Leung and Flores 1961:63].) The problem would have been compounded if young children were frequently underfed, as the ethnographic analogies suggest. As a result, all of the young children may well have been chronically undernourished.

Nutritional problems must have been even worse during the dry years after 1335 and especially during food shortages. At these times, the children's diet shrank just as the adults' did, although some special efforts may have been made to feed young children. At San Juan Pueblo, for example, the elderly abstained from meat during times of scarcity so that the children might have it (Ford 1968a:175), and when conditions were especially bad, old people went "without food for days on end so that children could eat . . ." (Ford 1968a:162). Such a practice would have lessened the sting of hunger at Arroyo Hondo but it probably could not have ensured a normal diet for each young child. Because the elderly usually represent a small portion of the population, their total share of food would not have gone very far toward nourishing the young, a much larger group. Indeed, at San Juan, the elderly's sacrifices were only partially successful: Ford's informants maintained that "when they were children they were often hungry, especially in late winter and early spring following a summer when insects attacked the corn" (Ford 1968a:161–62). Similarly, at Arroyo Hondo the adults probably never succeeded in keeping the young children adequately nourished during poor periods.

Malnutrition and Disease. The problem of nutritional deficiencies is compounded by the cycle linking disease and malnutrition in nonindustrial societies today, and this syndrome must have been prevalent in prehistoric times as well. Infectious ailments, to which young children are highly susceptible, make children even more vulnerable to malnutrition, which in turn predisposes them to infection if they are not already sick. The resulting combination of infection and malnutrition is deadly, even more devastating than either condition alone (Scrimshaw, Taylor, and Gordon 1968:16).

Almost any bacterial or viral infection can lead to malnutrition; for example, an attack of kwashiorkor is often preceded by diarrhea or measles (Scrimshaw, Taylor, and Gordon 1968:27). The infection apparently creates a new protein deficiency or aggravates malnutrition that had already developed (Scrimshaw, Taylor, and Gordon 1968:30, 32). It does this by increasing the rate at which the body loses nitrogen, an essential component of protein, and by suppressing the appetite. If the sick child refuses to eat, the lost nitrogen cannot be restored; daily nutrient needs are unsatisfied; and the little food the child does eat may be poorly absorbed because of the infection. It is not surprising, then, that other nutrient deficiencies often develop with an infectious disease. Scurvy, beriberi, and vitamin A deficiency can all be precipitated by infection, and it apparently aggravates rickets and anemia.

In like manner, malnutrition usually leads to infectious disease, which is often the final cause of death in PCM victims. It is not clear why malnutrition should reduce a child's resistance, but several factors have been implicated. First, a protein-deficient body cannot produce antibodies and phagocytes, essential for defense, at the same rate as a healthy body (Scrimshaw, Taylor, and Gordon 1968:152–57). Malnourished children may also be more vulnerable to invasions of bacteria and viruses because their tissues lose integrity. The gastrointestinal tract seems to be particularly susceptible to infections, possibly because of the changes in the number, type, and distribution of intestinal flora that accompany malnutrition. Finally, the body may be more vulnerable because of the alterations in its endocrine balance that accompany malnourishment.

Infections must have been a serious threat to the well-being of the Arroyo Hondo toddler. Sanitation and hygiene were certainly not up to contemporary standards. Water carried from the Arroyo Hondo spring probably sat for days in large jars where microorganisms could breed. Garbage, which was discarded in empty rooms, in the plazas, and at the edge of the pueblo, may have provided another breeding ground for infectious agents, which toddlers could easily have picked up while crawling across dirt floors and plazas.

Long-Term Effects of PCM. Having passed the most dangerous and vulnerable period of life, a malnourished child who is still alive at age four has a good chance of surviving into the adult years. After four years, protein requirements diminish relative to body size, while appetite increases. However, no matter how much the PCM victim eats later on, it is unlikely that recovery will ever be complete. The disease appears to leave a permanent record in the body by stunting growth and altering normal bone development (Graham 1967; Woodruff 1966:23–25). It frequently causes a variety of bone lesions, including growth arrest lines (Jones and Dean 1956:57, 60), and delayed ossification (Garn 1966:44). In addition, the bones of malnourished individuals often are thinner and have a smaller total mineral content than those of healthy people (Garn 1966:54–57). Two dental abnormalities have also been associated with PCM: delayed development and linear hypoplasia. The latter, a defect in the enamel, appears as a horizontal line of pits along the front and lateral upper incisors. Since the pits are highly susceptible to caries, they often stand out as a dark, decayed line (Sweeney, Saffir, and de Leon 1971:29).

These long-term developmental effects of PCM are particularly important for archaeological work since they leave a permanent record of deficiency in the skeleton. Although poor diet and the prevalence of infection at Arroyo Hondo Pueblo can never be fully verified, direct evidence for malnutrition if it did occur should be found in the skeletal remains from the pueblo. If young children suffered from protein-calorie malnutrition, their remains should display several distinctive characteristics. There should be a clustering of individuals in the newborn-to-four-years-old category, and many of these should have reduced quantities of cortical and compact bone, as well as other lesions. Skeletons of older individuals might also exhibit a variety of bone lesions.

If, on the other hand, PCM was not common at Arroyo Hondo, there would be many skeletons of babies less than six months old, but no concentration in the under-four category. The number of bone lesions would be few, and they would not cluster in single individuals or age groups. In the next chapter, these tests will be applied to the pueblo's skeletal population.

4

Diet, Death, and Demography

A drought in the 1330s inaugurated an era of highly variable rainfall at Arroyo Hondo. For the pueblo's inhabitants, the erratic rains and desiccated landscape almost certainly meant food shortages and hardship. Everyone would have suffered, but the greatest burden was borne by young children because they are highly susceptible to protein-calorie malnutrition (PCM). This chapter analyzes how the pueblo's demography may have been affected by the prevalence of PCM during dry years, and it considers the archaeological evidence for these effects.

DIET AND HEALTH

Imagine an experiment in which a group of marginally healthy toddlers is underfed for six months. At the end of this period, some subjects would probably show signs of PCM, and some might be dead. However, PCM is much too complex to allow predictions at the outset as to when symptoms would appear, who would be stricken, or what percentage would die.

At Arroyo Hondo Pueblo, the chronic underfeeding of small children was probably a reality at various times during the fourteenth century, but very little is known about the conditions under which this occurred, so there is no way to predict with any confidence what proportion of the children died as a result of PCM. It is possible, however, to examine the potential range of demographic effects.

As explained in the previous chapter, deprivation was worse during long droughts than in single dry years, presumably resulting in higher death rates. Extended dry periods were demographically important for another reason as well: spanning several years and followed by a recovery period that was also impoverished, they would have touched the lives of a large segment of a generation. For example, by the time normal conditions were restored, a two-year drought followed by two years of recovery would probably have affected all children between the ages of one and eight years. These children would have endured at least some malnutrition between the ages of six months and four years, their vulnerable period, with those born early in the drought suffering the most. Those who were three or four at the onset of the dry period and those born at its conclusion would have suffered less, but would still have been more likely to die than children born in better years.

DEMOGRAPHIC EFFECTS

During drought years, the people of Arroyo Hondo would have grieved over the many deaths of young children. The impact of these deaths on the community and its demographic patterns would probably have been even more sorely felt about 15 to 20 years later, when the surviving children reached adulthood. Their numbers depleted, they would not have added the normal cohort of new members to the adult age group and the work force, and this situation would have had some potentially important repercussions for the pueblo.

One way to explore these consequences is to examine how hypothetical populations are affected over time by deaths in the youngest age classes. For this purpose, three tables were prepared (tables 22–24) using, in part, figures from three model life tables selected from a set developed by Kenneth Weiss (1973) for anthropological demographic work. Weiss's generalized models attempt to describe the underlying demographic features of the nonindustrialized populations with which anthropologists and archaeologists usually work. Based on data from skeletal, historic, contemporary, and other anthropological populations, the life tables describe the mortality and longevity experiences of a population by age class. The age distribution of the population is indicated by the number of individuals in each age group, which also predicts the future experience of every cohort as it passes through the various stages of life (Weiss 1973:9). The 72 life tables Weiss devised were constructed by combining eight model adult and nine model juvenile mor-

TABLE 22.
Losses to the future adult population when probability of death between ages 1 and 5 is increased. MT:15–30 (Weiss 1973:115); stationary population of 400.

	Mortality Group				
	I	*II*	*III*	*IV*	V
(1) Births occurring over 5 years	186.80	186.80	186.80	186.80	186.80
(2) Expected survivors at age 15	56.04	56.04	56.04	56.04	56.04
(3) Probability of death between ages 1 and 5 ($_4q_1$)	0.40	0.50	0.60	0.70	0.80
(4) Survivors at age 5 according to specified level of $_4q_1$	67.25	56.04	44.83	33.62	22.42
(5) Survivors to age 10	56.08	46.74	37.39	28.04	18.70
(6) Survivors to age 15	48.03	40.03	32.02	24.02	16.02
(7) Difference between expected and actual survivors to age 15	8.01	16.01	24.02	32.02	40.02
(8) Expected adult population (15–50) after 20 years from year 0	158.00	158.00	158.00	158.00	158.00
(9) Actual adult population (15–50) after 20 years from year 0	149.99	141.99	133.98	125.98	117.98
(10) Percentage of adult population lost	5.07	10.13	15.20	20.26	25.33

Calculations:

(1) Based on crude birth rate (number of births per person per year) of 0.0934, as given by Weiss in MT:15–30.

(2) Number of births multiplied by 0.30, the figure given by Weiss in MT:15–30 for survivorship to age 15.

(3) Arbitrary value.

(4) Calculation begins with Weiss's figure of 40% for probability of death before age 1. Thus, 186.80 x [1 – 0.40] = 112.08 survivors at age 1; and
112.08 x [1 – $_4q_1$] = number of survivors at age 5.

(5) The figure obtained for row (4) is multiplied by [1 – 0.166]. In MT:15–30, 0.166 is the probability of death between ages 5 and 10 ($_5q_5$).

(6) The figure obtained for row (5) is multiplied by [1 – 0.1435]. In MT:15–30, 0.1435 is the probability of death between ages 10 and 15 ($_5q_{10}$).

(7) Row (2) minus row (6).

(8) Population size of 400 multiplied by 0.395, Weiss's figure in MT:15–30 for the proportion of the population between ages 15 and 50.

(9) Row (8) minus row (7).

(10) Row (7) divided by row (8).

TABLE 23.
Losses to the future adult population when probability of death between ages 1 and 5 is increased. MT:20–50 (Weiss 1973:128); stationary population of 400.

	Mortality Group						
	I	*II*	*III*	*IV*	V	VI	VII
(1) Births occurring over 5 years; crude birth rate = 0.0527	105.40	105.40	105.40	105.40	105.40	105.40	105.40
(2) Expected survivors at age 15, according to MT:20–50	52.70	52.70	52.70	52.70	52.70	52.70	52.70
(3) Probability of death between ages 1 and 5 ($_4q_1$)	0.20	0.30	0.40	0.50	0.60	0.70	0.80
(4) Survivors at age 5 according to specified level of $_4q_1$	61.81	54.08	46.36	38.63	30.90	23.18	15.45
(5) Survivors to age 10; $_5q_5$ = 0.1100 in MT:20–50	55.01	48.13	41.26	34.38	27.50	20.63	13.75
(6) Survivors to age 15; $_5q_{10}$ = 0.0876 in MT:20–50	50.19	43.92	37.64	31.37	25.10	18.82	12.55
(7) Difference between expected and actual survivors to age 15	2.51	8.78	15.06	21.33	27.60	33.88	40.15
(8) Expected adult population (15–50) after 20 years from year 0 (= 46.6% in MT:20–50)	186.40	186.40	186.40	186.40	186.40	186.40	186.40

	Mortality Group						
	I	*II*	*III*	*IV*	*V*	*VI*	*VII*
(9) Actual adult population (15–50) after 20 years from year 0	183.89	177.62	171.34	165.07	158.80	152.52	146.25
(10) Percentage of adult population lost	1.35	4.71	8.08	11.44	14.81	18.18	21.54

Calculations follow the same pattern as those for table 22, using Weiss's figures for MT:20–50.

TABLE 24.
Losses to the future adult population when probability of death between ages 1 and 5 is increased. MT:30–50 (Weiss 1973:164); stationary population of 400.

	Mortality Group						
	I	*II*	*III*	IV	V	VI	VII
(1) Births occurring over 5 years; crude birth rate = 0.0417	83.40	83.40	83.40	83.40	83.40	83.40	83.40
(2) Expected survivors at age 15, according to MT:30–50	41.67	41.67	41.67	41.67	41.67	41.67	41.67
(3) Probability of death between ages 1 and 5 ($_4q_1$)	0.20	0.30	0.40	0.50	0.60	0.70	0.80
(4) Survivors at age 5 according to specified level of $_4q_1$	48.90	42.79	36.68	30.57	24.45	18.34	12.22
(5) Survivors to age 10; $_5q_5$ = 0.1100 in MT:30–50	43.52	38.08	32.64	27.20	21.76	16.32	10.88
(6) Survivors to age 15; $_5q_{10}$ = 0.0876 in MT:30–50	39.71	34.75	29.78	24.82	19.86	14.89	9.93
(7) Difference between expected and actual survivors to age 15	1.96	6.92	11.89	16.85	21.81	26.78	31.76
(8) Expected adult population (15–50) after 20 years from year 0 (from MT:30–50)	193.20	193.20	193.20	193.20	193.20	193.20	193.20

	Mortality Group						
	I	*II*	*III*	*IV*	V	VI	VII
(9) Actual adult population (15–50) after 20 years from year 0	191.24	187.28	181.31	176.35	171.39	166.42	161.44
(10) Percentage of adult population lost	1.01	3.58	6.15	8.72	11.29	13.86	16.43

Calculations follow the same pattern as those for table 22, using Weiss's figures for MT:30–50.

tality schedules with model fertility schedules (Weiss 1973:29). They assume stationary population conditions; that is, constant vital (mortality and fertility) rates and an unchanging age distribution and census count (Weiss 1973:10). However, they can be used to explore how a change in one parameter might affect the others (Weiss 1973:72), as will be done below.

The three model life tables selected from Weiss's work span a range of adult and juvenile mortality patterns characteristic of nonindustrialized societies. They represent two extremes of mortality experience and a middle value that seems best to characterize the Arroyo Hondo population. Weiss designated his tables "MT:*i–j*," where MT stands for "Model Table"; *i* is life expectancy at age 15, and *j* is the percentage of the cohort surviving to age 15. Thus MT:15–30 indicates a population in which an individual can expect to live an additional 15 years after reaching age 15 and in which 30 percent of all infants born will survive to 15 years. MT:30–50 represents the opposite extreme, a population in which 50 percent survive to age 15 and then can expect to live another 30 years. The third table, MT:20–50, an intermediate population, appears to provide the best match for Arroyo Hondo Pueblo.

For this study, I substituted figures higher than Weiss's for mortality values in the age class one to five years. In each table, mortality in this age category was increased from an arbitrary starting value up to 80 percent in 10-percent increments. Survivorship at age five was then determined for all cases, assuming a stationary base population of 400. It was assumed that after age five, the mortality experience of each cohort returned to the normal values as given in Weiss's table. This assumption seems to be a reasonable model of the events that may have occurred at Arroyo Hondo. During a severe drought, malnutrition and death would be expected to strike most heavily among the vulnerable young; but by the time the surviving members of this group reached age five, their death rates would have fallen, for two reasons. First, they would no longer be as vulnerable, as explained in the preceding chapter. In addition, those who had suffered PCM and recovered probably would not have had a greater death rate than other children: evidence from modern nonindustrialized societies indicates that PCM survivors fare as well as their age mates (Martorell et al. 1978:149).

The next step, then, was to calculate the number of survivors, out of those reaching age 5, to reach age 15, using Weiss's probability-of-death figures for the age groups 5–10 and 10–15. This would presumably simulate the demographic effects 15 years later of a drought during which toddler mortality was high for five years. The number of individuals normally reaching 15, according to Weiss's figures, was also calculated for a population of 400, and this estimate was compared with that for the drought cohort for all mortality levels. The percentage loss to the population for each case was then determined by dividing the difference between these two values by the expected number of adults (individuals 15 to 50) in a population of 400. These calculations are summarized in tables 22–24; the last row of each model table shows the percentage loss to the adult population.

The percentage lost varies with juvenile mortality and adult life expectancy. Populations with high juvenile mortality are more strongly affected than those with lower levels, and the percentage lost also increases as the adult life expectancy declines. The largest percentage losses occur in populations with a survival rate of 30 percent to age 15 years.

However, the pattern is the same for the three model cases; a small increase in toddler deaths has a negligible effect, whereas a mortality rate of 50 percent to 60 percent produces up to a 15 percent decline or more in the adult population. When the probability of dying reaches 80 percent for young children, the effect is large in all model populations, with the reduction in numbers of adults ranging from 16 percent to 25 percent. These calculations suggest that if Arroyo Hondo Pueblo lost 50 percent or more of its toddlers for several years, the adult population could have been significantly affected.

Demographic Effects on Growing Populations

The effect of increasing mortality among young children for five years in an expanding population was also investigated for one case, MT: 20–50. A growth rate of 0.5 percent per year was selected because it is considered a realistic rate for ancient populations (Barclay 1958:209) and is probably the maximum pace at which Arroyo Hondo Pueblo could have grown internally. The new population parameters were calculated using the method Weiss (1973:71) outlined for applying his model tables to an expanding population, and the number of survivors of a five-year-drought cohort to reach age 15 was determined using the new survivorship figures. The sizes of the expected adult and total populations after 20 years of constant growth were then estimated. Finally, the percentage loss to the adult population for different levels of mortality among young children was computed, using a procedure similar to the one outlined above. The calculations are summarized in table 25.

It can be seen that the losses to the expanding population are only slightly greater than those to the stationary community, meaning that an increase in the death rate of young children over a five-year period would have almost the same effect on the number of future adults whether the population of Arroyo Hondo were stable or growing.

Effect of a One-Year Drought

A one-year drought or any other short-term environmental disaster would not have had a significant impact on the population. A child's probability of developing PCM and dying would have been lower in this case than during an extended period of deprivation, and even if the losses were large they would have created only a small perturbation in the population, as illustrated in table 26. The values indicate the change in mortality in the one-to-five-year age category when the annual rate doubles or triples for a single year. The change is small in all cases and would not greatly affect the future adult population. For example, doubling or tripling of mortality for one year when ${}_4Q_1 = 16$ percent results in a ${}_4Q_1 = 20$ percent or 24 percent, which means a loss of only an additional 1.3 percent or 2.3 percent of the predicted adult population in a community with the characteristics of MT:20–50. Only events that caused an increase in deaths for several years, therefore, can be considered demographically important.

Long-Range Effects

Tables 22–25 demonstrate that five years of very high death rates for toddlers could have a significant impact on the future adult population. Whether or not these effects actually occurred would have depended on the behavior of the population following recovery from the drought. If, for example, the people of Arroyo Hondo compensated for their losses by having additional children, the net change 30 years later would have been insignificant. However, it seems unlikely that the pueblo

TABLE 25.
Losses to the future adult population when probability of death between ages 1 and 5 is increased. MT:20–50 (Weiss 1973:128); stable population expanding 0.5 percent per year starting with 400 individuals.

	Mortality Group						
	I	*II*	*III*	*IV*	V	*VI*	*VII*
(1) Births occurring over 5 years; crude birth rate = 0.0580	117.76	117.76	117.76	117.76	117.76	117.76	117.76
(2) Expected survivors at age 15, according to model table	58.88	58.88	58.88	58.88	58.88	58.88	58.88
(3) Probability of death between ages 1 and 5 ($_4q_1$)	0.20	0.30	0.40	0.50	0.60	0.70	0.80
(4) Survivors at age 5 according to specified level of $_4q_1$	69.05	60.42	51.79	43.16	34.53	25.89	17.26
(5) Survivors to age 10; $_5q_5$ = 0.1100 in MT:20–50	61.46	53.78	46.09	38.41	30.73	23.05	15.36
(6) Survivors to age 15; $_5q_{10}$ = 0.0876 in MT:20–50	56.07	49.06	42.06	35.05	28.04	21.03	14.02
(7) Difference between expected and actual survivors to age 15	2.81	9.82	16.82	23.83	30.84	37.85	44.86
(8) Expected adult population (15–50) after 20 years from year 0	205.73	205.73	205.73	205.73	205.73	205.73	205.73

TABLE 25. *(continued)*

	Mortality Group						
	I	*II*	*III*	*IV*	V	VI	VII
(9) Actual adult population (15–50) after 20 years from year 0	202.92	195.91	188.91	181.90	174.89	167.88	160.87
(10) Percentage of adult population lost	1.37	4.77	8.18	11.58	14.99	18.40	21.81

Calculations:

(1) The crude birth rate (b) for an expanding population growing at 0.5 percent per year, starting with 400 people, was calculated using the following equation (Weiss 1976:71):

$$b = \frac{1}{\sum_{0}^{80} \hat{L}(x)\, e^{-r\bar{x}}}$$

where $\hat{L}$ = person-years lived in age class x,
r = growth rate,
$\bar{x}$ = midpoint of age class.

The new age distribution (C) is calculated using the following equation (Weiss 1976:73):

$$C = \frac{\hat{L}(x)\, e^{-r\bar{x}}}{\sum_{0}^{80} \hat{L}(x)\, e^{-r\bar{x}}}$$

(8) The expected adult population (15–50 years) was calculated using the new age distribution shown above and the new population size N calculated using the following equation (Weiss 1976:73):

$$N_t = Ne^{rt}$$

where t = time.

All other calculations follow the same pattern as those for table 22.

TABLE 26.
The effect on age class mortality of increasing annual mortality during one year.

Original Q(1)	*Annual Mortality for Age Class 1–5*	*New Q(1) if, in a Single Year, Annual Mortality:* Doubles	Triples
10%	2.6%	12.4%	14.8%
15%	4.0%	18.5%	22.0%
20%	5.4%	24.8%	29.3%
25%	6.9%	30.6%	36.2%
30%	8.5%	36.5%	43.1%

Definitions and calculations:
Q(1) = Probability of dying in the age class 1–5 for those reaching age 1.
Annual mortality = $1 - \sqrt[4]{P(1)}$ where P(1) = probability of surviving from 1 to 5 and is is calculated P(1) = 1 − Q(1) (Weiss 1973:73).
New Q(1) if annual mortality doubles =

$$1 - [(1 - [1 - \sqrt[4]{P(1)}])^3 (1 - 2[1 - \sqrt[4]{P(1)}])].$$

New Q(1) if annual mortality triples =

$$1 - [(1 - [1 - \sqrt[4]{P(1)}])^3 (1 - 3[1 - \sqrt[4]{P(1)}])].$$

could have replaced the lost individuals by any means except immigration. Any other form of replacement would have required a decline in mortality or an increase in fertility, neither of which is likely to have been possible.

The fertility rates of Arroyo Hondo women clearly cannot be determined, but they may have been similar to those of modern Tewa Pueblo Indians, among whom the average woman gave birth every 24 months for a period of 17 years (Aberle 1931). If this were the case at Arroyo Hondo, it seems improbable that the birth rate could have increased significantly after a drought. A child every 12 months might have been possible, but this appears unlikely in light of evidence from modern anthropological populations. For example, data compiled by Weiss (1973:33) show that among New Guinea agriculturists, women bear at most 1.5 children every two years during their most fertile period, 25–29 years of age. Among other anthropological populations for which Weiss found information, the rates were even lower. This suggests that the modern Pueblos' fertility rates may surpass those of their forebears. In any case, it seems unlikely that the women of Arroyo Hondo bore additional children to compensate for the ones lost during drought periods.

A decline in mortality to below-normal levels is also implausible since Arroyo Hondo nutrition, health care, and hygiene almost certainly returned to preexisting conditions after recovery from a drought. Survivorship among children in the one-to-five age category would have been higher only if the post-drought period were very moist, food were abundant, and the young were consistently well nourished.

While, as demonstrated, fertility and mortality probably returned to normal values after a drought period, the population may have felt one major change besides the deaths among toddlers. As mentioned earlier, many inhabitants may have abandoned the pueblo during the worst of the drought period between 1335 and 1350. The effects of this emigration will be considered later.

Time Range of Effects

If the community of Arroyo Hondo had stayed more or less intact except for possible minor losses to migration, it would have felt the reduced numbers among the drought cohort until everyone in this age group had died; that is, for 40 to 50 years after the drought period. However, the effects would have diminished through time, as shown in figure 6. In order to arrive at these estimates, the size of the cohort at each age interval was calculated, starting with five different mortality rates for one-to-five-year-olds and following the survivorship schedule of MT:20–50. The expected cohort for each age category was also determined, and the difference between this value and the figure for the drought cohort was used to compute the percentage loss to the adult population, which has been plotted in the figure as a solid line. The loss to an adjusted MT:20–50 with a growth rate of 0.5 percent per year was also calculated and is shown as a broken line. The pattern is the same in both the stationary and expanding populations: the greatest drop in the number of adults occurs when the drought cohort reaches adulthood, and the discrepancy between normal and drought-affected numbers diminishes as the cohort matures, dropping off more rapidly in the growing than in the stationary population.

Implications of an Adult Population Decline

As the drought cohort reached adulthood, the decline in the number of adults could have affected the functioning of the Arroyo Hondo com-

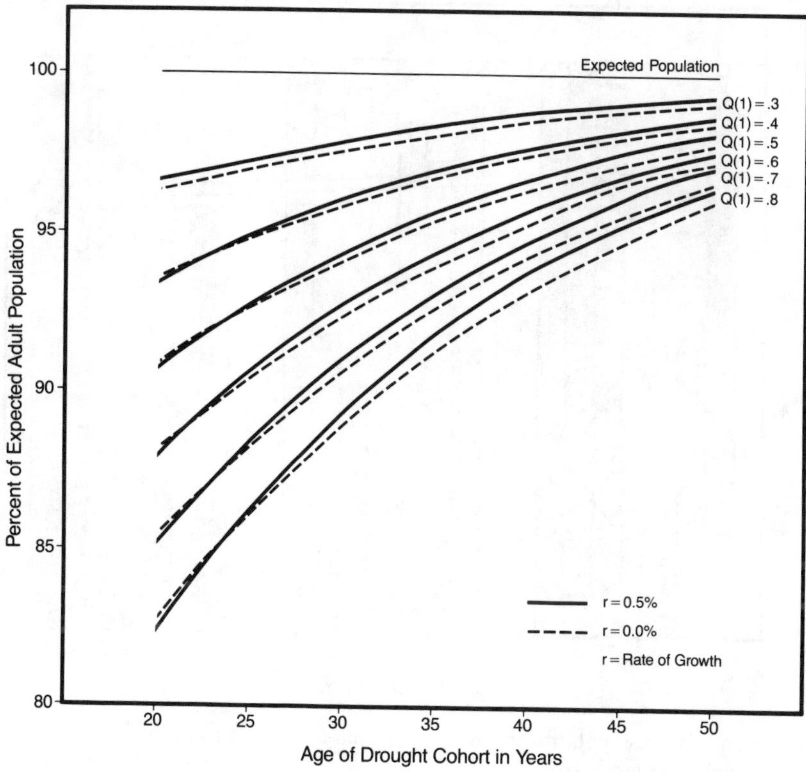

Fig. 6. Size of the adult population relative to expected population in MT:20–30 as the drought cohort matures.

munity in several important ways. First, the normal building rate of the pueblo would have dropped since fewer new households would have been established when the cohort married. The dependency ratio also would have shifted because each productive adult would have had more elderly, infirm, and young to support. As a result, the work load may have increased or the community's per-capita food production declined.

The children of the drought would have affected future demographic patterns by causing a reduction in the crude birth rate. The greatest change would have occurred while the females of the cohort were between 20 and 30 years of age, the most fertile period (Weiss 1973:35), but the decline would have been dispersed through time, as illustrated in figure 7 for one case example, MT:20–50. The histogram indicates

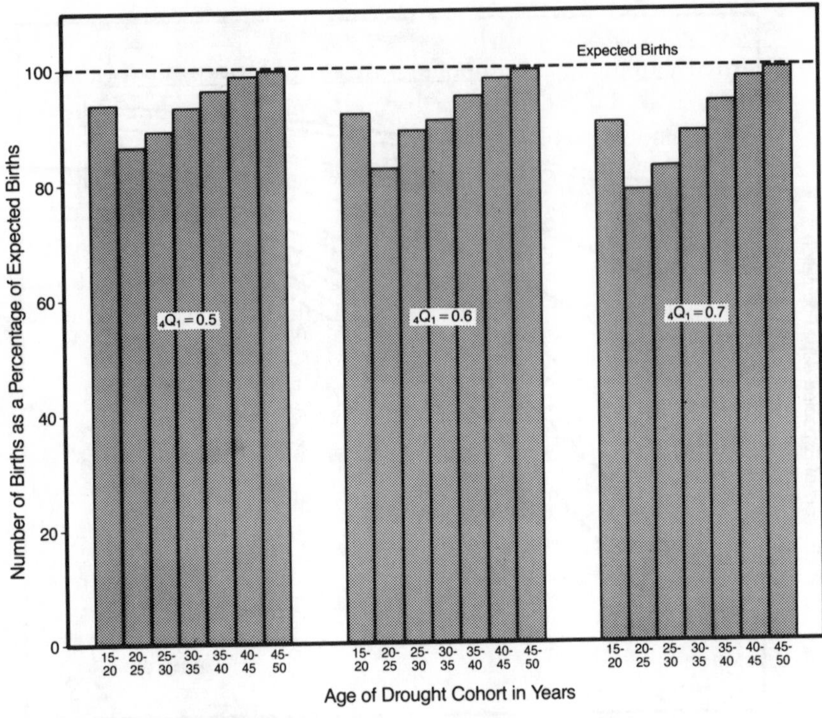

Fig. 7. Total number of births in five-year intervals as drought cohort females pass through their fertile years.

in five-year intervals the number of children born in a stationary population of 400 as a percentage of expected births over the 30-year span of the drought cohort's reproductive years. Three hypothetical cohorts that experienced mortality of 50, 60, and 70 percent rather than the normal 16 percent (Weiss 1973:128) are shown. The straight horizontal line represents expected births. The number of children born to the reduced adult population was calculated according to Weiss's (1973:124) fertility schedule and age distribution for MT:20–50. The numbers of women in the appropriate age intervals were adjusted for the population reduction, and births were then calculated and plotted. The pattern of the histograms would be the same for any other model life table since the shape is a function of the way in which human reproduction varies with age, but the magnitude would depend on the birth rate and the age distribution. For a smaller population, the same pattern would have occurred, but the total number of births would have been lower.

The result of this decline in the crude birth rate would be a second dip in the adult population 20 to 40 years later. An example is illustrated in figure 8 for MT:20–50. Here, the total adult population has been plotted for the period during which the second-generation drought cohort would be passing through adulthood. The curve represents the number of people as a percentage of the expected adult population in a stationary community. A figure for drought cohort offspring surviving at each age interval was calculated, and the total adult population for each five-year period was then determined.

A dotted line indicating the shape of the initial population dip resulting from the drought cohort has been superimposed over the figure, using the same time scale. The second fluctuation, caused by the cohort's offspring, is smaller and dispersed over a much longer time span.

The Effects of Migration

After some of the Arroyo Hondoans left the pueblo in the 1340s, a small community seems to have stayed on at the site. This remnant was ap-

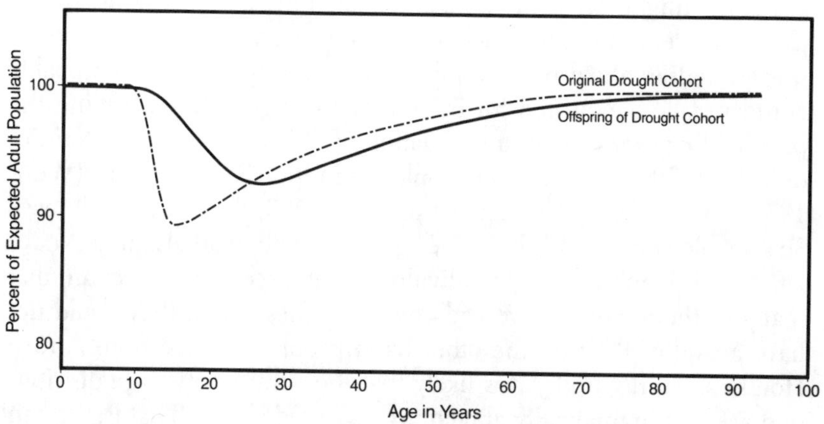

Fig. 8. Size of the adult population as the offspring of the drought cohort mature. (Calculated for MT:20–50.)

parently joined by additional settlers during a brief moist phase about 30 years later (Schwartz 1980:xvi). The archaeological evidence for these changes offers no precise information about the new, smaller population, but the natural resources of the area at this time probably supported no more than two to three hundred people, as suggested earlier. Neither do the archaeological remains give any clues as to who left, who remained behind, or who joined the pueblo in the 1370s. Did whole kinship groups move, or were the migrants single families or even lone individuals? Were some families forced out early because they had little access to farmlands in the canyons? Were others encouraged to leave because of convenient kinship ties with people in pueblos on the Rio Grande and the Santa Fe River?

It is impossible to find answers for these questions at present. However, we can consider how different patterns of migration might have affected demographic patterns. Whether family migrants were rich or poor in land and whether they were of the same or different kinship groups, they would have had the same impact on the age structure of the community. By removing individuals representing a wide range of ages, they could well have left the age distribution of the population relatively unchanged, although their departure would have reduced the size of the community. If, on the other hand, single individuals migrated, the population structure might have been dramatically altered. For example, if healthy young adults in their late teens abandoned the pueblo, they would have left a large gap in the age distribution.

Family migration is the more probable of these two patterns. Architectural evidence from the pueblo, consisting of many abandoned rooms, suggests a dramatic drop in numbers in the 1340s, a drop that probably could not be accounted for by one or two age cohorts leaving the pueblo. For example, in a population of 400 with the characteristics of MT:30–50, only about 35 people fall in the 15–20 age class (Weiss 1973:164). If all 35 abandoned a pueblo of 400, they would still leave 365 people behind. Adults in the age bracket 20 to 30 also might have left Arroyo Hondo as single individuals, but it seems fairly certain that many of them would have had young families whom they could not have abandoned. If on the other hand people migrated from Arroyo Hondo as family units, it is likely that the community's age distribution was not dramatically altered, as suggested above. That is, we can assume that a representative group of adults and children departed.

The one age class whose proportion may have changed is the elderly.

Unfit for the rigors of a several-days' journey, they may well have stayed behind, as a result of which the relative proportion of people 50 and over would have increased as population declined. The change could have been substantial, but would not have been long lasting. For example, in a group of 400 with MT:30–50 characteristics, about 56 people, or a little more than 14 percent, are over 50 (Weiss 1973:164). If the population declined to 200, with all the other age groups diminishing proportionately, the 50-plus class would represent nearly 30 percent of the community. This bulge in the age distribution would quickly begin to disappear, however, since mortality is especially high for the elderly, particularly in times of famine, as discussed in chapter 3.

In sum, migration probably had a dramatic impact on the size of the pueblo and possibly also on its demographic structure. However, it seems likely that the remaining inhabitants had roughly the same age distribution as the original population, at least after a few years. If this were the case, then Arroyo Hondo Pueblo may have suffered the effects of the 1335–45 dry spell, as described above: namely, the small drought cohort would have meant a dip in the adult population some 20 years later. Having endured a difficult decade, the pueblo's people probably would have been dramatically affected. A whole generation of children would have been touched by drought, leaving the community seriously short of productive adults during the period 1355–65. When another drought began in the 1360s, fit adults were sorely needed to gather, hunt, and scrounge all the farther for food. The second dry decade may have had a similar debilitating effect on the population between 1380 and 1390.

TESTING THE HYPOTHESIS

At this time it is impossible to muster the archaeological evidence necessary to demonstrate conclusively that climate, diet, and population were related in the ways outlined here. Clearly the most problematic issues are the size and stability of Arroyo Hondo's population after 1335 and the flow of migrants. Nonetheless, it is possible to explore other issues bearing on the population-food-climate relationship. We can examine in particular evidence for food stress at Arroyo Hondo, for nutritional stress in the population, for a demographic structure similar to those of nonindustrialized societies today, and for the proposed effects of a population dip resulting from an undersized drought cohort.

Archaeological Evidence of Food Stress

When Arroyo Hondo Pueblo suffered through the drought documented in the dendroclimatological record, its inhabitants presumably endured the food shortages and stresses discussed in the previous chapter. Unfortunately, the archaeological findings offer little substantial evidence to support or refute this hypothesis. The plant remains for the most part are too sparse to provide any clues to the relative quantities of food harvested; and differential preservation, poor recovery, sampling error, and lack of fine temporal control pose additional barriers to documenting food shortages at Arroyo Hondo.

An alternative approach is to look for traces of emergency or starvation foods, which could provide inferential evidence of dietary stress. These types of foods might be distinguished from regular dietary items on the basis of archaeological context as well as ethnographic and ecological data. Since an emergency food is not used frequently, it has a low probability of occurring in a flotation sample and should therefore appear only in a small number of samples, probably those taken from hearths and middens but not those from storage rooms. The plants producing such foods would most likely have small yields relative to the population's needs. In addition, a specimen's starvation-food status should be supported by ethnographic evidence.

No certain examples of emergency foods are among the Arroyo Hondo plant remains, but some of the 27 unknown seed types recovered from the ruins may have been starvation foods. Most occurred in fairly low frequencies (one to three seeds) in a small number of samples: 15 of the 27 came from midden deposits in plaza G, and the remaining specimens, from rooms in roomblocks 5, 9, and 18. One unknown was represented by 93 specimens, but all except one of these occurred in a single location, suggesting that the plant may have been used for only a short period in the pueblo's history.

Four unknown types do not meet the criteria proposed for starvation foods since they are abundant and widely dispersed. However, two of them may represent *several* emergency food sources because both are general categories for perhaps four or five different grass species that were grouped together in the initial analysis. These categories probably include *Sporobolus* sp., *Festuca* sp., *Agropyron* sp., *Bromus* sp., other grasses, and *Descurainia pinnata*, all of which could have been valuable starvation foods in poor years.

The unknown types cannot be confirmed as foods, emergency or otherwise, until they are positively identified. Some might prove to be no more than contaminants inadvertently gathered with the legitimate foods. However, the fact that some are concentrated, rather than scattered as intrusives would be, suggests that at least a few of these seeds were intentionally collected. In summary, the plant remains offer evidence of possible emergency foods that suggest periods of stress at Arroyo Hondo, but none of these items can be specifically tied to known droughts for lack of temporal controls.

Faunal Evidence for Food Stress

During drought periods, the people of Arroyo Hondo probably hunted more intensively than before in an effort to compensate for food shortages, as suggested in chapter 3. Both the large and small fauna from the site offer some evidence that this was the case.

The mule deer population in the Arroyo Hondo area apparently declined after 1330, as noted earlier. It appears that the hunters responded to this change and to the food shortages of 1335–45 by hunting the animals more intensively during the off season. In faunal samples dating prior to 1330, only 4 percent to 7 percent of the artiodactyl remains consisted of antler (Lang and Harris 1984:51). Between 1330 and 1345, the proportion of antler specimens rose to 11 percent, and between 1345 and 1355, the percentage climbed to 23. Lang and Harris (1984:51–52) believe this indicates a shift in seasonal hunting patterns: after 1330, a larger proportion of deer were apparently taken between August and mid-January, a season when they were concentrated in the higher foothills and mountains. If the Arroyo Hondo hunters had waited until spring, they could have stalked the same herds at lower elevations, which would have been easier. Lang and Harris (1984:52–53) suggest that facing poor weather and meager harvests, the Arroyo Hondoans resorted to more intensive hunting to compensate for their food shortages. Hunting in the fall, though it required more effort, provided food at a season when the once-plentiful crops were no longer adequate. In addition, it may have given Arroyo Hondo hunters an opportunity to cull a slightly larger number of animals, since more would have been available before the winter took its toll on them.

The remains of prairie dogs offer additional evidence of food stress during the period 1340–55. These large ground squirrels were apparently hunted throughout Arroyo Hondo's occupation, but their numbers and their relative contribution to the diet peaked between 1330 and 1355. In faunal samples dating from 1300 to 1315, prairie dogs represented about 9 percent of the minimum number of individual mammals identified, whereas between 1330 and 1345, they contributed approximately 19 percent, and about 18 percent between 1345 and 1355 (Lang and Harris 1984:60–61). As colonial animals, relatively easy to catch, prairie dogs would be the logical creatures to exploit if Arroyo Hondo hunters were trying to increase their kills. After the artiodactyls and lagomorphs, "prairie dogs formed the next level of productive potential among wild animal species of the piedmont" (Lang and Harris 1984:55).

The proportion of prairie dogs declined after 1355, but that of other small squirrels increased. As the prairie dogs were hunted out, the Arroyo Hondo people apparently turned to other meat sources including the spotted, rock, golden-mantled, and Richardson's ground squirrel (Lang and Harris 1984:56). Smaller than prairie dogs, these squirrels are less accessible, requiring trapping, but they offer an additional source of food in an environment where resources are becoming scarce (Lang and Harris 1984:56).

After the prairie dogs' decline, Arroyo Hondo hunters also turned to the small animals of the montane forest, especially the tree squirrels. These were an insignificant meat source in the early years of the pueblo, comprising only 1 percent of the minimum number of individuals found in the collection, but after 1355 their contribution rose to 4 percent. Trapping small squirrels required a large investment of time and energy and offered a small return (Lang and Harris 1984:59); however, they could be taken in the fall after the year's agricultural work was completed, and they offered another supplement to a meager diet. Their presence in the Arroyo Hondo collection says little about the most stressful periods at the site, but it does reflect the general difficulties of making a living in an unreliable, impoverished setting.

The bird remains in the collection show a pattern similar to that of the small mammals. In samples dating from 1330 to 1345, wild birds contributed a slightly larger share than in earlier periods, with raptors and small species such as quail and perching birds accounting for most of the increase. Lang and Harris (1984:63) believe this is another sign that Arroyo Hondo hunters tried to increase their wild food resources by taking a wider range of birds.

The faunal remains do not point specifically to drought and famine, but they do suggest stress. Facing food shortages, the pueblo's inhabitants apparently tried to intensify hunting through several means. By stalking a larger variety of animals, including species that offered relatively small returns, they increased the game available to them; and by traveling to the mountains, they found a greater variety of animals and may have taken a larger share of their most important meat source, the mule deer.

Demographic Structure

A total of 120 burials was recovered from Arroyo Hondo Pueblo of which 108 were associated with Component I, the occupation of 1300–70, and the remaining 12 dated from Component II, 1370–1425 (Palkovich 1980:7).

In order to determine the demographic characteristics of the population, Ann Palkovich, a physical anthropologist who analyzed the Arroyo Hondo material, prepared a composite life table. A special case of the life table, the composite form is constructed from skeletal data, using the age at death for each individual. Individuals from an unknown number of generations are treated as a single cohort under the assumption that population fluctuations over time will average out (Palkovich 1980:31).

Using the 108 burials from the earlier phase of the occupation, Palkovich constructed the life table shown in table 27. Individuals who could not be aged were distributed among the adult age categories according to the proportion of deaths in each group. To even out irregularities, the data were statistically smoothed (Palkovich 1980:31).

Palkovich then compared the Arroyo Hondo data with two of Weiss's model life tables that showed the closest correspondence to Arroyo Hondo, MT:27.5–40 and MT:25–40. She selected *qx*, the probability of death, for comparison since this is the only value in the life table that "does not exhibit cumulative error from one age category to the next" (Palkovich 1980:34). A comparison of the three sets of q_x values is shown in figure 9.

It is apparent that for the younger age groups, the Arroyo Hondo data agree well with the model life tables. The population shows the same general patterns as those of modern nonindustrialized societies—a high mortality among infants and young children. Only about 40 per-

TABLE 27.
Arroyo Hondo composite life table, smoothed.
After Palkovich 1980:Table 12.

Age	D_x	D_x *Smoothed*	d_x	l_x	q_x	L_x	T_x	$\overset{0}{e}_x$	Sq_x^2
0–1	29.00	29.00	26.35	100.00	0.2635	86.83	1623.17	16.23	0.0018
1–4.9	20.00	18.00	16.35	73.65	0.2220	261.90	1536.34	20.86	0.0021
5–9.9	5.00	11.00	9.99	57.30	0.1743	261.53	1274.44	22.24	0.0023
10–14.9	8.00	6.25	5.68	47.31	0.1201	222.35	1012.91	21.41	0.0020
15–19.9	5.75	6.02	5.47	41.63	0.1314	194.48	790.56	18.99	0.0025
20–24.9	4.31	4.79	4.35	36.16	0.1203	169.93	596.08	16.48	0.0027
25–29.9	4.31	4.79	4.35	31.81	0.1367	148.18	426.15	13.40	0.0034
30–34.9	5.75	8.15	7.41	27.46	0.2698	118.78	277.97	10.12	0.0065
35–39.9	14.38	7.67	6.97	20.05	0.3476	82.83	159.19	7.94	0.0103
40–44.9	2.88	7.67	6.97	13.08	0.5329	47.98	76.36	5.84	0.0173
45–49.9	5.75	3.84	3.49	6.11	0.5712	21.83	28.38	4.64	0.3640
50+	2.88	2.88	2.62	2.62	1.0000	6.55	6.55	2.50	

KEY
D_x = number of deaths in each age interval
d_x = proportion of deaths in each age interval

$$d_x = \frac{D_x}{\sum_{x=0} D_x}$$

L_x = number of years lived by survivors in each age interval

$$L_x = \frac{n(l_x + l_{x+1})}{2}$$

where n = number of years in each interval

T_x = total number of years lived by the survivors of each age interval

$$T_x = \sum_{x=0}^{i} L_x$$

l_x = survivorship for each age interval

$$l_{x+1} = l_x - d_x$$

q_x = probability of death for each age interval

$$q_x = \frac{d_x}{l_x}$$

$\overset{0}{e}_x$ = life expectancy for each interval

$$\overset{0}{e}_x = \frac{T_x}{l_x}$$

Sq_x^2 = sample variance for probability of death for each age interval

$$Sq_x^2 = \frac{q_x^2 - (1-q_x)}{D_x}$$

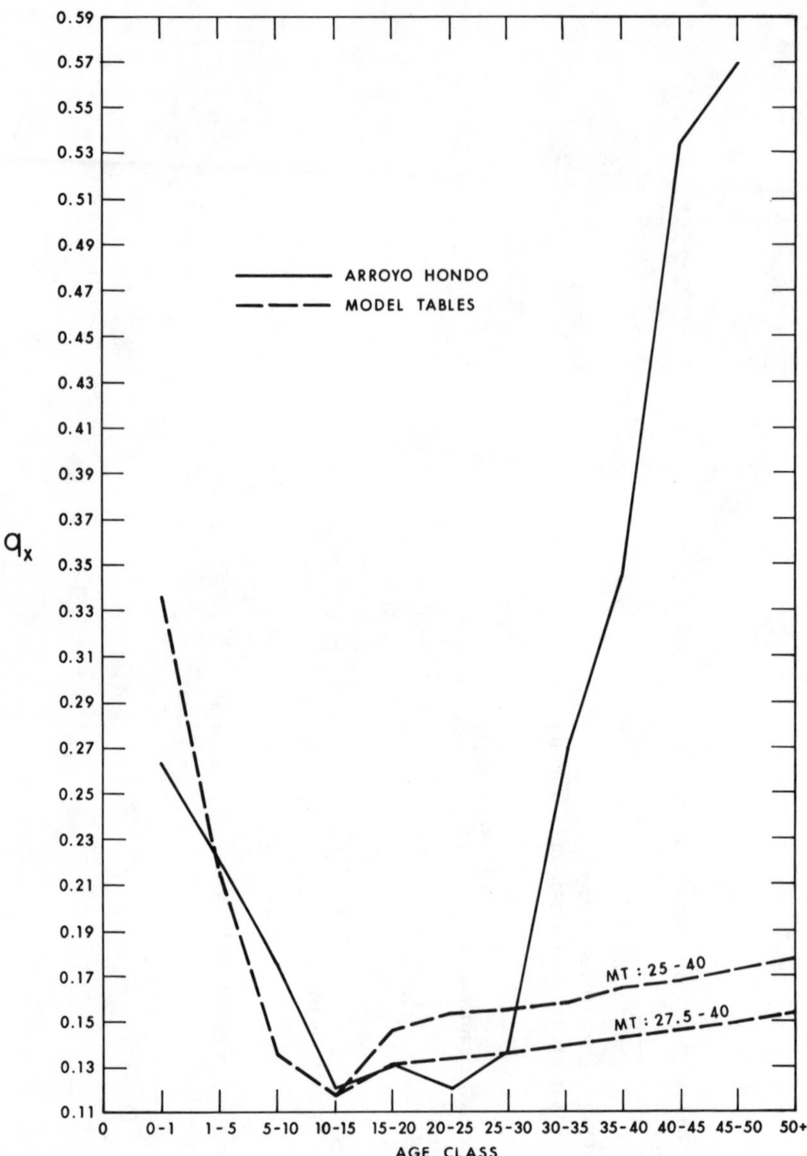

Fig. 9. The Arroyo Hondo composite life table, smoothed. (After Palkovich 1980.)

cent of the population survives to age 15, and the age group birth to five years accounts for roughly 42 percent of all deaths. Beyond age 15, however, the Arroyo Hondo population does not correspond closely to the model life tables, with the sharpest deviation occurring after age 30. Compared with the model tables, mortality seems to be exceptionally high.

In some skeletal collections, several types of bias might be responsible, including those introduced by burial practices, those resulting from aging criteria, and those stemming from sampling error, but Palkovich (1980:34, 36) rules these out. She points out that since the prehistoric Pueblos did not spatially segregate burials by age group, the Arroyo Hondo collection is probably not biased by burial practices. She also believes that bias was not introduced by aging because of the standard criteria she used. Sampling error could be a problem, but "at least a hundred individuals are considered adequate for paleodemographic studies" (Palkovich 1980:36).

Palkovich (1980:36–37) attributes Arroyo Hondo's unusual adult mortality patterns not to bias but to factors inherent in the prehistoric population. First, nine adults who were victims of accidental deaths fall into only four age classes, significantly inflating the death rate for groups over 30, especially the class 35 to 39.9 years of age. The below-expected death rate for the 20- to 24.9-year age group may simply reflect the above-average rates for the over-30 group; it might also reflect some out-migration, or perhaps a genuine increased survivorship for this age class. Those who survived exceptionally high childhood mortality may have been particularly well adapted to cope with disease as young adults.

Skeletal Indicators of Nutritional Stress

Some of the most compelling evidence for nutritional stress at Arroyo Hondo comes from the skeletal remains. In her study of this collection, Palkovich (1980:38–46) identified a variety of pathologies that are associated with malnutrition and cluster in the under-five age group. These abnormalities fall into two general categories: osteolysis, those involving "softening, resorption, and destruction of osseous tissue"; and osteosclerosis, those involving "abnormal hardening of bone substance" (Palkovich 1980:38).

In the Component I population, the only one large enough to be statistically significant, five pathologies predominated, each appearing in seven or more individuals. Bowing of the long bones was frequent among all age groups but most abundant in the adult categories. The other four abnormalities were commonest in the age groups 0 to 0.9 and 1 to 4.9 years, two of them, endocranial lesions and porotic hyperostosis, occurring exclusively among young children. Both of these involve destruction of the cranium, the former affecting the inner table and the latter the outer table (Palkovich 1980:41). The other two frequent pathologies, also most common among though not limited to children under five, were cribra orbitalia, resorption of bone in the orbital sockets, and generalized porosity, "small clustered points of cortical bone destruction in the postcranial skeleton" (Palkovich 1980:42). The remaining abnormalities occurred in only one or a few individuals.

The high incidence of these four conditions among young children and infants suggests that they are related to some underlying problem that was the cause of death in at least some cases. Palkovich's (1978:211–21) statistical studies of the pathologies and their distribution by age group lend support to this view. Her analysis of variance yielded a high statistical association between age distribution and age-specific skeletal abnormalities (Palkovich 1980:46).

The underlying problems that these pathologies reflect are almost certainly malnutrition and infectious disease. All four have been associated with nutritional problems, especially iron deficiency anemia (Palkovich 1980:43–44). Porotic hyperostosis, which has a controversial etiology, is believed to be of genetic or dietary origin, and in the present case it probably stems from a diet rich in maize. Known to inhibit iron absorption, maize is suspected of having caused iron deficiency anemia in other prehistoric Southwestern societies (El-Najjar 1977, cited in Palkovich 1980:44); societies which, moreover, exhibit the same pattern of endocranial lesions, cribra orbitalia, and generalized skeletal porosity associated with hyperostosis in individuals under five years of age (Palkovich 1980:45). "It is clear from clinical research and studies of extant and prehistoric populations that all of these skeletal manifestations are related to a synergism between malnutrition and infectious disease" (Palkovich 1980:45).

Further evidence for dietary problems comes from bowing of the long bones, the most common pathology among adults. All the bones of the afflicted individuals showed "thinner cortexes and less mineralization" (Palkovich 1980:45) than normal bones. Palkovich (1980:45) suggests that the pathology may have been the result of a dietary deficiency of minerals essential for bone maintenance and may be the "residual effect of dietary stress experienced at an earlier age."

In sum, the Arroyo Hondo skeletal remains offer good evidence for protein-calorie malnutrition. Most of the bone abnormalities associated with malnutrition and infectious disease cluster among children under five, and some older individuals, who may have been PCM survivors, show possible scars in the form of bowed long bones and thin cortexes. Unfortunately, it is impossible to determine how these deaths are distributed through time because they are not dated precisely. Although we would like to know whether deaths increased during drought periods, the best that can be said now is that the pueblo had a serious nutrition problem, which was probably exacerbated when food was scarce.

Archaeological Evidence for Population Dips

If the drought cohort meant an undersized adult population, the effects of this demographic blip might be seen archaeologically. Like much of the material described above, however, the evidence is suggestive but not substantial.

One would expect a decline in the adult population to have several physically visible effects on the community. First, the rate at which new households were established should have declined. With a reduced number of young drought-cohort adults marrying and beginning their own families, there should be evidence for less construction at the pueblo. Three building slumps have in fact been identified on the basis of archaeological evidence, occurring in 1340–55, 1360–70, and 1410–abandonment (Lang and Harris 1984:15), but only the second one can be associated with a possible drought cohort since the others are clearly correlated with drought and migration. The slump of 1360–70 follows the first great drought at Arroyo Hondo by about 20 years and coincides with the period when the first drought cohort would have been reaching adulthood and marrying. However, this decline could also be associated with another exodus prompted by drought since the 1360s were a dry period (Lang and Harris 1984:40). It might be possible, though, to rule out emigration by examining the households dating from this period. If residences had been abandoned by people leaving the pueblo, many of them would probably have been in the middle rather than at the end of the residence unit's cycle; that is, the households would probably show little evidence of sealed doors and vents, which appear to be common features of residence units occupied for a full generation. As the children grew up, the parents apparently sealed off rooms they no longer needed.

Another change one might expect to see in the wake of the drought cohort would be a shift in the residence unit structure. As the cohort's members matured, they would have found themselves assuming a larger number of elderly dependents than their predecessors since they perhaps had no siblings or cousins with whom they could share the responsibility. As a result, the number and size of extended household units should have increased during the period 20 to 30 years after a drought. Unfortunately, the information needed to test for residence units is not available because temporal controls are not adequate to specify when households were occupied.

In summary, the archaeological traces of the drought cohort as adults are faint at best. The building slump of the 1360s is suggestive of a decline in the adult population, but it cannot verify that the earlier drought of 1335–45 was responsible.

SUMMARY AND CONCLUSIONS

This chapter has examined the ways in which drought and other calamities might have affected the Arroyo Hondo population and its demographic patterns. Working with reference model life tables, we found that a drought's effect depended on its length and severity. A short dry spell resulting in a small increase in deaths among young children, even for five years, would have created only a minor, quickly absorbed perturbation in the population size. A large increase in deaths during one or two years would have been similarly damped. An extended and severe drought, however, could have had a dramatic impact on the population. Specifically, if the death rate among infants and young children increased to 50 or 60 percent during a five-year drought period, the future adult population could have been reduced roughly 10 to 15 percent, and the loss could have been as high as 25 percent if mortality among young children reached 80 percent. This would have held whether the Arroyo Hondo population was stationary or expanding.

The loss to the adult population would have been greatest when the cohort of survivors reached maturity, but it would have been felt until all members of the group were dead. During this time, the demographic change would have affected the construction of new households, the dependency ratio, the crude birth rate, and the size of the next generation.

In short, climate could have had a significant impact on Arroyo Hondo Pueblo's health and demographic patterns, according to the calculations used here. The archaeological data from the site offer some evidence that this may indeed have been the case. The plant remains include possible starvation foods, suggesting that the inhabitants suffered through lean times occasionally, and the faunal remains point to food shortages after the 1330s. Specifically, the latter provide evidence that the Arroyo Hondo hunters were working harder and traveling farther than before in order to bring home meat. They stalked a wider variety of game than in earlier periods, including small animals with a relatively meager return, and also traveled some distance into the foothills and mountains to hunt small game and to take deer during the off season. Neither of these lines of evidence points to specific famines, but the plant remains suggest food shortages, while the faunal remains indicate that these were probably more severe during the dry period after 1335.

Further evidence for dietary stress comes from the skeletal remains, which reveal a population with a high mortality rate among infants and young children that allowed only about 40 percent of the population to reach 15 years of age. These characteristics are common among nonindustrialized societies today, where a large number of children fall victim to a synergism of infection and malnutrition, maladies that were probably responsible for Arroyo Hondo's high death rate as well. Four bone pathologies that have been associated with nutritional problems were found clustered in the age groups under five years. Since only two of these appeared occasionally among older individuals, the pattern strongly suggests that malnutrition and disease may have been the underlying causes of death among young children. Further evidence for nutritional problems comes from the adults. The only pathology common in this age group, bowing of the long bones with reduced bone cortex, is believed to be a residual effect of malnutrition in early childhood.

Finally, the archaeological remains also provide evidence that droughts caused the predicted dip in the adult population 20 years later. Between

1360 and 1370, there was an apparent decline in construction at the pueblo, which could reflect a drop in the adult population resulting from the 1335–45 drought.

In summary, Arroyo Hondo's population appears to have suffered from food shortages and protein-calorie malnutrition. During drought periods, deaths from PCM were probably at their peak, with important consequences for the adult population 20 to 30 years later. The archaeological evidence suggests that the drought of 1335–45 may have had an effect on the pueblo, but the data now available can neither prove nor disprove this hypothesis. Until additional information is available, the proposed relationship among climate, health, and demography will have to remain a highly probable but unproven hypothesis.

Should this hypothesis be substantiated, its implications would raise questions about how Arroyo Hondo and other pueblos functioned over long time spans. Population fluctuations could have had far-reaching consequences for social organization and subsistence patterns. Indeed they may have contributed to the development of eastern Pueblo organization which has been the subject of study and controversy for several decades (Eggan 1950; Fox 1967, 1972; Ortiz 1969). Scholars have been particularly intrigued with the strikingly divergent social systems seen among the different Pueblo groups despite their great cultural and psychological unity (Eggan 1972:293). The western Pueblos "conform to a general pattern based on matrilineal clans and matrilocal households, with a Crow-type of kinship system," while the eastern Pueblos have "a dual division of the society and bilateral kinship system in which seniority, or relative age, is emphasized. . . . Between the two are the Keresan-speaking Pueblos, whose social systems partake of both western and eastern aspects" (Eggan 1972:293).

Eggan (1950) first attempted to account for this pattern by proposing that "the modern Pueblos might have a common ancestral source in the San Juan–Mesa Verde–Chaco region and that the divergence in social structure might be related to forced migrations to the Rio Grande and to the new adaptations and readjustments which were involved . . . the Tewa probably had a social structure of the western Pueblo type which was greatly modified during their sojourn in the east" (Eggan 1972:293). In the 1960s, Fox challenged the notion that the Keresan patterns of kinship were acculturated versions of a basic western Pueblo prototype. He proposed instead a rather elaborate original kinship system with exogamous patrilineal moieties cross-cut by matrilineal clans, from which the eastern, western, and Keresan systems diverged (Fox 1967, 1972:73–4).

This study cannot resolve the debate, but a knowledge of population dynamics may be useful in unraveling the development of Pueblo social organization since it suggests an impetus for change. Specifically, the periods of population dips may have placed strains on the society that could have eroded old systems and encouraged the rise of new. For example, at those times when the drought cohort was reaching adulthood, Arroyo Hondo Pueblo may have had problems filling all the ceremonial and political positions normally assumed by adults. Most seriously threatened would have been those posts for which the occupants were highly specified on the basis of descent. Unable to properly fill the roles, the Arroyo Hondoans may have left them vacant or bent the rules to find an occupant. This process has been observed among the Hopi, who have a very strong clan system intimately bound to the ritual cycle. Each ceremony in their annual calendar is "owned" by a particular clan "which furnished the officers and ritual equipment and provides for its continuance and transmission" (Eggan 1950:104). In the past, when a clan's membership dwindled, its ceremony might become extinct, as documented in several cases. But important ceremonies could not be dropped and were assumed by associated clans of the same phratry. "In extreme instances a ceremony may be offered to any individual who will take over the responsibilities and privileges of leadership" (Eggan 1950:90).

A related problem is sheer numbers. Even if all posts could have been filled by conventional or unconventional means, the community still may have been short the appropriate complement of individuals for all the posts. The result would probably have been a heavier load of ceremonial and political obligations for most adults, with some assuming more than one ceremonial role. The Hopi again illustrate how new arrangements might arise from such a situation. At Shongopovi, "there are but three members of the Kachina-Parrot clan and their ceremonial obligations are heavy. A way out was found. The office of Singers chief is made to rotate between the three men, each holding it for four years" (Parsons 1922:297, quoted in Eggan 1950:105). A similar pattern of rotating ceremonial positions, such as village chieftanship, has been seen in some of the other Hopi villages as well (Eggan 1950:105).

It is possible to imagine that repeated bending and breaking of rules in the past eventually led to their demise in communities such as Arroyo Hondo Pueblo.

Shortages of adults may have created problems in recruiting another form of personnel—appropriate spouses. Suitable mates may not have been available at times if highly specified by requirements for a cross-cousin or a member of a particular kinship group. Under such circumstances the members of the drought cohort would have again been encouraged to bend or break rules.

The drought cohort may have strained the social organization in still another way. If the pueblo had had some form of unilineal descent, the system may not have weathered periods of population decline. Clans are particularly vulnerable to demographic fluctuations, as Eggan noted (1950:110), and are taxed by both growth and decline. With the latter may come extinction, as in the Hopi case described above (Eggan 1950:90). Lineages likewise may disappear as a result of population fluctuations. In addition, some of their influence and strength may be dissipated during difficult times. Normally they are an effective mechanism for holding land and other possessions and passing them on to succeeding generations. But during periods of population dips such corporate groups would have faced several difficulties at Arroyo Hondo. For example, with a shortage of adult males some households may have failed to produce enough food, forcing them to seek help from many sources including kinsmen in other lineages. Those households well endowed with prime agricultural lands in the canyon but short on men may have tried to recruit new members through unconventional means. Residence rules, such as matrilocality, may well have been violated in order to effectively distribute productive adults, dependents, and land and water resources. A married couple, for example, might have combined their parental households to form one large extended family in order to support both sets of parents. Under these circumstances unilineal principles, if they had existed at Arroyo Hondo, may have given way to bilateral kinship.

Whatever principles first organized the early settlement at Arroyo Hondo Pueblo, it is clear that flexibility and adaptability were soon called for. With shortages of adults, the community needed a flexible system that made it possible to recruit personnel from a large if not open-ended pool. They needed a means to distribute responsibilities and privileges across the community in a flexible manner that could respond readily to population fluctuations. And they needed a system that allowed them access to the resources and support of as many other villagers as possible. If Arroyo Hondo Pueblo had begun with a more elaborate social structure than is presently known in this area, the demographic fluctuations would have threatened its stability. The rule bending and breaking necessary for adapting to varying numbers and deficits of adults could have gradually eroded the system. On the other hand, if Arroyo Hondo had been a simply organized community, on the lines of the present-day pueblos, the population fluctuations would have reinforced and helped perpetuate the system.

These periods of fluctuating population may have also stimulated new farming practices. Faced with feeding a disproportionately large number of dependents, the people of Arroyo Hondo may well have tried to increase yields through a variety of techniques. Where the canyon opens onto a flood plain, they may have improved water distribution across the fields by building dams and "water spreaders" of earth, stone, and brush, as did the Hopi and Zuni (Glassow 1980:48). If they already practiced these techniques they may have intensified them. Like the Zuni, they might have covered entire fields with a herringbone pattern of water spreaders or added "low dikes on the perimeters of the field to keep the floodwaters within the fields" (Glassow 1980:49). Like the western Pueblos, they might also have dug ditches to ensure that water went to every part of the field (Glassow 1980:49). On the piedmont they could have increased yields by building linear border fields, if they had not already done so. Known only through archaeological evidence, these "consist of parallel lines of rock, one or more courses high, that are placed so that each line is roughly at one elevation on a hillside slope" (Glassow 1980:52). Although simple, they are useful in catching soil washing down a slope and in retaining runoff (Glassow 1980:53). Simple reservoirs designed to catch runoff from the hillslopes just east of the village could also have improved yields.

Economic problems during these times of population fluctuations may have also prompted some households to find additional means for making a livelihood. For example, families that had problems raising enough crops may have begun to specialize in crafts which women and older individuals could produce and trade for food.

In sum, the periods of population flux following on the heels of droughts and other crises were undoubtedly felt at Arroyo Hondo in many ways. The shortages of productive adults about 20 to 30 years after the crisis could well have strained the community's social organization. Faced with a dearth of adults to fill all the ceremonial-political positions, the pueblo may well have had to bend and break rules in order to carry on its ceremonial life. Ultimately new, more flexible patterns for recruiting personnel and integrating the community may have emerged. The deficit of adults also may have caused economic hardship for many households, prompting them to turn to a wider range of kinsmen for support. As a result, new residence patterns might have appeared, while bilateral kinship principles may have been stressed. At the same time, the community may have tried to intensify agriculture and find additional ways to make a living.

We can imagine that at Arroyo Hondo, and many other villages in the area, these were periods of quiet turmoil with change and innovation creeping slowly into pueblo lifeways. They were not dramatic moments with severe hardship and heroic suffering. They were not the stuff of tales to tell the grandchildren—-the long remembered drought or locust plague. Yet their impact on Pueblo Indian life was probably far greater in the long run. During these times of mild hardship people had the strength to seek innovation, while the system was sufficiently intact to incorporate it. In contrast, the truly hard times with severe suffering were almost certainly periods in which social life dissipated or broke down altogether. At such times people would not have had the energy and motivation to improvise and invent. With attention focused on finding food today, they could not have troubled to locate a song leader for next winter's solstice celebration. Moreover, any changes that might have emerged were not likely to have been incorporated in the long haul since there was no system to absorb them at the time. Indeed, life during famines and other crises was most likely seen as anomalous, with patterns and customs that were quickly dropped once normal conditions resumed. The real makings for change in Pueblo social organization can probably be sought in the small incremental innovations and alterations that emerged during periods of minor stress such as these episodes of fluctuating numbers and shifts in age structure.

Appendix A

ENERGY REQUIREMENTS OF THE ARROYO HONDO PUEBLO POPULATION

Although we can never know precisely how much food the people of Arroyo Hondo Pueblo needed to sustain themselves, we can make a rough estimate of their collective energy requirement. A useful model of these needs can be found in the 1973 recommendations of the Food and Agriculture Organization (FAO) and the World Health Organization (WHO), intended for use in nonindustrialized countries. These agencies (1973) define their recommendations as the energy intake considered adequate to meet the needs of the average, healthy person in a specified age and size category. The values are not intended for any one individual but are designed to reflect the true requirement of the whole population.

The FAO-WHO recommendations, shown in table 28, are expressed in terms of the needs of a healthy, moderately active reference man and woman. The values are based on metabolic and food consumption studies, and can be applied to a subject population after being adjusted for size, age, and activity level with FAO-WHO correction factors. The values for children and older infants come from studies on healthy children in the United States and Canada, and those for infants under six months are based on the milk consumption of breast-fed infants.

The energy requirements for a whole community must be estimated on the basis of its age and sex structure and the specific needs of each

TABLE 28.
Human energy requirements.

Age in Years	*Calories per Kilogram Body Weight per Day*	*Calories per Day*
CHILDREN		
<1	112	
1–3	101	
4–6	91	
7–9	79	
Males		
10–12	71	
13–15	57	
16–19	49	
Females		
10–12	62	
13–15	50	
16–19	43	
ADULTS		
Males		3,000
Females		2,200

SOURCE: FAO-WHO 1973:28, 35.

group. The FAO and WHO have done this for a model nonindustrialized country, and their values can probably be applied to Arroyo Hondo with only minor modifications. The model population has a pyramid-shaped age distribution, with most individuals falling into the younger age categories, which would have been the case at Arroyo Hondo. The model adult males weigh 53 kilograms and the females 46 kilograms, figures which are probably close to those for the Arroyo Hondoans, who appear on the basis of the skeletal remains to have been relatively small. Using Trotter and Gleser's (1958) regression analysis techniques on eight individuals, Ann Palkovich (written communication) estimated mean adult stature as 172.6 centimeters for males and 159.5 centimeters for females. She believes, however, that males were on the average shorter than the value she calculated because her sample was skewed by several tall individuals.

Table 29 gives the estimated energy needs of the Arroyo Hondo pop-

TABLE 29.
Energy requirements of the Arroyo Hondo population. Based on FAO-WHO 1973:31, 82.

			Winter Requirement (calories)		Summer Requirement (calories)
Age in Years	*Percentage of Population Represented by Age Group*	*Average Weight of Individuals in Age Group (kilograms)*	*Per Person per Day*	*Contribution to Total Requirement per 100 Persons*	*Contribution to Total Requirement per 100 Persons*
1[a]	2.5	9.0	1,090	27.50	
1–3	11.4	13.4	1,360	155.04	
4–6	10.5	20.2	1,830	192.15	
7–9	8.7	28.1	2,190	190.53	
Males					
10–12	3.9	37.0	2,600	101.40	
13–15	3.4	51.0	2,370	80.58	94.28
16–19	3.8	53.0	2,490	94.62	110.71
20–39	13.6	53.0	2,440	331.84	338.25
40–49	3.8	53.0	2,318	88.08	103.05
50–59	2.6	53.0	2,196	57.10	
60–69	1.5	53.0	1,952	29.28	
70+	0.7	53.0	1,708	11.96	
Females					
10–12	3.9	37.0	2,350	91.65	
13–15	3.4	46.0	2,080	70.72	82.74
16–19	3.7	46.0	1,932	71.48	83.63
20–39	13.5	46.0	1,840	248.40	290.63
40–49	3.8	46.0	1,748	66.42	77.71
50–59	2.7	46.0	1,656	44.71	
60–69	1.6	46.0	1,472	23.55	
70+	0.9	46.0	1,288	11.59	
Total Calories per Person per Day:				1,989	2,107
Average = 2,048 Calories per Person per Day					

[a]Includes needs for pregnancy and lactation.

ulation based on the FAO-WHO model, with a few modifications. The column showing Arroyo Hondo's winter needs was calculated using the FAO-WHO figures for a moderately active life style. The last column indicates the pueblo's energy requirements during the summer months, with corrections for a very active life style applied to individuals 13 to 49 years of age. This adjustment seemed appropriate in light of the fact that these people would have been actively engaged in farming, hunting, collecting plants, building, and felling timber in the summer.

The FAO WHO have also included a correction for the additional energy needs of pregnancy and lactation by including these in the requirements for children under one year. It was assumed that during any year, the number of pregnant women exceeds that of children under one year by 10 percent, allowing for pregnancy wastage and perinatal mortality. The total energy supplement per pregnancy is 80,000 calories, which averages out to about 240 calories per child less than one year old per day. Infants under six months must be breast-fed, so lactating women, whose extra requirements are 750 calories per day, represent 50 percent of the population of children under one year. The additional needs for lactation after six months are incorporated into the caloric needs of children 6 to 12 months.

Appendix B

PROTEIN REQUIREMENTS OF THE ARROYO HONDO PUEBLO POPULATION

The FAO-WHO's (1973) recommendations for protein requirements, shown in table 30, provide a useful model for understanding the protein needs of the Arroyo Hondo population. Though they are based on several sources, most of the figures come from nitrogen balance studies—a technique for determining the amount of nitrogen, and hence protein, needed to maintain growth in children and to prevent loss of tissue protein in adults.

For infants under six months of age, the figures are based on the amount of protein that breast-fed infants consume. Interpolated values were used for some of the older age classes of children, due to a lack of appropriate nitrogen balance studies among these age groups. Values for the additional needs of pregnancy and lactation were based on analysis of fetal tissue and breast milk composition. In order to provide a small margin of safety, the FAO and WHO increased all of these figures by 30 percent, producing the recommendations shown in the table.

As in the case of the energy recommendations, these values are estimates of the average physiological requirement but are not applicable to any single individual. Using them for a group is valid, however, since the varying needs of individuals within the population should average out.

To calculate Arroyo Hondo Pueblo's protein needs, the FAO-WHO's

TABLE 30.
Human protein requirements.

Age	*Grams of Protein per Kilogram of Body Weight per Day*
CHILDREN	
6–11 months	1.18
1–3 years	0.92
4–6	0.78
7–9	0.68
MALES	
10–12	0.62
13–15	0.55
16–19	0.47
Adults	0.44
FEMALES	
10–12	0.59
13–15	0.49
16–19	0.43
Adults	0.40
Last half of pregnancy: add 6.5.	
First 6 months of lactation: add 13.0.	

SOURCE: FAO 1973:74.
NOTE: The FAO (1973:74) estimates for a safe level of protein intake were used here after corrections. The original figures include an extra margin of 30 percent to allow for individual variability and to cover the upper range of needs (FAO 1973:70). This 30 percent of the original value was subtracted to give a figure that more closely approximates average needs.

model population was again used to estimate the total requirement of each age class, as shown in table 31. The values are expressed in terms of milk or egg protein, a form that is considered nearly perfect for the human body (FAO-WHO 1973:67). When poorer quality protein, such as that derived from corn or beans, is included in the diet, the requirements must be increased to account for the fact that these are not utilized as well as those from milk or eggs. Accordingly, the last three

TABLE 31.
Protein requirements of the Arroyo Hondo population.

Age in Years	Percentage of Population Represented by Age Group	Average Weight of Individuals in Age Group (kilograms)	Requirements for Egg or Milk Protein		Individual Requirement for Different Quality Proteins		
			Individual Requirement (grams per day)	*Contribution to Total Requirement per 100 Persons (in grams)*	NPU = 80 *(in grams)*	NPU = 70 *(in grams)*	NPU = 60 *(in grams)*
Children							
<1	2.5	9.0	10.62[a]	26.55			
1–3	11.4	13.4	12.33	140.56	15.41	17.61	20.55
4–6	10.5	20.2	15.76	165.48	19.70	22.51	26.27
7–9	8.7	28.1	19.11	166.26	23.88	27.30	31.85
Males							
10–12	3.9	37.0	22.94	89.47	28.68	32.77	38.23
13–15	3.4	51.0	28.05	95.37	35.06	40.07	46.75
16–19	3.8	53.0	24.91	94.66	31.14	35.59	41.52
20–39	13.6	53.0	23.32	317.15	29.15	33.31	38.87
40–49	3.8	53.0	23.32	88.62	31.80	36.34	42.42
50–59	2.6	53.0	23.32	60.63	31.80	36.34	42.42
60–69	1.5	53.0	23.32	34.98	31.80	36.34	42.42
70+	0.7	53.0	23.32	16.32	31.80	36.34	42.42

TABLE 31. *(continued)*

Age in Years	Percentage of Population Represented by Age Group	Average Weight of Individuals in Age Group (kilograms)	Requirements for Egg or Milk Protein: Individual Requirement (grams per day)	Requirements for Egg or Milk Protein: Contribution to Total Requirement per 100 Persons (in grams)	Individual Requirement for Different Quality Proteins: NPU = 80 (in grams)	Individual Requirement for Different Quality Proteins: NPU = 70 (in grams)	Individual Requirement for Different Quality Proteins: NPU = 60 (in grams)
Females							
10–12	3.9	37.0	21.83	80.77	27.29	31.19	36.38
13–15	3.4	46.0	22.54	76.63	28.18	32.20	37.57
16–19	3.7	46.0	19.78	73.19	24.73	28.26	32.97
20–39	13.5	46.0	18.40	248.40	23.00	26.29	30.67
40–49	3.8	46.0	18.40	69.92	23.00	26.29	30.67
50–59	2.7	46.0	18.40	49.68	23.00	26.29	30.67
60–69	1.6	46.0	18.40	29.44	23.00	26.29	30.67
70+	0.9	46.0	18.40	16.56	23.00	26.29	30.67

Average = 19.41 grams protein per person per day.

[a]14.09 grams for pregnancy and lactation.

columns express the requirement in terms of slightly poorer proteins. The three types are classified according to the Net Protein Utilization (NPU) value, a combined measure of a protein's digestibility and the efficiency with which it is utilized. For example, a protein with an NPU of 100 is fully utilized by the body, whereas one with an NPU of 60 is only 60 percent utilized.

Appendix C

THE CALORIE CONTENT OF ARROYO HONDO FOODS

TABLE 32.
Calorie content of plant foods.

Plant	*Calories per Kilogram*	*Source*[a]	*Comments*
Maize (*Zea mays*)	3,600	L&F:14	Whole kernel, dried yellow corn
Beans (*Phaseolus vulgaris*)	3,370	L&F:60	Whole seeds
Prickly pear fruit (*Opuntia* spp.)	2,175	L&F:57	The L&F value was adjusted for the same moisture content as the prickly pear collected in the productivity studies—dried fruit with 25% moisture.

TABLE 32. *(continued)*

Plant	*Calories per Kilogram*	*Source*[a]	*Comments*
Yucca fruit[b] (*Yucca baccata*)	3,900	Wetterstrom, unpublished data	Dry fruit
Weed seeds	3,400	L&F: 13, 17, 18	Median value of L&F figures for *Chenopodium pallidicaule, C. quinoa,* and teosinte (*Zea mexicana*).
Indian rice grass[b] (*Oryzopsis hymenoides*)	4,100	Wetterstrom, unpublished data	Dry seeds

[a]L&F = Leung and Flores 1961.
[b]The author assayed yucca fruit and Indian rice grass for a variety of constituents. Total nitrogen, and indirectly protein, was determined by means of the micro-Kjeldahl technique (Lillevik 1970; Horowitz 1965). Lipids were removed by means of a Soxlet-type extractor and measured by weight loss. The carbohydrate content was calculated by subtracting the protein and lipid content and correcting for ash. The caloric value was then determined by summing the energy contribution of each of these constituents. These were estimated on the basis of Atwater's physiological fuel values for nutrients (Merrill and Watt 1955).

TABLE 33.
Caloric value of animal foods.

Animal	*Meat Weight (kilograms)*	*Source*	*Calories per Kilogram*	*Source*[a]
Deer (*Odocoileus hemionus*)	45.50	Ford 1968a:159	1,460	L&F:70, roasted venison

TABLE 33. *(continued)*

Animal	*Meat Weight (kilograms)*	*Source*	*Calories per Kilogram*	*Source*[a]
Pronghorn (*Antilocapra americana*)	27.20	Estimated as 50% of the live weight of 55 kg (Russell 1964:7).	1,460	Caloric value of deer used in absence of published data on pronghorn.
Rabbits and hares (*Sylvilagus audoboni, Lepus californicus*)	0.38	Estimated as 55% of the combined live weight of cottontails and jackrabbits in a 1-to-3 ratio. Cottontails = 1.0 kg (Hall and Kelson 1959:265), jackrabbits = 2.75 kg (Bailey 1931:48).	1,350	L&F:67, hare, flesh only
Turkeys (*Meleagris gallopavo merriami*)	2.30	Live weight estimated at 4.5 kg (Schorger 1966:86–89); 50% taken for meat weight.	1,700	L&F:68, young chicken, raw, total edible

[a]L&F = Leung and Flores 1961.

Appendix D

FOOD PLANT REMAINS FOUND AT ARROYO HONDO PUEBLO

TABLE 34
Number of seeds and seedlike structures by provenience.

NOTE: In the following provenience designations, the first number refers to a roomblock, the second to a room in that roomblock, and the third to a specific level or feature within the room; the fourth number is usually a sample number. Thus 4-2-5-2 refers to roomblock 4, room 2, level 5, sample 2. Designations that begin with a letter instead of a number refer to grid squares or other features excavated in plazas.

These data are based on materials excavated during 1972 and 1973.

	Corn (present)	Beans	Squash	Cheno-ams	Purslane	Winged Pig-weed	Ground Cherry	Indian Rice Grass	Hedgehog Cactus	Other
4-2-5-2	x									
4-2-6-3	x									
5-4-7-36	x									
5-5-5				1						
5-5-6E-2				3						
5-8-VE-1	x		1	36	2		5	465		
5-8-6E-2	x							38		
5-9-1W	x									
5-9-2	x									
5-9-2E-4	x									
5-9-2E-6	x				6			3	1	
5-9-2E-9	x			2						
5-9-2E-3W	x									
5-9-14-3	x			195	46	1	43		1	1 pincushion cactus seed
5-11-IVS-8	x			1	2					1 bee plant seed
5-12-IVW-1	x			16	2					
5-13-IIW-1	x								1	
5-14-3-2	x		1							
7-7-3-1	x									
7-8-IE	x									
8-5-2-10	x									
8-5-4-1	x									
8-5-12				1						

	Corn (present)	Beans	Squash	Cheno-ams	Purslane	Winged Pig-weed	Ground Cherry	Indian Rice Grass	Hedgehog Cactus	Other
9-2-3-22	x			5		1			1	
9-6-3	x	75								
9-6-III	x			7		2				1 pinyon nut
9-7-V	x									
9-7-8	x									
9-8-6	x									
9-8-7	x			4						
9-9-1W	x									
9-9-2W-4	x									
9-10-II	x									
9-10-2	x									
9-10-2S	x									
9-10-IIN-10	x			4						
9-10-IIN-11				1						1 yucca seed
9-10-II-8	x									
9-10-3	x									
9-10-3-1-1	x									
9-11-2N	x									
9-11-III	x									
9-11-IIIS-1	x			6	2			1	2	
9-11-7-1	x			3						
9-12-1W	x	1								
9-12-IIE	x	26								
9-12-II	x									

TABLE 34. (continued)

	Corn (present)	Beans	Squash	Cheno-ams	Purslane	Winged Pig-weed	Ground Cherry	Indian Rice Grass	Hedgehog Cactus	Other
9-12-4-5	x									
9-13-2	x									
9-13-IIIW	x	2								
9-13-5-1	x								1	
10-3-3,4,5-2	x			2						
10-3-3,4,5-3	x									Fragments of 1 pinyon nut shell 1 yucca seed
10-3-6-3										
10-3-10,12,13-2	x			1						
10-3-14-2				1						
10-3-16-2	x									
10-4-2	x									
10-4-3	x									
10-4-3S-1	x			8	1	1				
10-4-III-5	x									1 squash seed impression
10-4-4	x									
10-5-1	x									
10-5-1N	x									
10-5-2	x									
10-5-2N-2	x			21	1					
10-5-3	x									
10-5-IIIS-1					5				1	

	Corn (present)	Beans	Squash	Cheno-ams	Purslane	Winged Pig-weed	Ground Cherry	Indian Rice Grass	Hedgehog Cactus	Other
10-6-1	x									
10-6-2S-11	x									
10-6-3	x									
10-6-IIIN-2	x			4						1 pincushion cactus seed
10-6-IVS-9	x			2		2				
11-6-1-2	x									
12-4-1-1										1 yucca seed
12-4-1-3				1						
12-4-2-2	x			4	1					1 bee plant seed
12-4-2-3	x							1		
12-4-5-2	x			1						
12-4-8-2	x									
12-4-9-3	x									
12-6-1-1	x			1						
14-5-1-3	x									
14-5-2-3	x									
14-5-3	x			2						1 yucca seed
14-5-3-5	x				2					
14-5-3-21	x			1						
14-5-5	x									
14-5-6	x			1						1 sunflower seed
14-5-8	x									
14-5-10	x			2						

TABLE 34. *(continued)*

	Corn (present)	Beans	Squash	Cheno-ams	Purslane	Winged Pig-weed	Ground Cherry	Indian Rice Grass	Hedgehog Cactus	Other
15-6-1	x		4							3.3 grams carbonized squash flesh
15-6-1-1	x	71	4						1	94 pinyon nuts
15-7-1	x									
15-7-3	x									
15A-7-1-1	x									1 bee plant seed
15A-7-4-1	x			2						
15A-8-1	x									
15A-8-1-4	x			4						
15A-8-6-1	x			2						
15A-8-11-2	x			1						
15A-9-1	x									
15A-9-3	x									
15A-9-4				3	1					
15A-9-4-2	x			1						
15A-9-5	x									
16-38-3				1						
16-38-4	x									
16-38-5	x			2						
18-5-3-4	x									
18-5-IV-8	x			7	6					
18-5-5-3				4	1				3	
18-6-2N&S	x			3						1 sunflower seed

	Corn (present)	Beans	Squash	Cheno-ams	Purslane	Winged Pig-weed	Ground Cherry	Indian Rice Grass	Hedgehog Cactus	Other
18-7-5-2	x			4						
18-8-III-5	x									
18-8-5N-1	x			2	1				1	
18-8-6-6-1	x									
18-8-8N&S-7-1	x									
18-9-2N&S-1				1						
18-14-1S&W-1	x	1		3	5					
18-14-2N&S-1	x			5	1					
18-14-3N&S-1				4		1				
18-14-IVN&S-1	x			23	1					
18-14-V-2	x			7						
18-15-II	x	218								
18-15-II-1	x									
18-15-II-2	x			18	162					
18-15-III		90	7							
18-15-5-2	x			1						
18-32-3E-3					1					
18-32-IIIE&W-1				14	1	59	7			1 prickly pear cactus seed 1 possible bee plant seed 2 sunflower seeds
18-38-3N&S-1	x			15	655					
18-39-IIS-3	x									
18-39-2N&S-8	x									

TABLE 34. *(continued)*

	Corn (present)	Beans	Squash	Cheno-ams	Purslane	Winged Pig-weed	Ground Cherry	Indian Rice Grass	Hedgehog Cactus	Other
18-39-4N&S-1				1						
18-39-5N&S-1	x			1						
18-39-5-7	x	1		81	619			2		4 sunflower seeds 4 pincushion cactus seeds
18-42-IVN&S	x									
18-49-IN-4	x									
18-49-IIS-1	x									
18-49-4N&S-1	x							1	1	
18-49-7N&S-1		2		6	1				1	
21-3-5-3	x									
21-4-1-4								1		
21-6-2	x			9						
21-6-2-1	x				1					
21-6-2-5	x									
21-6-5-6	x			1	3					
24-3-6-1							1			
24-3-6-2				131	7	7		1		1 yucca seed pinyon nut shell fragments
C-3-11		92								
D-1-7-2	x			4		1				
G-1-2				131	approx. 1,200			3		9 sunflower seeds
G-1-2-1							1			
G-1-3	x		7	20						

	Corn (present)	Beans	Squash	Cheno-ams	Purslane	Winged Pig-weed	Ground Cherry	Indian Rice Grass	Hedgehog Cactus	Other
G-1-3-1	x	1			231					1 bee plant seed
G-2-3-22				1						
G-2-3-23	x			18	1	1	1			1 pinyon nut
G-2-3-29	x	5		9	28			1	17	1 squash rind fragment
G-2-3-32	x	2		15	6	3		1	13	3 bee plant seeds
G-2-3-86	x									1 chokecherry pit and fragments of 2 pits pinyon nut shell fragments
G-2-3-95	x			1	1				4	
G-19A-2					1					
G-25A-III-1	x			26	5	14	1			
G-25C-2-3	x				1				1	1 prickly pear cactus seed
G-25C-3				40						
G-28A	x			3						
G-34A-4-1	x			3						
G-35A-1				33						
G-35A-4-1	x				3	6				
G-102B-2				121	4	5	19		4	1 bee plant seed
G-102B-4-1	x									1 pinyon nut shell
G-103B-2-1				141	22	10			8	3 bee plant seeds
H-2-7	x	1								
TOTAL		588	20	1,260	3,039	114	78	518	62	

Part 2

Additional Reports

I

The Ethnobotanical Pollen Record At Arroyo Hondo Pueblo

Vorsila L. Bohrer

ACKNOWLEDGMENTS

The interest and guidance of Douglas W. Schwartz, President of the School of American Research, is gratefully acknowledged in helping this manuscript reach publication. Richard W. Lang, also of the School of American Research, was pivotal in developing a research design, securing samples, and maintaining communication that helped us both to evaluate the results more carefully and to improve the quality of our interpretation. Close cooperation has not only secured better results but has also distinctly enhanced my sense of satisfaction in helping find solutions to problems relating to the plant world.

Many individuals have made direct contributions to aspects of research described in this paper. Wilma Wetterstrom secured samples of pollen from living pinyon trees at Arroyo Hondo, and Richard Lang obtained modern pollen samples from surface transects at the site. Lucile Housely procured numerous specimens of modern cholla. The conservation efforts of Bertha P. Dutton during her years of residence in Santa Fe allowed comparisons of lichen ground cover and cholla pollen with that from Arroyo Hondo.

INTRODUCTION

Prehistoric pollen survives in exposed archaeological sites in better condition and generally in greater abundance than other plant remains. The coats, or exines, of pollen grains preserve well naturally, whereas the seeds, fruits, and stems of plants are usually preserved only by carbonization. Morphological characteristics of the pollen exines allow most of them to be identified at the species, genus, or family level. The preserved pollen encompasses species that are carried by the wind as well as those distributed by animals. Consequently, many of the identified pollen types differ from the types recognized through seeds, most of which are brought into a site by humans.

Because pollen preserves well, is abundant and identifiable, and represents a wide range of plants, it is a useful source of information about prehistoric climate, vegetation, and human subsistence practices. Fossil pollen comes from plants once living in varying proportions in particular kinds of habitats. These plants produced different amounts of pollen, and some, such as the pinyon, varied in pollen production from year to year. To estimate the proportions of the various pollen types in the overall rain of pollen to the ground, pollen is extracted from the soil matrix, and a random sample of 200 grains is identified and tabulated under magnification. The frequencies of all the pollen types in a sample are known collectively as a pollen spectrum. From examining the pollen spectra, one begins to derive insights about the past environment and economy that may be supplemented through other interpretive techniques. Often, the pathways by which conclusions are reached in pollen studies are as important as the conclusions themselves.

Several assumptions are basic to two methods designed to reconstruct fluctuations in climate. For the small pine percentage (Bohrer 1968, 1972; Hevly 1964), it is necessary to assume that the small-pine pollen rain was uniform across Arroyo Hondo residential areas. For the arboreal pollen percentage (Hevly 1964; Schoenwetter 1964), it is necessary to recognize the reciprocal nature of the arboreal and nonarboreal fractions to the total pollen rain. Since most cultivated crops and many gathered plants are nonarboreal, the herbaceous fraction is likely to be affected by human economic activity. If the nonarboreal percentage changes, the complementary arboreal percentage also changes. Therefore, one would expect that the arboreal pollen percentage too might be skewed from normal by the impact of human economic activity on the pollen rain. Thus the detection of and explanation for the presence of ethnobotanical pollen became research objectives. The search for ethnobotanical pollen produced insights into the diet, ecology, and economy of the Arroyo Hondo inhabitants.

In order to be cognizant of pollen spectra skewed by cultural activity, it is essential to recognize a normal spectrum. Many pollen analysts have interpreted a paraphrase of Hutton's 1795 doctrine of uniformitarianism, "the present is the key to the past," literally to represent the following equation:

$$\frac{\text{modern plant community}}{\text{modern pollen count}} = \frac{\text{prehistoric plant community}}{\text{fossil pollen count}}$$

Because the elaborate language used in 1795 to explain the doctrine has been telescoped into so few words, the vital message has been obscured. Hutton was concerned that the principle used to explain a past event be the same as that operating in the present: "no powers [are] to be employed that are not natural to the globe, no action to be admitted of except those of which we know the *principle* [italics mine], and no extraordinary events to be alleged in order to explain a common appearance" (Mather and Mason 1964:95).

At Arroyo Hondo, the principles influencing the formation of the modern and prehistoric plant communities differ. Two biotic factors of prime impact on the development and expression of the vegetation historically—domestic grazing animals and alien weeds—were absent prehistorically. A brief description of the present environment of Arroyo Hondo and the changes that have occurred historically will demonstrate why the local, modern pollen spectra could not be used in this study as a norm for interpreting the prehistoric pollen data.

HISTORIC CHANGES IN VEGETATION

Arroyo Hondo ruin, located slightly more than four miles south of the main plaza of Santa Fe, New Mexico, lies on the western margin of the foothills of the Sangre de Cristo Mountains at an elevation of 7,090 feet. The site occupies a rise on the piedmont overlooking the deep Arroyo Hondo. Although the arroyo is classified as an intermittent stream, its sandy bottom stays sufficiently moist to support vigorous stands of rabbit brush *(Chrysothamnus nauseosus)*.[1] A permanent spring in the bottom of the arroyo immediately below the site creates subsurface moisture downstream. Cattail *(Typha latifolia)*, sedges (Cyperaceae), and willow (*Salix* spp.) grow near the spring.

The vegetation immediately around the Arroyo Hondo site today is typical of a juniper savanna, except where vegetation to the south was disturbed by an earthen reservoir in the 1930s (Kelley 1980:73). A few one-seeded junipers *(Juniperus monosperma)* and a scatter of cholla and prickly pear cactus (*Opuntia* spp.) interrupt what would otherwise be a shortgrass prairie dominated by grama grass (*Bouteloua* spp.). The juniper savanna extends for some 2½ miles west of the pueblo, gradually becoming shortgrass prairie. For the same distance east and north of the site, an increasingly dense coniferous woodland covers the foothills of the Sangre de Cristo Mountains. Pinyon *(Pinus edulis)* and one-seeded juniper dominate in nearly equal numbers, with cholla *(Opuntia imbricata)* and blue grama grass *(Bouteloua gracilis)* most abundant among the shrubs and herbs, respectively (Kelley 1980:62–63). A few young ponderosa pines *(Pinus ponderosa)* grow in Arroyo Hondo canyon near the site today, but ponderosas become numerous only on shaded, north-facing slopes about two miles east of the site. A true ponderosa forest begins about 4¼ miles east of Arroyo Hondo Pueblo.

Although many of the same kinds of plants grew in the Arroyo Hondo area in prehistoric times as at present, there is good reason to believe that the character of the woodland and grassland has changed substantially. The factor chiefly responsible for the change is grazing by domestic animals. For more than 300 years since the founding of Santa Fe in 1610, the Arroyo Hondo area has furnished forage for sheep, goats, burros, horses, and cattle. In 1849, Captain Marcy (1850:196) described the five miles south of Santa Fe as a succession of barren hills covered in places with dwarf cedar but destitute of grass. The nearest place where immigrants could find grass for their teams was Galisteo, 24 miles south of Santa Fe (Marcy 1850:196). Weather records suggest that the landscape seen by Marcy was a product of drought in addition to overgrazing (Tuan et al. 1973:7).

Overgrazing has altered the abundance and proportions of certain native grasses, annuals, and shrubs in the vicinity of Arroyo Hondo Pueblo. The most striking aspect of the present grassland composition is the rarity of cool-season grasses such as wheatgrass *(Agropyron smithii)*, Indian ricegrass *(Oryzopsis hymenoides)*, mutton grass *(Poa fendleriana)*, squirreltail *(Sitanion hystrix)*, and needle-and-thread *(Stipa comata)*. Studies of areas unaffected by domestic grazing suggest that the low visibility of these species near Arroyo Hondo results from a history of year-round grazing (Baxter 1977; Bohrer 1975a; Schmutz, Michaels, and Judd 1967). Explanations for the decline of cool season grasses under domestic grazing include (1) generally tall growth that makes much of the plant readily accessible to grazing animals, (2) the demand for succulent plants early in the spring after their winter dormancy, and (3) the long exposure of the plants to grazing while they are still immature because of slower growth in the spring (Schmutz, Michaels, and Judd 1967:368).

Overgrazing has also lowered the overall abundance (Kelley 1980:82, 84), and therefore the contribution to the pollen rain, of native annuals like sunflower *(Helianthus annuus)* and goosefoot (*Chenopodium* spp.). In the vicinity of Santa Fe, these highly palatable genera (Smith 1896; Wooton 1908) do not play as great a role as would be deduced from observations of early plant succession in disturbed habitats elsewhere (Erdman 1970:18; Weaver and Albertson 1956:145).[2] A native shrub now rare in the Arroyo Hondo area is winterfat *(Eurotia lanata)* (Kelley 1980); its infrequence there and elsewhere in the Southwest is a result of historic grazing pressure (Dayton 1931:32).

Another effect of overgrazing has been the establishment and spread of introduced alien annuals, many of which are members of the goosefoot family (Chenopodiaceae). For example, summer cypress *(Kochia scoparia)* is now abundant in disturbed areas such as fields and pastures (Kelley 1980:83), and it became well established on the Arroyo Hondo site itself after two summers of excavation. Russian thistle *(Salsola kali)*, or tumbleweed, is another introduced species common in domestic areas near Arroyo Hondo (Kelley 1980:83). All undoubtedly contribute to the high cheno-am percentage in modern soil samples (table 35).

Even moderate grazing can induce losses in the ground cover of nonflowering plants, or cryptogams (Kleiner and Harper 1972). A heavy cryptogamic soil crust is common in undisturbed pinyon-juniper woodlands (West, Rea, and Tausch 1975:43), where it minimizes the erosive effect of hard rains and serves as an organic mulch on which higher plants can become established. At Arroyo Hondo, small patches of lichen crust are found only infrequently on the barren soil of north-exposed slopes. In contrast, the B. P. Dutton property near Santa Fe has been spared trampling and grazing for 22 years; there, stiff cushions of ground

TABLE 35.
Percentages of cheno-am and arboreal pollen in modern surface samples from Arroyo Hondo Pueblo.

Sample	*Cheno-ams (%)*	*Arboreal pollen*	*Arboreal pollen (%)*
16 (farthest from pines)	52.0	41/179	22.9
17 (intermediate to pines)	71.0	19/184	10.3
18 (nearest to pines)	47.0	60/189	31.7
16, 17, and 18 combined	56.6	120/552	21.7

lichen occupy substantial areas not closed by grama grass. Spores of cryptogams occur only in archaeological sediments at Arroyo Hondo (appendix C).

Finally, overgrazing has fostered an increase in the density of trees in the pinyon-juniper woodland around Arroyo Hondo Pueblo. Current estimates of tree density in the area run as high as 284 per acre (0.4 ha), although south of Arroyo Hondo, extensive agricultural clearance has counteracted the trend of increased tree density (Kelley 1980:61, 73). Studies of pinyon-juniper woodlands indicate that the loss of competition from herbs and grasses of the understory promotes the establishment of trees (Stevens, Giunta, and Plummer 1975:78; West, Rea, and Tausch 1975:50). Plots protected from grazing show that in the absence of fire, high tree density is of long duration—25 years or more (Potter and Krenetsky 1967). In historic times, the Arroyo Hondo area has been protected from forest fires by the human inhabitants, and overgrazing also contributes to the reduction of fires by diminishing the combustible grass understory.

FIELD AND LABORATORY METHODS

Since the objective of the initial pollen investigation at Arroyo Hondo was the reconstruction of climate,[3] the investigators did not wish a temporally fragmented pollen record that might better reflect social organization as expressed either by mortuary practices or feature functions. Consequently, the ideal sampling location was judged to be within plaza C. Sediments from such an open area would have the greatest probability of representing average values; also, it was believed that sediments from the entire occupation were deposited in plaza C. A stratigraphic column of pollen samples was obtained from south of gate 12-C-3, 1.3 m west of the inner corner of room block 16 (fig. 10). Differences in soil color and composition in the stratigraphy (from gravels to loamy sands flecked with carbon), along with the contrasting texture of the initial hardpacked plaza surface of each occupation, delineated in the column the various periods of occupation and abandonment. Richard Lang recognized and dated the stratigraphic units by their association with adjacent architecture and trash deposits that had been dated through a study of painted pottery and its association with tree-ring specimens (Lang 1975).

To serve as a cross-check on the first stratigraphically continuous column, another stratigraphic column from the north side of the plaza (12-C-A) was sampled (fig. 10). If both plaza locations received average pollen deposition, their pollen spectra should compare closely. To supplement the two sampling columns from plaza C, an artificial sample series was formed out of spatially different sampling units that could be chronologically arranged on the basis of their relative physical contexts and material culture contents (Richard Lang, correspondence 10/3/72).

In order to determine whether the modern frequency of small-pine pollen differed from the prehistoric frequency, surface samples were taken along three transects at Arroyo Hondo on March 7, 1973, following two field seasons of excavation. By that time, the overburden had been stripped from most of the site, and winter storms had averaged and mixed the pollen on the soil surface. The three transects were located where modern vegetation had been least disturbed by the excavation process. They ran parallel to the band of pinyon trees stretching across the western slopes of the Sangre de Cristo Mountain foothills, but at three different distances from the site. Transect 12-D-0-1 was nearest the pinyons, 12-J-0-1 was intermediate, and 12-0-0-1 was farthest from the trees (fig. 10). Each transect, 100 paces long, was the source of 40 subsamples of soil casually taken as two-finger pinches from places undisturbed by excavation.

To help the excavators secure pollen samples in which contamination from modern pollen was at a minimum, the author visited Arroyo Hondo close to the start of excavations in June 1972. Excavators were asked to secure pollen samples with a clean trowel immediately upon exposure of the sediments and to record the date on which the sample

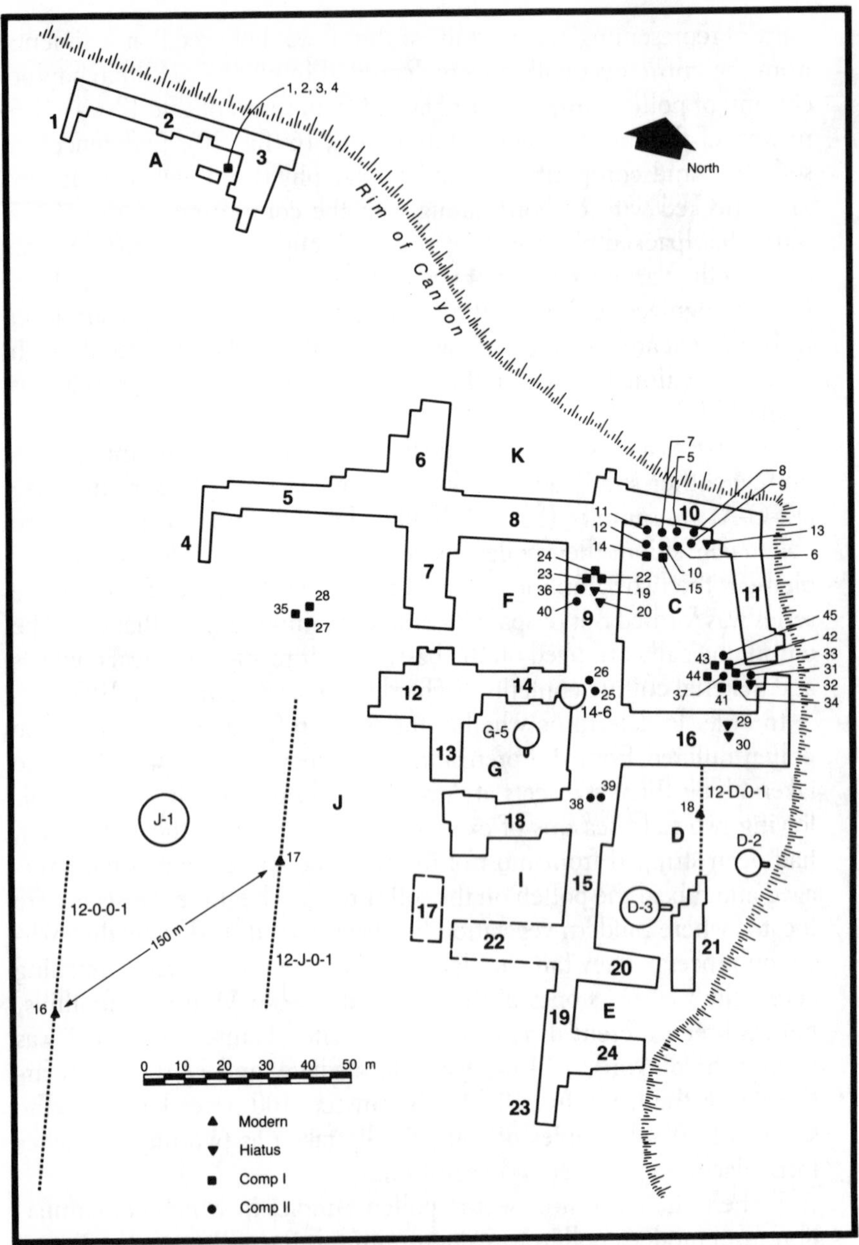

Fig. 10. Locations where analyzed pollen samples were taken from Arroyo Hondo Pueblo. Dashed lines mark transects where modern pollen samples were collected.

was taken. The latter step helped identify samples that were particularly vulnerable to modern pine pollen contamination, since the excavators were exposing prehistoric structures in early June, when local pinyons release their pollen. Pollen samples from the stratigraphic columns (12-C-3 and 12-C-A), so vital to climatic interpretation, were obtained after the season of pine pollination, in October 1972.

Throughout this study, the author extracted pollen from prehistoric sediments using procedures outlined by Mehringer (1967:137), with the exception of using 50% hydrofluoric acid exclusively and acetolyzing samples following their treatment with hot hydrochloric acid. In the final steps, alcohol was used to dehydrate and stain followed by a benzene wash preparatory to the addition of 12,500-centistoke silicon oil. The contents of each vial were thoroughly mixed before a portion was mounted on a microslide for examination. A 200-grain count was attempted for each sample. In addition, the pine pollen saccus breadth was measured with a Filar eyepiece micrometer for a maximum of around 100 grains per sample.

From a total of 454 prehistoric pollen samples obtained, 61 were selected for their potential ability to contribute to the research objectives. Forty-one of these were extracted, and pollen counts obtained on all but two (samples 12 and 29). Adding the three modern surface samples that were taken, a total of 42 samples constitute the data base of the present study.

Pollen extraction began in November of 1972 and resulted in a report on 19 samples the following year. Pollen studies resumed late in 1974 with the analysis of 23 additional samples. In 1975 all analyzed samples were studied to reveal ethnobotanical pollen types and their distribution. The following pages represent that report supplemented by the pollen spectra and catalog of specimens that were documented the next year.

The pollen sample number bears no clue to the sample's provenience, except by coincidence. In contrast, the School of American Research field specimen number codifies part of the information. For example, the number 12-7-7-7 translates as LA 12 (Arroyo Hondo's Laboratory of Anthropology number), roomblock 7, room 7, level 7 of the first half of the room to be excavated. If the level belonged to the second half of the room excavated, the last number would be expressed as roman numeral VII. The full contextual information supplied with each sample appears in appendix B.

The pollen counts are given in appendix A. Each 200-grain pollen count was separated into totals for the first and second hundred grains, columns *a* and *b* in the appendix. If a full count of 100 grains was not possible, the column is headed by the letter p to indicate a partial count. The pollen category dicotyledon is a taxonomically broad group of nonarboreal pollen that serves to improve the estimate of nonarboreal pollen; the poor preservation of these pollen grains did not allow further identification.

ETHNOBOTANICAL POLLEN

The recognition of culturally introduced pollen enhances one's understanding of plant use and distribution in the past. In order to recognize ethnobotanical pollen, one must first understand differences in pollination modes. Flowers pollinated by insects tend to produce relatively little pollen. The grains vary in size but are sticky and often highly ornamented (Proctor and Yeo 1972:258). In contrast, flowers fertilized by wind-transported pollen produce large quantities of pollen. The grains are generally small and lack protuberances that would seriously interfere with wind transportation (Proctor and Yeo 1972:258). Because of the apparent dichotomy in pollination mechanisms, we tend to divide plants into those having wind-carried and those having insect-carried pollen.

In nature, some entomophilous, or insect-pollinated, species produce enough pollen to permit small-scale wind pollination (Proctor and Yeo 1972:275). Although it is difficult to demonstrate, it can be asserted that such deviations form the building blocks of natural selection when insect pollination declines in effectiveness. A possible example of limited wind pollination may be found in the genus *Eriogonum*, in which all pollen grains are relatively smooth and some species possess pollen small enough to be wind carried.

One can recognize a single pollen grain from the insect-pollinated cholla in a fire pit as being due to human activity with more certainty than one can a cheno-am pollen grain, which normally is wind-borne. Wind-transported pollen can land anywhere, but the probability of bees transporting cholla pollen to a fire pit seems relatively low. The recovery of pollen from insect-pollinated plants in abnormal contexts may suggest ethnobotanical relationships.

The recognition of wind-carried pollen as being overconcentrated by human activity can be difficult. A method of identifying pollen spectral distortion at the Hay Hollow site (Bohrer 1972) could be used at Arroyo Hondo only with modification. Originally, pollen spectra derived from modern surface samples were used to establish the upper percentage limits for various pollen types (Bohrer 1972). An interpretation of prehistoric pollen spectral distortion seemed justified when a percentage failed to come within the 95 percent confidence interval[4] of the highest percentage of occurrence in a modern spectrum (Bohrer 1972). However, at Arroyo Hondo, foreign species contribute pollen to the modern spectra at the expense of native pollen producers. Tumbleweed *(Salsola)* and summer cypress *(Kochia)* typify modern, introduced cheno-ams whose local pollen production may exceed that of native *Chenopodium* and *Eurotia*. For this and other reasons outlined in the discussion of historic changes in vegetation, it was felt that the modern pollen rain at Arroyo Hondo provided an unreliable analogy to the past pollen rain.

As an aid in recognizing inflated percentages of the wind-pollinated categories, pollen samples from comparatively undisturbed prehistoric contexts were substituted for modern surface samples. Three pollen samples (15, 24, and 35) from an old A-zonal soil surface dating to the earliest, lightest occupation of Arroyo Hondo were used to estimate a normal pollen rain. The pollen spectra of these samples were least likely to reflect disturbance or the economic activity of large numbers of people. In addition, a good, loamy soil such as this should have buffered the local vegetation from drought better than degraded soils promoted by erosion and trampling (see Pieper, Montoya, and Grace 1971). The Arroyo Hondo prehistoric control samples deviated no more than two percentage points from twenty-five in their cheno-am content, whereas soil disturbance and erosion later in the site's history often accentuated the magnitude of oscillations in the cheno-am (and other pollen) percentages. Prehistoric samples with significantly higher percentages than those of the control samples (nonoverlapping 95 percent confidence intervals) were examined for possible ethnobotanical usage.

Actual determination of ethnobotanical use of wind-pollinated species results from evaluating contextual factors. For example, sediments deriving from periods of full or partial abandonment seem especially likely to show surges of early successional species such as cheno-ams. Water standing in unroofed rooms or barren ground formed by eroding adobe walls would also be prime targets for colonization by weedy annuals, as would sediments associated with burrows or rodent rummaging. When such contexts were recognized, ethnobotanical pollen was eliminated as a possibility.

While not used to a significant extent in the present study, observations on the numbers and sizes of clumps of wind-carried pollen grains help to evaluate ethnobotanical pollen. Mature pollen of wind-pollinated species is normally dry and not self-adherent. When somewhat immature pollen is knocked from the plant by wind or other forces, any grains that still adhere to one another tend to fall close to the plant producing them, because together they are too large and heavy for wind transport.

It is important to determine the context in which clumping occurs. When small clumps (two to four grains) are observed frequently in samples of noncultural fill, it seems reasonable to suppose that the plants bearing the pollen grew directly upon the fill. When pollen derived from cultural contexts also shows clumping, ethnobotanical use may be suspected and supplementary information sought. Extremely large clumps of pollen (from six to thirty grains, for example) seem unnatural.[5] Such accumulations of sticky, immature pollen most likely derive from the direct gathering of the pollen-bearing structures or perhaps from beating the seeds (and immature pollen) from a plant of economic importance. If beaten seeds are believed to account for the pollen clumps, the hypothesis can sometimes be supported by the recovery of seeds, preferably from the same stratigraphic unit. Clumps of wind-carried pollen do not usually constitute strong evidence for ethnobotanical usage unless supplementary sources of information point toward the same conclusion.

ETHNOBOTANICAL POLLEN AT ARROYO HONDO

This section describes the pollen types thought to represent plants that were used in the subsistence economy of Arroyo Hondo Pueblo. It provides notes on the known distribution of such pollen in other archaeological sites and presents ethnobotanical information of interpretive value. With the exception of jimsonweed *(Datura)* pollen, the pollen types described here occurred as at least two grains in at least one pollen sample at Arroyo Hondo. The number of grains in each pollen spectrum of 200 is listed in appendix A. The pollen counts given in the following descriptions are sometimes higher because they include additional grains encountered as the slides were scanned after the 200-grain samples were completed. The criteria used to recognize certain pollen types are given in appendix C.

Cheno-ams

Palynologists who reconstruct past environments do not separate most chenopod and amaranth pollen, a morphological group frequently termed cheno-ams. Cheno-ams form part of all pollen spectra, for the wind easily transports the small pollen grains. It is only when cheno-am values are highly inflated that one may consider these plants possibly to have been a food source. The roles of cheno-ams as early successional species on disturbed ground and as gathered plants become interrelated factors in interpreting samples when cheno-ams show frequencies above 40 percent.

Several lines of evidence at Arroyo Hondo indicated that cheno-am frequencies above 40 percent were unlikely to be produced by climatic variables. First, when a histogram of cheno-am frequencies arranged in 5-percent intervals was constructed, the expected continuous distribution and approximation of a bell-shaped curve were not realized. There

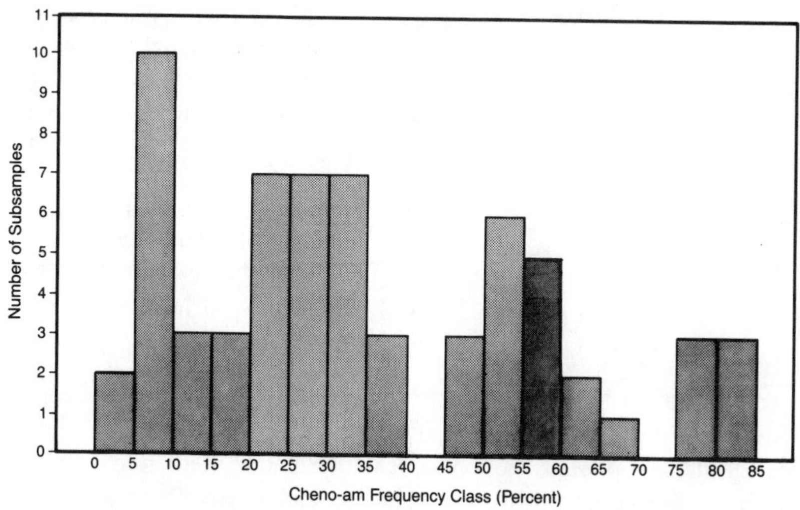

Fig. 11. Number of subsamples in cheno-am frequency classes at Arroyo Hondo. One subsample consists of 100 grains in a sample of 200 pollen grains.

were no samples with frequencies between 41 and 45 percent, and the conformation appeared bimodal (fig. 11). An inspection of the 12 samples with frequencies above 40 percent revealed that every one either represented human economic activities (trash, floor contact, living surface of plaza) or resulted from a proliferation of weedy plant pioneers (that is, a wall fall lens and post-abandonment samples; see table 36). Conversely, of the 23 samples with less than 40 percent cheno-ams, 7 consisted entirely or partly of trash.

TABLE 36.
Prehistoric samples with cheno-am percentages above 40.

Sample Number	*SAR Number*	*Cheno-ams (%)*	*Remarks*
1	12-A2-18-III	72.5	Shallow clay-lined basin in plaza A.
3	12-A2-18-IV-4	51.5	Shallow clay-lined basin in plaza A.
5	12-C-A-16-1	59.0	Plaza C, layer 2. Wall fall lens with limited trash.
6	12-C-A-16-2	58.5	Plaza C, layer 2. Wall-fall lens marking burning of roomblock 10 and previous use of plaza.
25	12-9-15-A	76.0	Upper room fill of washed adobe and wind-blown sand. Complete abandonment.
26	12-9-15-B2	70.5	Beneath sample 25, loam washed from wall of burned room. Complete or partial abandonment.
27	12-H-2-I-1	83.5	Trash deposit in plaza H.
31	12-C-3-1	61.5	Plaza C, layer 1. Buff, gravelly wash. Complete abandonment.
37	12-C-3-II	48.0	Trash deposit in plaza C.
38	12-15A-87-3-2	54.5	Floor contact.
39	12-15A-8-5-1	42.0	Floor contact.
40	12-9-12-A	54.0	Upper room fill of buff washed adobe and sand. Complete abandonment.

Second, analysis of seeds from flotation samples revealed that *Chenopodium* and *Amaranthus* were the most widely distributed and among the most important genera of wild plants at Arroyo Hondo (Wetterstrom, this volume). The ubiquitous seeds supported the belief that samples from floor contact, trash, and living surfaces of the plaza might contain excessive amounts of cheno-am pollen due to seed processing.

Third, the two Arroyo Hondo pollen samples (24 and 35) from pre-occupation (or earliest occupation) levels on A-zonal soils had cheno-am values that deviated no more than two points from 25 percent. The 95-percent confidence limits that should contain the true mean for each sample ranged between 19 percent and 32 percent. These samples are the least likely of any from Arroyo Hondo to reflect disturbance or the economic activity of large numbers of people.

Certain samples with elevated cheno-am values are especially likely to represent economic use of cheno-ams at Arroyo Hondo. These are samples 27 and 37 from trash deposits, samples 38 and 39 from floor contact, and sample 5 from the last well-defined surface in plaza C; all except sample 27 date from Component II. All these deposits are related to human cultural and economic activities. High counts in sample 6, from a wall-fall lens; sample 26, deriving from post-abandonment wall wash; and samples 25, 31, and 40, again from post-abandonment times, seem better interpreted as resulting from an abundance of weedy plant pioneers that grew near where the pollen samples were obtained.

Sample 6 holds particular interest since it comes from one room in a series that was gutted by fire between A.D. 1415 and 1425 (R. W. Lang, correspondence 1975). One wonders if the adjacent woodland was decimated by fire as well, causing the annuals to develop more vigorously in the three or four years following the fire (Barney and Frischknecht 1974:91). At the very least, cheno-ams would grow in the bare spots in the grass cover following the drought of 1415 to 1425 (Rose, Dean, and Robinson 1981). Partial abandonment of the pueblo might also have fostered the establishment of weeds.

Beeweed (Cleome)

The three grains of this insect-pollinated type all derived from a single pollen sample, number 33, containing a loamy sand with carbon flecks from plaza C. The sample dates from the time of a possible Component I population peak in the plaza C area.

Ethnographic accounts refer to boiled *Cleome* greens as a food item at Zuni (Stevenson 1915:69), Hopi (Whiting 1939:77), Isleta (Jones 1931), Cochiti (Lange 1959:147), and Zia (White 1962:107). The dried flowers, leaves, and stems have been ground into flour and mixed with cornmeal for bread (Clark 1972:49). The plants have been used for poultices and for pottery pigment (Robbins, Harrington, and Freire-Marreco 1916:58, 59), and the seeds have been used for food (Jones 1931; White 1962:107).

Cleome pollen has been reported from Rosa phase features (A.D. 700–850) in the Navajo Reservoir District (Schoenwetter 1964); from samples taken during a site survey in the Chuska Valley and on the Chaco Plateau (Harris, Schoenwetter, and Warren 1967); from Broken K Pueblo in east-central Arizona in amounts reaching 25 percent in one sample (Hill and Hevly 1968:205); from Hooper Ranch Pueblo in eastern Arizona (Schoenwetter 1962:183); and both farming terraces and trash slopes at Wetherill Mesa, where counts reached a maximum of 45 percent (Martin and Byers 1965).

Beeweed, though insect pollinated, produces relatively large amounts of pollen. The few grains recovered at Arroyo Hondo do not suggest intensive use of the flowers. It is more likely that the grains were transported indirectly on beeweed pods or leaves or on human clothing to the point where the pollen samples were taken. Carbonized seeds of *Cleome* were recovered from 11 locations during the Arroyo Hondo excavations (Wetterstrom 1976:93).

Squash (Cucurbita spp.)

Five grains of squash, an insect-pollinated genus, were distributed among three plaza samples that date from Component II times (table 37). One sample (10) containing three grains originated in a mixture of trash and turkey dung, perhaps reflecting the prehistoric value of the flowers for food.

The Hopis (Beaglehole 1937:68) and Navajos (Bailey 1940:289; Vestal 1952:46) have been reported to boil squash blossoms with water, salt, and grease into a soup. Both the Navajos and the Rio Grande Pueblos add the blossoms to meat stew as a seasoning (Bailey 1940:289; Hughes

TABLE 37.
Squash (*Cucurbita*) pollen at Arroyo Hondo Pueblo, Components I and II.

Sample	SAR No.	*Diameter excl. spines (micrometers)*	*Spine Length (micrometers)*	*Source*
10	12-C-A-12-3	59.60 66.15 70.25	4–5 8–10 9.45	Mixed trash and turkey dung.
37	12-C-3-II	59.04	3.50	Associated with extensive burning during phase of part-time residence.
45	12-C-3-III	135.00	8.10	Loamy sand with carbon flecks.

1972:25), and the Pueblos believed that squash blossoms ensured fertility (Española Hospital Auxiliary 1975:26). By stringing the blossoms in the shade to dry, the Navajos preserved them for later cooking (Bailey 1940:289). The Hopis often brought squash blossoms to the villages for use in ceremonial contests and wrangles (Voth in Whiting 1939:93). At Zuni, people applied the blossoms externally to relieve the pain of being whipped with cactus and incorporated them into medicinal pats or cakes for rheumatism and swellings (Stevenson 1915:46).

The blossoms of the buffalo gourd *(Cucurbita foetidissima)* were employed for dye by the Cahuilla of southeastern California (Bean and Saubel 1972:58). The Hopis use the buffalo gourd blossoms as baking containers for cornmeal cake (Cutler and Whitaker 1961:474). The Pimas and Papagos gathered pumpkin flowers for drying, stored them in sealed ollas, and later cooked them with mesquite beans or boiled them to eat with pinole (Castetter and Bell 1942:191).

Judging from the many uses of squash flowers, it is evident that the blossoms might become part of the archaeological record for a variety of reasons. A reader who does not garden may be unaware that the pollen-bearing flower and the fruit-bearing flower are separate entities on the same vine. The pollen-bearing flowers bloom earliest and most abundantly, and hence would most likely be selected for use.

Prehistoric squash pollen has also been found in Arizona at Grasshopper Ruin (Bohrer 1982), Snaketown (Bohrer 1970:428), Broken K Pueblo (Hill and Hevly 1968:205), Glen Canyon (Martin and Sharrock 1964:177, Cutler 1966:21), and Hooper Ranch Pueblo (Schoenwetter 1962:183); in New Mexico at Navajo Reservoir (Schoenwetter 1964), and Chuska Valley and Chaco Plateau (Harris, Schoenwetter, and Warren 1967); and in Colorado at Wetherill Mesa (Martin and Byers 1965:130).

Jimsonweed (Datura)

A single grain of jimsonweed pollen was recovered from a large, shallow basin in plaza A at Arroyo Hondo (sample 3). Datura plants, which are insect pollinated, often grow near Pueblo Indian ruins located near talus slopes (Yarnell 1965:667), and the seeds and pods are sometimes found in southwestern archaeological contexts (Yarnell 1959). A combination of extra moisture in masonry ruins or canyons and the disturbance created by erosion or rodents could serve to perpetuate the species. Careful investigations of the possibility of rodent introduction of jimsonweed seeds into archaeological contexts would better establish the reason for the seeds' presence. Because of questions about rodents, I am not convinced by Yarnell's (1959) summary of evidence for the widespread use of *Datura* in the greater Pueblo area (Anasazi, Rio Grande, Mimbres, Sinagua) from early Pueblo III times through early Pueblo IV. Yarnell could be on the right track, but his generalization seems premature.

Ethnographic accounts of the use of jimsonweed among the Hopis (Whiting 1939), Zunis (Stevenson 1915), Tewas (Curtis 1970:17–22), and the Acomas and Lagunas (Swank 1932:41) emphasize the drug properties of the root but offer little information to account for the presence of pollen from the flowers. However, Stevenson (1915:47) asserts that the Zunis ground the root and flower together into a meal that was applied to wounds of every description. The medicine was the property of the rain priests and the directors of the Little Fire and Cimex fraternities. The Navajos use a cold infusion prepared from the flowers as an eyewash for blindness in horses (Vestal 1952:42). From this scant information, I assume that *Datura* flowers probably were an ingredient in medicine water that was sprinkled into the basin in plaza A from which the grain of jimsonweed pollen came.

Buckwheat (Eriogonum)

Eriogonum pollen, a type both wind- and insect-carried, was found at Arroyo Hondo in samples from pre-occupation levels, Component I, Component II, post-abandonment deposits, and modern soil surface transects (table 38). When the *Eriogonum* pollen is arranged according to size and its distributional contexts are studied, it appears that the first 14 grains listed in table 38 have no ethnobotanical meaning. Not only are the grains relatively homogeneous in size (equatorial diameter 15.42 micrometers, standard deviation 1.20; polar height 22.54 micrometers, standard deviation 0.71), but also they derive from contexts with little cultural significance. However, four other sizes of *Eriogonum* pollen seem to indicate some cultural use, based on their twice-observed presence in cultural contexts; these are marked with asterisks in table 38. The remaining three grains come from the same sediments as the first fourteen, sediments that are not obviously cultural in origin. Yet each seems unique in its proportions. Such singular occurrences could represent insect-pollinated species which have entered sediments through human activity. I see no way to distinguish between either explanation.

The various ways in which Pueblo Indians use *Eriogonum* provide too wide a choice to allow one to decide precisely how it was employed at Arroyo Hondo. The Zunis, for example, store the powdered blossoms of *Eriogonum jamesii* in a sack with a pencil-shaped applicator stone, and the powder clinging to the moistened stone is rubbed over the body and clothing of the dancers in a ceremony (Stevenson 1915:91). The Hopis employ a brushy species with yellow-green flowers as menstruation medicine and to expedite childbirth (Whiting 1939:73). They used *E. hookeri* to impart flavor to boiled mush and pressed the boiled stalks of *E. corymbosum* into cakes that were dried and eaten with salt (Vestal 1940:160).

Eriogonum recovered in other archaeological sites suggests ethnobotanical usage. At Broken K Pueblo in east-central Arizona, higher-than-average amounts of *Eriogonum* pollen were found in two of the kivas, as contrasted with rooms, suggesting prehistoric ceremonial use (Hill and Hevly 1968:207). At Point of Pines, Arizona, carbonized seed and perianth parts comparing closely to *E. pharnaceoides* were recovered from a corrugated storage vessel (Bohrer 1973:429).

TABLE 38.
Buckwheat (*Eriogonum*) pollen at Arroyo Hondo Pueblo.

Sample	SAR No.	*Equatorial Diameter*	*Polar Height*	*Source*
35	12-H-3-D	16.20	23.94	Subsoil, floor or arroyo. Pre-occupation and Component I.
7	12-C-A-16-3	16.20	23.85	Sandy wash of wall surface. Component II.
34	12-C-3-XII	16.74	22.32	Plaza C, A-zone soil horizon.
25	12-9-15-A	16.56	22.14	Washed adobe, blown sand. Post-Component II.
31	12-C-3-1	16.56	22.14	Plaza C, postdates Component II abandonment.
18	12-D-0-1	16.65	22.50	Modern surface transect.
27	12-H-2-I-1	15.52	22.50	Component I terminal trash, possibly some Component II.
23	12-9-7-9-4	15.30	22.50	Floor contact. Terminal Component I.
34	12-C-3-XII	14.94	23.40	Plaza C, A-zone soil horizon.
40	12-9-12-A	14.04	22.86	Washed adobe and sand. Post-Component II.
18	12-D-0-1	14.62	22.50	Modern surface transect.
14	12-C-A-12-7	13.95	21.37	Turkey pen area and sand. Terminal Component I.
34	12-C-3-XII	13.34	22.86	Plaza C, A-zone soil horizon, pre-occupation and Component I.
25	12-9-9-A	13.14	22.50	Blown sand and washed adobe in uppermost layer of fill of burned Component II. Post-Component II occupation.
38*	12-15A-7-3-2	11.88	18.00	Room reoccupation, Component II.
3*	12-A-2-18-IV-4	12.15 12.27	18.00 19.80	Basin A. Component I.
8*	12-C-A-16-4	19.57	30.37	Turkey dung, sand, trash. Component II.
27*	12-H-2-I-1	19.80	30.60	Terminal Component I trash with a few Component II sherds.

Sample	SAR No.	*Equatorial Diameter*	*Polar Height*	*Source*
14	12-C-A-12-7	15.75	27.00	Turkey pen area, sand. Terminal Component I.
25	12-9-15-A	13.68	24.12	Washed adobe, sand. Post-Component II.
18	12-D-0-1	16.89	20.47	Modern surface transect.
Mean		14.43	22.99	
S.D.		3.39	3.11	
N		22.00	22.00	

Sunflower (Helianthus)

Helianthus-type pollen was recovered in eight prehistoric samples from Arroyo Hondo, some of which represent possibly disturbed deposits such as gravel, washed adobe and sand, the floor of an arroyo, and part of a plaza associated with roof and wall fall. Other grains came from trash deposits and plaza surfaces (table 39).

Numerous cultural pathways can lead to the deposition of the insect-born *Helianthus* pollen. Stevenson (1915:93) reported that the Zunis employed the blossoms extensively in various kivas. The Jemez make

TABLE 39.
Sunflower (*Helianthus*) pollen at Arroyo Hondo Pueblo.

Sample	SAR No.	*Diameter excl. spines (micrometers)*	*Spine Length (micrometers)*	*Source*
1	12-A2-18-III-1	16.20	4.90	Plaza surface near shallow basin. Component I.
6	12-C-A-16-2	19.35	4.10	Roof and wall fall lens in plaza. Component II.

TABLE 39. *(continued)*

Sample	SAR No.	*Diameter excl. spines (micrometers)*	*Spine Length (micrometers)*	*Source*
35	12-H-3-D	18.00	4.40	A-zone soil in floor of probable arroyo, later occupied Component I.
37	12-C-3-III	18.00	3.06	Component II trash.
40	12-9-12-A	18.00	3.96 4.32	Clump of 3 grains. Washed adobe and sand in room. Post-Component II.
41	12-C-3-V	21.38 20.25 21.60	4.95 4.50 6.08	Terminal Component I, plaza.
43	12-C-3-X	21.60	4.95	Component I occupation, plaza.
44	12-C-3-XI	20.03 21.15 20.70	4.95 5.17 4.50	Component I occupation, earliest plaza surface.

NOTE: *Helianthus* pollen has been subsumed under long-spine Compositae in appendix A.

plaster from clay mixed with sunflowers, which serve to bind the clay particles together, and they also use the flower as a decoration in dances (Cook 1930:23). The Hopis dry the petals and grind them into a powder that is an ingredient in yellow face powder used in the women's basket dance (Whiting 1939:97). The Navajos sprinkle a cold infusion from the flowers onto the clothes of hunters for good luck (Vestal 1952:52).

Helianthus blossoms dry and shrivel but persist on the apex of the ripening achene. Wind and moisture may transfer pollen from the old flower to the developing fruit. Even more probably, the achenes are dusted by pollen when the heads are flailed or hand-abraded to release the seeds from the long bracts in the head. When wild sunflower seeds are rinsed, the water contains abundant pollen (Bohrer 1972a:26). Pollen and seeds show a positive correlation in coprolites (Williams-Dean and Bryant 1975:104). Sunflower seeds were recovered in five locations at Arroyo Hondo in association with other edible plants (Wetterstrom 1976:99–100).

At Arroyo Hondo, *Helianthus* pollen in samples 35 and 40 could have derived from plants growing naturally on the spot (table 39). The pollen from the plaza surface near the broad shallow basin (sample 1) and from the trash deposit (sample 37) might easily have resulted from the threshing or winnowing of sunflower heads. None of the pollen from plaza samples is apt to have derived from sunflowers growing in place, but instead it probably represents human religious or economic activities.

Pincushion Cactus (Mammillaria)

A single grain of *Mammillaria* pollen, an insect-carried type, was found in each of two samples (numbers 24 and 34) from soil horizons on which cultural deposits were laid. The combination of cholla and *Mammillaria*-type pollen in each sample suggests that some cultural activities led to the deposition of economic pollen. Normal surface samples rarely carry any cactus pollen; the presence of two types is indeed unusual.

Eleven trash samples from various locations at Arroyo Hondo contained carbonized seeds of *Echinocereus triglochidiatus* or *Mammillaria* sp. (Wetterstrom, this volume), indicating that the fruits of these species were eaten. Since the modern ethnographic use of fruits has been mentioned (Wetterstrom, this volume), the following remarks are confined to the prehistoric utilization of the body of the plant. The recovery of single pollen grains suggests that they were lodged fortuitously either on the fruit or on the plant body. Plant remains from Pindi Pueblo include the charred outer rinds of *Echinocereus* (Stubbs and Stallings 1953:141). The spines of both *Echinocereus* and *Mammillaria* have been reported from Tonto National Monument (Bohrer 1962). *Echinocereus* has been reported from Jemez Cave (Alexander and Reiter 1935:64) and from Tularosa Cave (Cutler 1952:479). Fragments of shoot and root crowns of *Echinocereus* come from Cordova Cave, near Tularosa Cave, in New Mexico (Kaplan 1963:354). In southwestern Texas, middle and late archaic horizons of a rock shelter yielded fecal samples containing *Mammillaria*-type pollen indicative of flower consumption (Bryant 1974:413). The use of these genera may have been more widespread than the ethnographic record indicates.

Cholla (Cylindropuntia)

Cholla pollen, normally insect carried, was recovered in 16 prehistoric samples from Arroyo Hondo, representing time periods ranging from pre-occupation to post-abandonment (table 40). The number of pollen grains in each sample was small, never exceeding 2 percent of any one sample (appendix A).

In order to obtain cholla pollen in a modern surface sample, it is necessary to take soil from directly beneath a living cholla. Thus, the presence of cholla pollen on work surfaces and in trash suggests economic use, but one can only speculate about whether or not the pollen was deposited as a result of the roasting of cholla buds. The Pimas, Papagos (Castetter and Bell 1942:63; Curtin 1949:58), and Hopis (Nequatewa 1943:19) like cholla buds as a cooked vegetable but generally use the roasted joints and fruits as food during hard times (Castetter 1935:35). Both Bohrer (1972:26) and Bryant (1974:412–13) found that pollen adheres to the joints and stems of *Opuntia* in small amounts. The extremely low frequencies of cholla pollen at Arroyo Hondo seem unlikely to represent the roasting of buds, for a single discarded bud should carry a concentration of pollen. The churning of trash and sediments during or following deposition, however, might have broken up the pollen concentrations. Alternatively, the pollen might have come

TABLE 40.
Cholla (*Cylindropuntia*) pollen at Arroyo Hondo Pueblo.
Samples are arranged chronologically.

Sample	*SAR No.*	*Diameter (micrometers)*	*Source*
24	12-9-7-10-1	86.94	Soil horizon below ash deposit. Pre-occupation or Component I.
34	12-C-3-XII	87.48 60.30 68.04	A-zone soil on which plaza formed. Pre-occupation or Component I.
44	12-C-3-XI	57.38 92.93	Earliest plaza surface, Component I.
33	12-C-3-IX	76.34 80.64	Component I.

Sample	*SAR No.*	*Diameter (micrometers)*	*Source*
42	12-C-3-VI	60.98 54.23	Sand with carbon flecks. Late Component I.
13	12-C-A-12-6	72.00 90.00	Occupational hiatus; fill derives from Component I structures.
8	12-C-A-16-4	67.50 77.62	Component II, former work area converted to turkey pen.
9	12-C-A-12-2	54.67	Plaza work surface during Component II population peak.
10	12-C-A-12-3	63.62 55.12 85.50 57.60 75.83 56.93 62.55	Component II trash and turkey dung.
11	12-C-A-13-4	71.75	Component II turkey dung.
37	12-C-3-II	75.96	Component II trash.
38	12-15A-7-3-2	59.22 47.70	Floor of Component II room with hearth.
39	12-15A-8-5-1	69.84	Floor of Component II room with hearth.
36	12-9-10-C	78.12	Terminal Component II.
31	13-C-3-I	57.47	Post-Component II abandonment.
40	12-9-12-A	66.42 59.22	Washed adobe and sand, post-Component II abandonment.

Mean diameter = 68.74 micrometers; s.d. = 12.80.

from water in which fruits or joints were boiled. Assuming some antiquity for the Pueblo practice of sweeping plazas and doorways clean of plant life, the chances that the pollen derived from chollas growing as weeds seem low, at least for the period before the site was partially abandoned.

An investigation was launched to determine what cholla species might have once grown near Arroyo Hondo, since the size distribution of the prehistoric pollen has a higher standard deviation than that found in modern samples from any single species (table 41). Cane cholla (*O. imbricata*), a species that grows throughout the Santa Fe area, was removed from the Arroyo Hondo site before excavation began. In 1849, *O. clavata* was reported growing on the plains to the south and southwest of Santa Fe (Gray 1849:2, 52), and more recently it has been observed in the Ortiz Mountains southwest of Santa Fe (Lucile Housely, correspondence, 1975). A small population of *O. viridiflora*, which is thought to have genetic affinities with both *O. whipplei* and *O. imbricata* (Tierney 1978), grows in Santa Fe. *O. whipplei* grows in western New Mexico near the Arizona border (Wooton and Standley 1915:442).

Prehistoric cholla pollen diameters were compared with the mean diameters of modern species. Thirty grains of freshly acetolysed pollen were measured from at least one blossom of each species that, on the basis of geographic distribution or taxonomic relationship, might have grown at Arroyo Hondo. One plant of *O. imbricata* was sampled from Arroyo Hondo and another from the B. P. Dutton property, while 12 different plants of *O. viridiflora* from Santa Fe were sampled (table 41). It is apparent the prehistoric mean lies nearest that of *O. whipplei*, but the diameters overlap those of *O. imbricata* and exhibit far more variability than do those of any modern species, including *O. viridiflora*.

TABLE 41.
Diameter in micrometers of cholla (*Cylindropuntia*) pollen from various locations.

Type	*Mean*	*s.d.*	*Variance*	*Range*	*Sample Size*	χ^2
LA 12 prehistoric	68.74	12.80	163.80	45.23	32	
LA 12, modern *O. imbricata*	77.82	3.40	11.58	17.55	60	186.90
Ft. Marcy, *O. viridiflora* hybrids	74.26	6.27	38.76	42.62	360	188.85
O. clavata	75.28	4.88	23.86	20.02	30	18.30
O. whipplei	66.06	6.47	41.94	28.30	30	12.90
O. imbricata	85.78	4.77	22.75	25.86	30	143.70

The chi-square statistic was used to test the null hypothesis that there was no significant difference between the prehistoric population and (a) modern Arroyo Hondo O. *imbricata*, (b) O. *viridiflora*, (c) O. *clavata*, (d) O. *whipplei*, (e) O. *imbricata* from the B. P. Dutton residence, and (f) an artificial population of O. *whipplei* and O. *imbricata*. In each instance, the null hypothesis was rejected at the 0.5 level of significance using the critical value of 9.48 with 4 degrees of freedom. Thus no single modern species seems likely to have been the source of the pollen at Arroyo Hondo.

I remain puzzled by this anomalous prehistoric record, as well as by evidence found at Salmon Ruin in northwestern New Mexico and at three sites in Arizona. Preliminary pollen investigations at the Salmon site revealed a cholla pollen grain 90 microns in diameter (sample 31W052). The grain exceeds the normal size range of the one cholla, *Opuntia whipplei*, known to grow in the vicinity today. The Hay Hollow site in east-central Arizona has also produced a record of cholla pollen diameters (mean 58.5 micrometers, standard deviation 22.2, n = 24) that are much more variable than those of O. *whipplei*, the sole cholla species in the area today (mean 63 micrometers, standard deviation 6.0, n = 24) (Bohrer 1972:24).

At Point of Pines Ruin (Arizona W:10:50) carbonized cholla buds and joints were recovered, even though the nearest cholla grows about 6 miles from the ruin, 500 feet up and 1,000 feet over the other side of the Nantack Ridge (Bohrer 1973:431). Round-trip travel to this site would probably have required more than a day's journey, if one uses for comparison the practices of modern gathering cultures (Silberbauer 1972:287; Schrire 1972:659; Gardner 1969:209).

At Grasshopper Ruin (Arizona P:14:1), also in east-central Arizona, the archaeological cholla pollen is unique, for cholla does not grow in the valley today. In order to find cholla, one must go eastward to Spring Canyon where O. *spinosior* appears to be a recent introduction, or some 5 miles to the southwest and 400 feet lower in elevation, where a few scattered plants of O. *spinosior* grow near the ruin of Red Rock House. In the Jemez Mountains, O. *imbricata* was found growing in certain archaeological sites at elevations higher than the natural limits of the species (Housely 1974). It would not be surprising if the record of discrepancies between prehistoric and modern cholla pollen grows larger.

What factors accounted for the prehistoric distribution of cholla? We are told that the Zunis cultivated a bed of O. *imbricata* on Corn Mountain for use in whipping ceremonies (Curtis 1970:17:153; Stevenson 1915:95). The Zunis believed that their ceremony derived from the Hopis (Curtis 1970:17:154). It is conceivable that the Hopis cultivated *O. imbricata* as well, because Hopi land lies outside of the cholla's normal range. But if so, who gave *O. imbricata* to the Hopis? Ford (1968a) has suggested that new plants originated from seeds distributed in feces near habitations. My observations of young *O. spinosior* plants growing near the perimeter of an abandoned Apache encampment in Spring Canyon, near Grasshopper Ruin, support Ford's hypothesis. The plants might also have been propagated through the Hopi practice of planting cacti at the corners of house foundations (Beaglehole 1937:58). Wildfires tend to destroy chollas temporarily (Wright 1974:6), but one wonders whether the fire's burning the seed, breaking the sod, or reducing the tree overstory might eventually aid in cholla reestablishment. Rodents may also help spread cholla colonies by accumulating joints or storing seeds.

Today, humans seldom serve as direct agents of cactus seed reintroduction into areas where disease or unfavorable climatic conditions have decimated plant populations. When native ceremonies disappear, the need for maintaining the required plants also wanes. Other factors such as trade or methods of processing may help explain the anomalies in cholla pollen size and distribution in the prehistoric record.[6]

Prickly Pear (Platyopuntia)

Pollen from prickly pear, another insect-pollinated genus, appeared in only three samples from Component I and two from Component II (table 42). The record of prickly pear pollen is far more limited than is that of cholla pollen.

TABLE 42.
Prickly-pear cactus (*Platyopuntia*) pollen at Arroyo Hondo Pueblo.

Sample	*SAR No.*	*Diameter (micrometers)*	*Source*
9	12-C-A-12-2	82.35	Plaza C, adobe mixed with ash and some trash. Component II.

Sample	*SAR No.*	*Diameter (micrometers)*	*Source*
10	12-C-A-12-3	102.00	Plaza C, mixed trash and turkey dung with ash lenses. Component II.
13	12-C-A-12-6	70.87	Washed adobe from Component I structures of roomblock 10.
43	12-C-3-X	99.45	Loamy sand with carbon flecks. Component I.
44	12-C-3-XI	45.00	Earliest plaza C surface, Component I.

Navajo youngsters have shown me how much the petals of prickly pear flowers taste like lettuce. The consumption of flowers may be indicated by counts of 13 percent prickly pear pollen at Broken K Pueblo (Hill and Hevly 1968:205) and more than 25 percent in Glen Canyon fecal samples (Martin and Sharrock 1964:177). Prickly pear buds were found at Tonto National Monument (Bohrer 1962:97). No high concentrations of prickly pear pollen were found at Arroyo Hondo (table 42). The Arroyo Hondo counts resemble those of Cactaceae (cf. prickly pear) at Hooper Ranch Pueblo, Arizona; that is, from 1 to 4 grains per sample (Schoenwetter 1962). The scarcity of prickly pear pollen at Arroyo Hondo contrasts with its prevalence at Broken K Pueblo, where 42 of 44 samples contained *Opuntia* pollen. (However, cholla pollen may have been included as at Broken K.)

Unless pollen concentrations contained in feces were dispersed through trash mixing or lost, the grains in the Arroyo Hondo samples probably were retained on pads or joints brought home to be cooked. The mechanisms for introducing both cholla and prickly pear pollen into the Arroyo Hondo record could have been very similar.

Cattail (Typha)

The record of cattail pollen at Arroyo Hondo comes from six samples, together spanning a period of population growth, a hiatus, and another

TABLE 43.
Cattail (*Typha*) pollen at Arroyo Hondo Pueblo. Samples are arranged chronologically, earliest to latest.

Sample	*SAR No.*	*Source*
3	12-A-2-18-IV-4	Floor scrapings from trash-filled basin in plaza A. Three tetrads, one dyad, one monad. Component I.
13	12-C-A-12-6	Culturally sterile wash from Component I structures in plaza C. Post-Component I. Two monads.
19	12-9-7-1-1	Layer of water-deposited sand from period of occupational hiatus. One tetrad.
11	12-C-A-12-4	Turkey dung with no obvious trash. Component II.
10	12-C-A-12-3	Sample associated with Component II population growth, 1386–87. Three tetrads.
38	12-15A-7-3-2	Floor contact. Casts of *Typha* stems were found in adobe roofing. Post-Component II burning.

brief period of occupation (table 43). Presumably, intensive agriculture was practiced during the two periods of occupation, and the pollen derives from a deposit waterlaid during the intervening period. Cattail pollen appears to be absent from sediments dating to the earliest occupation of the site and from those sediments post-dating the burning of Component II rooms, including the modern surface samples.

Today cattail, a wind-pollinated plant, grows on the floor of the Arroyo Hondo below the site and north of it. Apparently the pollen is neither abundant nor light enough to travel in sufficient quantity to be observed in samples from the three surface transects on the western side of the site. The prevailing southwesterly winds may also decrease the probability of deposition on the site. If prehistoric *Typha* pollen had been carried on stalks and leaves to be used in matting or for ceremonial purposes, as at Acoma (Parsons 1939:883), then the pollen should appear in samples from all time periods and all levels of cultural activity. Since it does not, one might speculate that an irrigation ditch or reservoir near the village held cattails during the period in question.

Upon reading the preceding information in an interim report, Richard Lang, then of the School of American Research, wrote to me as follows (correspondence, 1975):

> As casts of *Typha* stems have been found in adobe roofing materials, this could explain its [room] 12-15a-7 occurrence . . . . Although our sampling was heavily weighted toward the north/northeast sections of Arroyo Hondo, it is interesting that in all cases except that of 12-15a-7, the locations of *Typha* occurrence are to the north/northeast of the only feature which we found on the site promontory which might have supplied suitable habitat for cattail. While no evidence for a prehistoric irrigation ditch near the site came out of the five years of work there, and geography makes the existence of an undetected one improbable, there is a case for an impoundment area. The now deeply silted drainage line into which runoff from about 8 acres of the site would have drained is blocked just southwest of the plaza A complex by a dam formed of andesite rubble. The dam is presently 1.72 m high, 8.4 m wide, and 19.9 m long, although its extreme south end has been removed by arroyo cutting. Since the dam's construction, about 1.4 m of soil has deposited (vertically) behind it. Although trenching at the dam's base produced no artifacts which could be used to date it, a likelihood exists that it is a prehistoric feature, and there is no evidence to the contrary. In fact, the *Typha* pollen occurrence and distribution could be taken as evidence that this dam existed by the late 1330s and continued to function as a water catchment in Component II times whenever immediate precipitation was great enough over the area drained to result in standing water. At any rate, this dam represents both the appropriate kind of feature and the right location required to explain the former presence of *Typha* in the on-site pollen rain.

Maize (Zea mays)

Of a total of 38 samples in which a minimum count of 100 pollen grains could be made, slightly over half (21 samples) contained at least one pollen grain of the wind-pollinated cultigen maize (appendix A). Omitting four samples in which maize pollen exceeded 13 percent, the mean percentage was 2.4 and the mode 1.

Concentrations of maize pollen greater than 15 percent seem likely to represent human introductions exclusively, because this percentage far exceeds the upper 95 percent confidence limit (4 percent) of the highest mean value (1 percent) reported for maize pollen in cultivated fields (Berlin et al. 1977:588). Concentrations of maize pollen higher than those found in cultivated fields probably reflect activities such as husking (Bohrer 1972), grinding, and the offering of prayer meal composed of corn pollen. Cornmeal and pollen seem to be interchangeable as prayer offerings, although meal may have been used more frequently (Goldfrank 1927:67). One can gain an impression of the myriad uses for this sacred dust by exploring the many references to it in the index to Parsons's (1939) book on Pueblo religion.

SOME INTERPRETATIONS FROM ETHNOBOTANIC POLLEN

Two Shallow Basins in Plaza A

Four pollen samples were taken from two superimposed shallow basins (features C and A) in plaza A in the hope of gaining more information about how the basins had been used. Basin C is associated with the occupation of the earliest, northern room alignment of roomblock 2, dating to Component I. Analysis of sediments from basin C (sample 4) revealed an abundance of lower fungi that appeared badly degraded. Insufficient pollen prevented a count of 200 grains. The fungi must have flourished on accumulated organic debris and puddled rainwater. Because they collect fungal spores capable of degrading organic material, such basins might possess short life spans for processing foodstuffs. If seeds, for example, were threshed or winnowed in old, contaminated basins, they would soon become dusted with fungal spores. During subsequent storage, a slight build up in moisture would promote fungal growth and foster early decay of the seeds.

Basin A was built superimposed on basin C. One pollen sample (sample 2) was taken after the basin had been exposed for perhaps half a day during the season of pine pollination. This sample contained 57 percent pine pollen. By contrast, sample 3, taken just after the basin had been exposed, contained only 20 percent pine and juniper pollen. The difference illustrates how arboreal percentages can be skewed if insufficient care is taken in obtaining samples. Only sample 3 was fully analyzed. A control sample was taken from southwest of basin A, from a subsurface believed to have been contemporaneous with the use of the basin.

The control sample from outside the basin contained a significantly higher percentage of cheno-am pollen (72.5 percent) than was found in the sample from inside the basin (51.5 percent). This observation is consistent with the supposition that the basin was used for winnowing seeds, inasmuch as the heavier seeds would have fallen into the basin and the lighter chaff (and pollen) would have been deposited outside. These results were not consistent, however, with my expectation that the prevailing winds would have come from the southwest, which would have tended to diminish the cheno-am pollen rain on the southwest side of the basin. Factors such as the modification of wind patterns by the construction of houses or even by local storms may make such expectations too unrealistic.

The only large percentage differences between the basin sample and its control seem to be in the cheno-am category. I have demonstrated experimentally that when *Chenopodium dessicatum* seeds are collected by being beaten into a container and are then washed in water, they yield abundant pollen (Bohrer 1972:26). Partly mature stalks of *Chenopodium* bear flowers and seeds simultaneously, permitting one unintentionally to collect the pollen while gathering seeds. Judging from the pollen evidence alone, basin A could have been used for processing *Chenopodium* or *Amaranthus* seeds. The seeds of these two genera were the most widely distributed in flotation samples at Arroyo Hondo (Wetterstrom 1976:75). In fact, the recovery of both seed types in the trash fill of the basin (R. W. Lang, correspondence 1976) may help to explain the ambiguous pollen record. Cheno-am pollen percolating with rainwater down through the trash to the basin floor might have skewed the original pollen spectrum deposited during use of the basin.

A number of pollen types were unique to basin A: five unknown types plus *Eriogonum*, *Typha*, and *Datura*. In the previous discussion of *Datura*, it was suggested that medicine water containing the flower may have been sprinkled on the basin. Medicines typically contain numerous ingredients, and it seems reasonable to suppose that other pollen types originated in medicine water as well. Since the basin itself might transmit disease (fungal decay) to the seeds processed within it, in my opinion some "medicine" would be necessary to counteract such tendencies. Some of the pollen types could, of course, have derived from the processing of other seeds or fruits besides *Chenopodium*. It is also possible that pollen originating in the trash fill of the basin was inadvertently incorporated into the sample, and that the unique pollen types derived from this trash deposit.

Pollen From Turkey Dung Samples

Palynological investigations of turkey dung provide some insights into the dietary habits of domestic turkeys. Sample 14 derived from a terminal Component I layer of mixed turkey dung and brown sand. It contained an unusually high percentage of pine pollen (64.5 percent) with low percentages of cheno-ams (8.4 percent) and maize (2.5 percent). The high percentages of pine in sample 14 may indicate that the turkeys were driven into the denser pine forests to forage for food, and in their pens at night they deposited dung rich in pollen from the grit acquired on the forest floor. (In her story *Turkey Girl* [1960], Pablita Velarde from Santa Clara Pueblo tells the tale of a girl taking turkeys out to forage for food.) Another possible interpretation is that the pollen sample represents a concentration of pine pollen during June when pollen is ubiquitous, though I consider this less likely because of the tendency of pollen to disburse in sediments.

Sample 11, from the Component II occupation, consisted of light greenish brown turkey dung. The count of 42.5 percent pine pollen in this sample is not unusual for the time period. Sample 11 was relatively high in maize pollen (19.5 percent), which could represent either prayer offerings in the pen area or the accumulation of pollen from maize leaves that might have been fed to the turkeys. The presence of five unidentified pollen types unique to the sample again suggests that foraging took place outside the village.

Two other samples (8 and 10), because they contained trash mixed with dung, are not easily interpreted. For example, the *Cucurbita* pollen in these samples might reflect either human use of cucurbits or human tolerance for turkeys foraging in cultivated fields. The 60.5 percent maize count in sample 10 could represent a humanly concentrated amount possibly religious in nature.

Appendix A

TABLE 44

POLLEN COUNTS FOR EACH NUMBERED SAMPLE

NOTE: Samples 12, 21, and 29 were omitted from the data matrix, as they were not extracted.

KEY TO SYMBOLS:
a = count of first 100 grains
b = count of second 100 grains
p = partial count
* = deleted from adjusted arboreal sum

Sample Number:	1		2	3		4	5		6		7	8	
Nature of Count:	a	b	a	a	b	p	a	b	a	b	p	a	b
Pinus	21	06	57	17	08	08	26	32	20	22	03	29	37
Juniperus	02	02		03	02			02				03	01
Abies/Picea type												01	
Quercus													
*Alnus													
Cheno-ams	66	79	34	52	51	10	60	58	60	57	10	23	30
*Sarcobatus													
Long-spine Compositae	02	02	01	04	02		05	03	05	06		09	03
Ambrosia type	02	01	02	04	04	03	06	01	07	03	01	03	04
Artemisia	01			04	01			01	02	03		01	01
Ephedra torreyana type			02										
Ephedra nevadensis type				01	01	01					01		
Gramineae	02	02		01	03	03			01	02	05	06	06
Sphaeralcea type													
Eriogonum		01		02								01	
*Cylindropuntia												02	01
Mammillaria type													
*Zea mays	03		01		02	01			01		01	01	07
Oenothera type													
*Typha		01		04	02								
Dicotyledon	01	06	02	03	09	04	03	03	02	06		11	09
Platyopuntia													
*Cucurbita													
Datura													
Cleome													
*Unknown type 1			01	02					01		02	03	01
*Unknown type 2				03	01					01		04	
Unknowns					04				01			03	
Small Pine Fraction	4/12			9/24			17/38		9/26		3/17	13/50	
Arboreal Fraction	31/193		57/97	40/186			60/193		42/189			71/182	

Sample Number:	*9*		*10*		*11*		*13*		*14*		*15*	*16*	
Nature of Count:	a	b	a	b	a	b	a	b	a	b	p	a	b
Pinus	37	35	17	28	36	49	59	74	67	62	10	13	18
Juniperus									01			06	04
Abies/Picea type													
Quercus													
*Alnus													
Cheno-ams	25	34	07	05	14	07	07	08	07	10		52	52
*Sarcobatus													
Long-spine Compositae		02	01	01	03	05	02	03	04	01		13	14
*Ambrosia type	01	03			02	02		01	01	01		11	10
Artemisia					02	02	02	01	01	03			
Ephedra torreyana type										01			
Ephedra nevadensis type													
Gramineae	08	01	05	07	08	08	07	04	11	07	01	03	02
Sphaeralcea type				01		02	07						
Eriogonum									01	01			
*Cylindropuntia	01			03		01	02	02					
Mammillaria type													
*Zea mays	24	25	67	53	19	20	06	04	01	04			
Oenothera type	01			01									
*Typha			02		01		01	01					
Dicotyledon	01				09	02	04	02	05	08		01	
Platyopuntia	01						02						
*Cucurbita			01										
Datura													
Cleome													
*Unknown type 1	01						01		01	02		01	
*Unknown type 2					02	02							
Unknowns					04								
Small Pine Fraction	28/62		16/36		25/65		36/102		40/107		4/8	24/100	
Arboreal Fraction	72/146		45/73		85/155		133/183		130/193			41/179	

Sample Number:	17		18		19		20		22		23	24	
Nature of Count:	a	b	a	b	a	p	a	p	a	b	a	a	b
Pinus	04	11	25	21	73	21	44	32	21	18	29	45	43
Juniperus	01	02	04	10	01		17	11	02		03	02	
Abies/Picea type													
Quercus	01												
*Alnus													
Cheno-ams	70	72	45	49	06		18	12	18	23	30	25	23
*Sarcobatus													
Long-spine Compositae	05	04			03	03			02		10		05
*Ambrosia type	10	06	06	05	04		04	05	03	01	05	04	01
Artemisia										02	02	02	01
Ephedra torreyana type												01	02
Ephedra nevadensis type	01							01					
Gramineae	05	04	16	13	02		06	06	04	03	07	12	15
Sphaeralcea type													
Eriogonum			02	02						01	02		01
*Cylindropuntia													
Mammillaria type													01
*Zea mays					01							01	
Oenothera type													
*Typha													
Dicotyledon	01	01	02		09	01	11	07		01	10	08	08
Platyopuntia													
*Cucurbita													
Datura													
Cleome													
*Unknown type 1	01				01				49	50	02		
*Unknown type 2	01								01	01			
Unknowns													
Small Pine Fraction	31/100		21/100		41/76		36/62		24/47		17/26	74/133	
Arboreal Fraction	19/184		69/189		95/120		104/165		41/145		32/95	90/194	

Sample Number:	25		26		27		28	30		31		32	
Nature of Count:	a	b	a	b	a	b	p	a	b	a	b	a	p
Pinus	04	05	05	20	03	03	27	37	40	20	26	34	23
Juniperus	01		02		01	01	18	08	12	01	02	06	03
Abies/Picea type													
Quercus													
*Alnus		01											
Cheno-ams	76	76	81	60	82	85		39	34	62	61	29	23
*Sarcobatus													
Long-spine Compositae	01		05	04	06	06	05	04	01	04	06	07	03
*Ambrosia type	06	06	01	09	05	03	01	08	08	07	01	04	02
Artemisia			05	02			03	01	01				
Ephedra torreyana type				01								01	01
Ephedra nevadensis type													
Gramineae	04	04		04	03	02	01	02	02	02		09	04
Sphaeralcea type													
Eriogonum		02							01	01			
*Cylindropuntia													
Mammillaria type													
*Zea mays							09				01		
Oenothera type													
*Typha													
Dicotyledon	06	05	01				05	01	01	03	03	07	05
Platyopuntia													
*Cucurbita													
Datura													
Cleome													
*Unknown type 1	02	01										03	02
*Unknown type 2													
Unknowns													
Small Pine Fraction			28/55		27/47		4/20	42/63		36/64		16/52	
Arboreal Fraction	10/187		27/140		8/192			97/184		49/191		66/160	

Sample Number:	33		34		35		36		37		38		39	
Nature of Count:	a	b	a	b	a	b	a	b	a	b	a	b	a	b
Pinus	36	23	32	28	31	36	33	35	28	26	10	11	15	21
Juniperus	01			06	03	02	03	06	03	06	03	04	03	02
Abies/Picea type														
Quercus	03	03	01	03										
*Alnus														
Cheno-ams	02	07	25	25	27	26	36	32	46	50	55	54	48	36
*Sarcobatus													04	
Long-spine Compositae	03	05	06	03	12	06	10	04	01	07	12	11	09	14
*Ambrosia type	05	02	04	07	07	03		04	05	04	02	02	01	03
Artemisia			07	07	03	10	02	02	03					01
Ephedra torreyana type				02			01							
Ephedra nevadensis type								01						
Gramineae	10	06	12	07	07	05	02	06	01		02	03		
Sphaeralcea type														
Eriogonum				02		01		01						
*Cylindropuntia		01	02					01		01			01	
Mammillaria type														
*Zea mays	02	02	03	04	04	09			02		01	01	04	04
Oenothera type														
*Typha	06	06									01	01		
Dicotyledon	07	08	08	06	06	02	10	03	03	02	09	08	14	16
Platyopuntia														
*Cucurbita														
Datura														
Cleome														
*Unknown type 1	16	19					03	05	08	03	05	05	01	03
*Unknown type 2	09	18								01				
Unknowns														
Small Pine Fraction	41/114		38/100		23/87		35/105		40/86		17/55		12/42	
Arboreal Fraction	66/188		70/180		72/177		77/195		63/188		28/192		41/187	

Sample Number:	*40*		*41*		*42*		*43*		*44*		*45*	
Nature of Count:	a	b	a	b	a	b	a	b	a	b	a	b
Pinus	20	15	24	24	38	50	42	26	21	29	46	56
Juniperus	06	06	03	03	02	04	01	01		01	06	04
Abies/Picea type						01						
Quercus												
*Alnus				02				01				
Cheno-ams	53	55	33	32	34	27	12	09	13	09	28	19
*Sarcobatus												
Long-spine Compositae	07	08	05	06	01		04	07	05	04	02	04
*Ambrosia type	05	01	06	10	10	06	08	05	12	05	07	05
Artemisia			01	01	01							
Ephedra torreyana type		01	01	01		03		01			01	01
Ephedra nevadensis type												
Gramineae	02	04	06	05	05		03	06	20	10	03	08
Sphaeralcea type								02				
Eriogonum		01			01				01	02	02	
*Cylindropuntia		01						01				
Mammillaria type												
*Zea mays	01	01	01	01			09	18	03	03		
Oenothera type												
*Typha		01										
Dicotyledon	06	01	10	12	07	08	21	22	22	35	04	03
Platyopuntia												
*Cucurbita												
Datura												
Cleome												
*Unknown type 1		05	08	03	01	01		01	01		01	
*Unknown type 2			01									
Unknowns			01						02	02		
Small Pine Fraction	30/54		31/77		43/112		40/150		41/140		57/120	
Arboreal Fraction	47/190		54/182		95/184		70/159		51/177		112/188	

Appendix B

DATA ON POLLEN SAMPLES FROM ARROYO HONDO PUEBLO

SAMPLE 1

SAR number: 12-A2-18-III-1. Date taken: June 6, 1974.
Comments: Plaza A, surface 2 (first major surface accumulation), subsurface B (latest deposition during accumulation of surface 2). Sample taken from this surface and to the southwest of basins A and C (see below). Component I; precise date unknown. Associated with occupation of earliest (i.e., northern) alignment of roomblock 2 and initial construction of southern alignment.

SAMPLE 2

SAR number: 12-A2-18-IV-2. Date taken: June 7, 1974.
Comments: Basin A in plaza A. Later of two superimposed basins. Associated with subsurface B of surface 2. Sample taken from floor scrapings after basin had stood open for some time. Component I. Associated with the occupation of the northern room alignment of roomblock 2. Abandoned and trash-filled upon construction of southern room alignment.

SAMPLE 3

SAR number: 12-A2-18-IV-4. Date taken: June 6, 1974.
Comments: As above. Sample taken from floor scrapings before basin had stood open for long. Alternate sample.

SAMPLE 4

SAR number: 12-A2-18-VI-1. Date taken: June 7, 1974.
Comments: Basin C in plaza A. Earlier of two superimposed basins, overlain by basin A. Associated with surface 2, subsurface A (earliest deposition during accumulation of surface 2). Trash filled. Component I. Associated with occupation of earliest (northern) room alignment of roomblock 2. Pre-dates samples 1, 2, and 3.

SAMPLE 5

SAR number: 12-C-A-16-1. Date taken: July 3, 1974.
Comments: North side of plaza C, layer 2. Deposit of wall-fall and adobe wash with limited trash, 10–15 cm above plaza surface 2 (the last well-defined surface of plaza C). Associated with latest activity in plaza C. Sample post-dates burning of Component II roomblock 10. Probably correlates with sample 37.

SAMPLE 6

SAR number: 12-C-A-16-2. Date taken: July 3, 1974.
Comments: North side of plaza C, lower layer 2, and plaza surface 2. Taken from burned wood and wall-fall lens. Component II. Associated with burning of roomblock 10 and with previous use of plaza surface 2. This surface apparently saw seasonal use after most hearths in roomblock 10 were sealed. Probably correlates with sample 37.

SAMPLE 7

SAR number: 12-C-A-16-3. Date taken: July 3, 1974.
Comments: North side of plaza C, layer 3, underlying surface 2. Lens

of very light brown, sandy wash with very little trash. Derived from erosion of wall surfaces of roomblock 10. Component II. Probably associated with population decline in this area of site, but before the fire. Sample probably correlates with 37.

SAMPLE 8

SAR number: 12-C-A-16-4. Date taken: July 3, 1974.
Comments: North side of plaza C, layer 4. Primarily light greenish brown turkey dung mixed with sand. Occasional eggshell fragments, decomposed plant materials, and some trash. Component II. Associated with abandonment of work area along south side of roomblock 10, removal of portal, and installation of turkey pens. Layer 4 should correspond temporally with the lower portion of layer 12-C-3-II (sample 37).

SAMPLE 9

SAR number: 12-C-A-12-2. Date taken: July 3, 1974.
Comments: North side of plaza C, layer 5. Sample is from 6-cm-thick deposit of adobe soil mixed with ash and containing small quantities of trash. Deposit is possibly wash formed, but may represent dumping of relatively clean soil along roomblock 10 in order to provide a fresh surface. Component II. Surface 4 forms the top of layer 5; this surface is associated with the primary Component II occupation of roomblock 10 and the peak of Component II population. Sample probably correlates with sample 45.

SAMPLE 10

SAR number: 12-C-A-12-3. Date taken: July 3, 1974.
Comments: North side of plaza C, layer 6. Mixed trash and turkey dung with ash lenses. Thickness 10–11 cm. Component II. Pre-dates surface 4. Associated with terminal use of earliest Component II turkey pens and trash dumping after construction of rooms in roomblock 10. Forms base for surface 5. Dates about A.D. 1386–87.

SAMPLE 11

SAR number: 12-C-A-12-4. Date taken: July 3, 1974.
Comments: North side of plaza C, layer 7. Turkey dung with no obvious trash. Thickness 12–14 cm. Component II. Pre-dates surface 5. Associated with turkey penning in this area. Accumulated between A.D. 1374 and 1386. No clear correlation with 12-C-3 series.

SAMPLE 12

SAR number: 12-C-A-12-5. Date taken: July 3, 1974.
Comments: North side of plaza C, layer 8. Sand lens containing small amount of trash. Probably derived from erosion of walls and room fill of abandoned Component I structures of roomblock 10, with limited trash deposition. Thickness 15–17 cm. Probably early Component II, overlapping with late hiatus phase. No clear correlation with 12-C-3 series.

SAMPLE 13

SAR number: 12-C-A-12-6. Date taken: July 3, 1974.
Comments: North side of plaza C, layer 9. Gravelly, sandy, culturally sterile orange-tan wash derived from Component I structures of roomblock 10. Hiatus phase between Component I and II occupations. Correlates with sample 32.

SAMPLE 14

SAR number: 12-C-A-12-7. Date taken: July 3, 1974.
Comments: North side of plaza C, layer 10. Mixed turkey dung and brown sand, 10 cm thick. Presumably terminal Component I occupation in roomblock 10 area. Area used for turkey penning at that time. Appears to correlate temporally with sample 41 through perhaps 33, 43, and 44.

SAMPLE 15

SAR number: 12-C-A-12-8. Date taken: July 3, 1974.
Comments: North side of plaza C, layer 11. Medium-brown loamy sand and gravel with limited trash and hard plaza surface at soil horizon. Thickness 7–10 cm. Component I. Appears to be an old A-zone mixed with trash. Footings of walls of roomblock 10 rest upon this surface. Layer 11 is underlain by layer 12, a culturally sterile orange-tan subsoil deposit. Sample correlates with sample 34 or 44.

SAMPLE 16

SAR number: 12-0-0-1. Date taken: March 7, 1973.
Comments: Modern surface. North-south transect 100 paces long, across pasture of McKinley Ranch. Approximately 150 m southwest of the 12-J-0 sample area and 250 m southwest of the 12-D-0 sample area. Cover consisted of grass, cholla, and a few snakeweed plants.

SAMPLE 17

SAR number: 12-J-0-1. Date taken: March 7, 1973.
Comments: Modern surface. North-south transect 100 paces long, at southwestern end of site. Transect runs across the eastern end of plaza J between kiva 12-J-1 and the west face of the dirt "tank," beginning at the south face of roomblock 12. Grass cover with cholla, prickly pear, and a few junipers.

SAMPLE 18

SAR number: 12-D-0-1. Date taken: March 7, 1973.
Comments: Modern surface. North-south transect 100 paces long, at eastern end of site. Transect runs across the eastern side of plaza D, between the north end of roomblock 21 and the south face of roomblock 16. Subsamples collected only from surfaces undisturbed by excavation. Grass cover with cholla, a few junipers, and scattered snakeweed, chamisa, and prickly pear.

SAMPLE 19

SAR number: 12-9-7-1-1. Date taken: June 30, 1972.
Comments: Post-abandonment fill of Component I room. Uppermost layer of fill directly below adobe base of Component II room floor. Layer composed of laminated tan sand, apparently water deposited, possibly derived from eroded walls. Hiatus phase.

SAMPLE 20

SAR number: 12-9-7-3-1. Date taken: June 30, 1972.
Comments: Post-abandonment fill of Component I room. Third layer of fill, 5–20 cm thick. Composed of laminated tan sand, apparently water deposited (possibly derived from eroded walls), with large fragments of second-story wall-fall on east side. Sample taken at center of deposit (vertically and horizontally). Hiatus phase.

(No sample was assigned number 21.)

SAMPLE 22

SAR number: 12-9-7-8-1. Date taken: June 30, 1972.
Comments: Terminal Component I, after abandonment of room. Layer 8 of fill represented mixed roof and second-story floor fall. Sample was taken from upper portion of layer, directly below ash deposit from fallen second story hearth.

SAMPLE 23

SAR number: 12-9-7-9-4. Date taken: July 10, 1972.
Comments: Floor contact in southwest corner of room. Terminal Component I.

SAMPLE 24

SAR number: 12-9-7-10-1. Date taken: July 11, 1972.

Old A-zone soil horizon below ash deposit. Pre-dates roomblock 9. Pre-occupation or early Component I.

SAMPLE 25

SAR number: 12-9-15-A (formerly 12-9-9-A). Date taken: October 3, 1972.
Comments: Layer of gravelly washed buff adobe and wind-blown sand, 9 cm thick, forming uppermost level of fill in burned Component II room. Postdates Component II occupation. Sample taken from 7 cm below surface.

SAMPLE 26

SAR number: 12-9-15-B2 (formerly 12-9-9-B2). Date taken: October 3, 1972.
Comments: Layer below that described for sample 25; 28 cm thick. Primarily composed of medium-brown sandy loam washed from wall of burned room. Probably postdates Component II occupation. Sample taken at 30 cm below surface.

SAMPLE 27

SAR number: 12-H-2-I-1. Date taken: June 13, 1972.
Comments: Uppermost stratigraphic layer of Component I trash deposit in plaza H. Washed, fine gray soil high in ash and cultural debris. Sample taken at 29 cm below datum (about 9 cm below surface) in upper portion of layer. Layer I represents end of Component I occupation. Glaze I ceramics are present but extremely rare, suggesting that layer I dates to the Component I–II transition, though specimens could be intrusive.

SAMPLE 28

SAR number: 12-H-2-IV-1. Date taken: June 13, 1972.
Comments: Layer IV is composed of culturally sterile red clay and ca-

liche. A discontinuous deposit interposed between layers III and V. Sample taken at 76 cm below datum. Component I.

SAMPLE 29

SAR number: 12-16-8-6-1. Date taken: June 23, 1971.
Comments: Post-abandonment fill of Component I room. Uppermost layer of fill directly below level of eroded Component II floor. Tan laminated sand with pebbles and caliche fragments, located below layer of adobe chunks. Presumably comparable to upper deposits of room 12-9-7. Sample taken at 26–28 cm below datum in layer 2. Hiatus phase.

SAMPLE 30

SAR number: 12-16-8-6-2. Date taken: June 23, 1971.
Comments: Post-abandonment fill of Component I room. Layer 3, 37–40 cm below datum. Dark brown sandy soil with pebbles and small adobe chunks. Presumably comparable to upper deposits of room 12-9-7. Hiatus phase.

SAMPLE 31

SAR number: 12-C-3-I. Date taken: October 3, 1972.
Comments: Layer I in plaza C, 1.3 m west of the interior northwest corner of room 12-16-38. Buff-colored gravelly wash post-dating the Component II abandonment. Layer 10 cm thick.

SAMPLE 32

SAR number: 12-C-3-IV. Date taken: October 3, 1972.
Comments: Layer IV in plaza C. Deposit of washed, gravelly, orange adobe, 15 cm thick, from abandoned Component I rooms of roomblock 16. Hiatus phase.

SAMPLE 33

SAR number: 12-C-3-IX. Date taken: October 3, 1972.
Comments: Layer IX in plaza C. Layer is 8 cm thick and composed of dark brown loamy sand with carbon flecks. Possibly contemporaneous with population peak in plaza C area, Component I. Dates about A.D. 1325–1335.

SAMPLE 34

SAR number: 12-C-3-XII. Date taken: October 3, 1972.
Comments: Layer XII in plaza C. Represents the old A-zone soil horizon and is underlain by culturally sterile reddish gravelly sand. Layer is 6 cm thick and composed of light reddish-brown sandy loam. Preoccupation.

SAMPLE 35

SAR number: 12-H-3-D. Date taken: July 21, 1972.
Comments: Layer D in plaza H. Buff-tan subsoil beneath layer C; contains a few sherds and flecks of carbon. Very earliest Component I. Floor of probable arroyo.

SAMPLE 36

SAR number: 12-9-12-C (formerly 12-9-10-C). Date taken: October 3, 1972.
Comments: Layer 3 of fill in Component II room. Loamy sand with carbon flecks and trash, 7 cm thick. Sample taken at 45 cm below surface, 4 cm above floor. Comparable to layer 3 of 12-9-9. Terminal Component II.

SAMPLE 37

SAR number: 12-C-3-II. Date taken: October 3, 1972.
Comments: Layer II in plaza C. Light brown loamy sand with carbon

flecks; 17 cm thick. Represents Component II soil and trash accumulation.

SAMPLE 38

SAR number: 12-15A-7-3-2. Date taken: June 8, 1972.
Comments: Floor contact in Component II room with hearth. Room burned along with others in the main north-south spine of the Component II complex.

SAMPLE 39

SAR number: 12-15A-8-5-1. Date taken: June 13, 1972.
Comments: Floor contact of Component II room with hearth, ventilator, and loom or ladder holes. Floor layer 5, below floor of 12-15A-7.

SAMPLE 40

SAR number: 12-9-12-A (formerly 12-9-10-A). Date taken: October 3, 1972.
Comments: Layer 1 of Component II room. Composed of buff-colored gravelly washed adobe and sand, 17 cm thick; comparable to layer 1 of 12-9-9. Sample taken at 15 cm below surface. Postdates Component II occupation.

SAMPLE 41

SAR number: 12-C-3-V. Date taken: October 3, 1972.
Comments: "Layer" V in plaza C. Lens of medium-brown loamy sand with carbon flecks, 1–1.5 cm thick. Terminal Component I.

SAMPLE 42

SAR number: 12-C-3-VI. Date taken: October 3, 1972.

Comments: Layer VI in plaza C. Layer is 9 cm thick and composed of reddish-brown loamy sand with carbon flecks. Late Component I.

SAMPLE 43

SAR number: 12-C-3-X. Date taken: October 3, 1972.
Comments: Layer X in plaza C. Layer is 12 cm thick and composed of medium-brown loamy sand with carbon flecks. Component I.

SAMPLE 44

SAR number: 12-C-3-XI. Date taken: October 3, 1972.
Comments: Layer XI in plaza C. Composed of light reddish brown sandy loam with carbon flecks; 9–10 cm thick. Layer is hard and compact and represents the earliest plaza surface. Component I.

SAMPLE 45

SAR number: 12-C-3-III. Date taken: October 3, 1972.
Comments: "Layer" III in plaza C. Lens of medium-brown loamy sand with carbon flecks; 1–1.5 cm thick. Early Component II accumulation.

Appendix C

DESCRIPTIONS OF ETHNOBOTANICAL POLLEN

CHENO-AMS

Chenopod and amaranth pollen with periporate grains usually between 20 and 35 micrometers form the morphological group termed cheno-ams. Differences in pore number in relation to grain diameter have been helpful in isolating certain genera for identification as have electron microscope studies (Kapp 1969). However, for most southwestern pollen analysts, the frequencies of the wind-borne grains are so high that the time needed for detailed classification is prohibitive.

Prehistoric pollen grains differ little from acetolized modern counterparts, except that two morphological states are seen in the fossil record. One remains thin-walled in appearance with pore rims close to the surface of the grain. The other type has pores sunken into the surface, providing the grain with a bony, hard appearance. I do not know if these differences are typical of certain genera or instead are degradation states within the morphological group.

CLEOME (BEEWEED)

Prolate, tricolporate pollen grains. Reticulate sculptoring has been reported (Martin and Byers 1965:125), but two different acetolyzed modern sources (microslide 343 and 664) failed to show this characteristic.

The polar height averages 15 micrometers (standard deviation 1.33 micrometers), and the equatorial diameter 11.7 micrometers (standard deviation 0.6 micrometers) in 10 measured grains. Dimorphism in pollen size has been reported for the genus (Vuilleumier 1967:212). Poorly preserved pollen resembles other genera in the Capparidaceae, i.e., *Polanisia*, *Wislizenia*, and *Cleomella* (Martin and Byers 1965:125).

CUCURBITA (SQUASH)

Periporate grains with operculate pores, variable in size, and bearing spines that differ in shape and in the presence or absence of smaller protrusions between spines. At Arroyo Hondo a *Cucurbita* grain of 70.25 micrometers has spines that sharply constrict near the tip and bears fine hairs or setae between spines. The largest grain, 135 micrometers, has broad (4.5 micrometers at the base), sturdy spines with scabrate sculptoring between spines. In sample 37 the spine tips were blunt and fingerlike; the presence of pores was uncertain. Published species descriptions of pollen based on herbarium vouchers of dubious identification (Cutler 1966:21) have little practical application.

DATURA (JIMSONWEED)

Subspheroidal grains average 34.31 micrometers (standard deviation 1.91 micrometers) in equatorial diameter and 32.58 micrometers (standard deviation 2.91 micrometers) in polar height (n = 10). The grain varies from tricolpate to tricolporate with a pore as elongated as 8.7 micrometers and culpae ranging from 4.95 to 16.65 micrometers. Striae radiate from the poles but are obscured in the polar areas by intrareticular sculptoring. In acetolyzed material, a tirelike equatorical bulge was frequently observed. Here the striae seemed most pronounced. Some grains lack the equatorial bulge and show intrareticular sculptoring in the equatorial region. The amount of equatorial bulge influences the variation found in the polar height of the grain. The foregoing description derives from the acetolyzed pollen of *Datura meteloides* (microslide 519) in my own pollen reference collection.

The single grain from the large basin in plaza A at Arroyo Hondo (sample 3) was tricolpate with striae over the swollen equatorial region and showed intrareticular sculptoring in the pole. The diameter measured 35.77 micrometers and the polar height remained undetermined due to the invagination of the grain.

ERIOGONUM (BUCKWHEAT)

The prolate (or sometimes subspheroidal), tectate grains have three slender furrows. Pores vary in size and shape. Pollen of *E. jamesii* ranges up to 50 micrometers in polar height, but many species are smaller. The lobes of fossilized grains belonging to this genus tend to deflate to form an interlobate grain as defined by Faegri and Iverson (1975:20). From a polar view the grain has the appearance of a three-bladed airplane propeller. The furrows apparently fold inward and obscure the pore in the process, for these features are seldom clear. The proportions of polar height to equatorial breadth (P/E index) in four modern species range from 1.17 to 1.66 and average 1.36 (n = 20). In the Arroyo Hondo material the P/E index ranges from 1.33 to 1.73.

HELIANTHUS (SUNFLOWER)

Spheroidal pollen grains of modern *H. petiolaris* and *H. annus* resemble each other closely in the diameter of the body and the length of the spines (table 45). No doubt depositional conditions influence the amount of shrinkage of the fossil pollen, but closing of the furrows or even invagination may contribute to size reduction in fossil pollen. In the 12 measurable prehistoric grains, the shrinkage of the body of the grain was more apparent than the reduction in the length of the spine (see table 39). In the one instance when both pore and furrow were open, the grain body was larger (21.15 micrometers).

Comparative work on the Compositae—the sunflower family—indicates that pollen from other southwestern genera may resemble *Helianthus* pollen. These genera include *Bidens, Helenium, Tagetes, Zinnia* (Kapp 1969:154), *Verbesina*, and *Chaenactis* (Martin and Drew 1970:146). At Acoma and Laguna, *Zinnia grandiflora* (as *Crassina grandiflora* in Swank 1932) flowers were ground with white clay to make yellow dye and were used to color buckskin and as body paint. *Verbesina* (as *Ximenesia* in Swank 1932) has similar uses and, like *Helian-*

TABLE 45.
Size in micrometers of sunflower (*Helianthus*) pollen.

Type	*Mean Diameter excl. spines*	*s.d.*	*Mean length of spines*	*s.d.*	*n*
Modern					
H. petiolaris	22.19	0.547	5.44	0.55	5
H. annus	23.10	0.982	5.35	0.54	5
Combined *H. petiolaris* and *H. annuus*	22.64	0.90	5.40	0.53	
Prehistoric	19.68	1.77	5.04	0.73	12

thus, grows in disturbed habitats. Except for these two genera, the prehistoric record of *Helianthus*-type pollen should represent this genus alone.

MAMMILLARIA (PINCUSHION CACTUS)

The oblate to spheroidal grains of the *Mammillaria* type include *Coryphantha*, *Echinocereus*, and certain genera found in southern New Mexico and Arizona, such as *Cereus* and *Echinocactus*. All bear tricolpate grains 41 to 42 micrometers (table 46) in diameter with finely pitted exines (Kurtz 1948). Tsukada (1964:56) suggests that *Echinocereus* can be distinguished from the other genera because of the blunted tips of two of the colpi, in contrast to the sharply pointed tips in the other genera. Pollen of *Echinocereus triglochidiatus* from Arroyo Hondo in the author's collection (microslide 487) fails to show this characteristic sufficiently to warrant any distinctions between genera.

OPUNTIA

Polyporate grains in the genus *Opuntia* can be classified into the prickly pear *(Platyopuntia)* or cholla *(Cylindropuntia)* types. In prickly pear, each pore is surrounded by a margo more than 5 micrometers in breadth,

TABLE 46.
Size in micrometers and sources of *Mammillaria* pollen at Arroyo Hondo Pueblo.

Sample	*SAR No.*	*Diameter*	*Source*
24	12-9-7-10-1	41.58	Old A-zone soil horizon below ash deposit. Polar height of grain. is 29.88 micrometers.
34	12-C-3-XII	42.72	Old A-zone soil horizon in plaza.

which forms a reticulum. Cholla pollen grains are more spherical in shape, lack the reticulum, and possess a punctibaculate ektexine (Tsukada 1964:70). In modern and some archaeological prickly-pear pollen, the margo itself may bear finer reticulations. Other prehistoric samples lack the finer sculptoring, probably due to diagenetic factors. Similar factors may cause prehistoric cholla pollen exines to appear thin and delicate.

TYPHA (CATTAIL)

Monoporate, reticulate grains, more or less spherical. When occurring singly, the grains may not be distinguishable from *Sparganium* (Kapp 1969:73). *Typha augustifolia* and *T. domingensis* typically produce single grains, while *Typha latifolia* grains remain in tetrads. When the two species hybridize, or when the tetrads break apart, dyads and monads will result (Mehringer 1967:172).

ZEA MAYS (MAIZE)

Large spheroidal pollen bearing a single pore surrounded by a distinct annulus or ring. At Arroyo Hondo, pollen from 57 to 59 micrometers in diameter, with a pore of 4.7 micrometers and annulus of 11 micrometers in diameter, was considered large enough to be classified as maize. The larger pollen grains of maize were sufficiently collapsed, wrinkled, or convoluted to prevent accurate measurement. The largest grain that could be measured accurately was 88 micrometers in diameter. Large grass pollen can also be found in the grass tribe to which the cultivated cereal grasses belong and among close relatives of maize. Neither cultivated cereals nor relatives of maize were expected at Arroyo Hondo for the time period in question. Schoenwetter (1974) has summarized some of the complications of maize pollen identification in Mexico.

UNIDENTIFIED POLLEN

Unknown Type 1

The grain, tricolpate and finely scabrate, sometimes appears tectate. It retains safranin stain poorly. Equatorial diameter averages 9.7 micrometers (standard deviation 0.5, n = 55), and polar height, 13.9 micrometers (standard deviation 2.0, n = 59).

Concentrations of 50 percent pollen in a sample taken directly beneath an ash pit (sample 22, table 47) and frequencies as high as 18 percent in trash (sample 33) strongly suggest economic utilization. The type might have been normally present in the environment shortly after abandonment (sample 40). It does not appear in modern surface samples. I would not be surprised if the plant were an annual that thrives in disturbed habitats created by humans or nature, particularly following recovery from drought.

Unknown Type 2

For the number and distribution of this type, see table 48. The tricolpate, spherical grains have a thickened wall and slightly roughened exine. The sturdy wall stains solidly with safranin and gives no indication of being tectate. Were columellae in the walls discernable, it would look much like *Artemesia* pollen, although pores seem to be lacking and it seems abnormally small. Equatorial diameter ranges from 14.5 to 15.5 micrometers (n = 9).

I find the tendency of a wall to stain solidly with safranin suspiciously like a highly fossilized, poorly preserved grain. During the current study I recall seeing only one pine pollen grain in this condition; none of the intrareticulations in the bladders could be seen. This unknown

TABLE 47.
Distribution of unknown type 1 pollen at Arroyo Hondo Pueblo.

Sample	*SAR No.*	*No. of Grains*	*Source*
22	12-9-7-8-1	99	Component I, probably terminal abandonment. Sampled directly below ash deposit from fallen second-story hearth.
23	12-9-7-9-4	2	Component I. Floor contact, zone of second-story floor fall.
33	12-C-3-IX	35	Component I. Loamy sand with carbon flecks. Possible population peak in plaza C area.
36	12-9-12-C	8	Terminal Component II. Loamy sand with carbon flecks and trash.
37	12-C-3-II	11	Component II. Sandy loam with trash, carbon flecks, plaza C.
38	12-15A-7-3-2	10	Component II. Floor contact.
39	12-15A-8-5-1	4	Component II. Floor layer 5, beneath floor of 12-15A-7 (sample 38).
40	12-9-10-A	5	Post-Component II. Washed adobe and sand.
41	12-C-3-V	1	Terminal Component I. Loamy sand with carbon flecks.

TABLE 48.
Distribution of unknown type 2 pollen at Arroyo Hondo Pueblo.

Sample	*SAR No.*	*No. of Grains*	*Source*
3	12-A-2-18-IV-4	1	Component I. Basin A in plaza A.
11	12-C-A-12-4	1	Component II, plaza C. Turkey dung with no obvious trash.
33	12-C-3-IX	27	Component I. Loamy sand with carbon flecks. Possible population peak in plaza C area.

pollen type may relate to extremely poor preservation conditions in the sediments or could represent fossilized grains redeposited from older sediments.

Unknown Type 3

This is a large, insect-pollinated type with an intrareticulate exine forming a pattern of angular to rounded polygons. A spine protrudes from the center of each polygon, or the spine base is present as a circular scar. See table 49 for dimensions and distribution. I have no explanation for its presence; its restriction to Component II times is intriguing.

ASTEROID POLYGON PLANT MICROFOSSIL

A polygonal plate highly variable in size with a series of cell walls radiating out from a common locus. The walls stain deeply and readily with safranin O, a good indicator of cellulose (plant) origin.

For the distribution of this type at Arroyo Hondo, see table 50. The

TABLE 49.
Size in micrometers and distribution of unknown type 3 pollen at Arroyo Hondo Pueblo.

Sample	SAR *No.*	*Diam. excl. spines*	*Spine l*	*Diam. of polygon*	*Source*
6	12-C-A-16-2	79.77	3.8	3–4	Component II, plaza C. Base of lens of burned wood and wall fall from roomblock 10.
37	12-C-3-II	130.78	4.5	6	Component II trash. Loamy sand with carbon flecks.
45	12-C-3-III	88.00	4.5	5–6	Early Component II occupation. Loamy sand with carbon flecks.

TABLE 50.
Distribution of asteroid polygon plant microfossil at Arroyo Hondo Pueblo.

Sample	*SAR No.*	*Source*
9	12-C-A-12-2	Component II, plaza C. Adobe soil mixed with limited trash. Associated with peak of Component II occupation.
27	12-H-2-I-1	Terminal Component I trash deposit.
36	12-9-10-C	Terminal Component II occupation. Loamy sand with carbon flecks and trash.
55	12-C-A-16-1	Component II. Associated with latest activity in plaza C. Washed adobe wall-fall with limited trash.

microfossil has also been found at Hay Hollow, a site in the earliest stages of agriculture dating from 300 B.C. to A.D. 300; at the Salmon Ruin in northwestern New Mexico; and at AZ T:4:8, a site north of Phoenix, near New River, Arizona. All sites but the latter are on the lower border of the pinyon-juniper plant community. AZ T:4:8 is an upper bajada site in the saguaro-paloverde plant community.

A surface sample from Mesita del Buey near Los Alamos, New Mexico (Transect 1, Station B), contained whole microfossils resembling a pottery water jar with a constricted neck. The bottom of the "vessel" resembled the above described microfossils and accepted safranin stain in a similar manner. The morphology is that of a sporangium or a container of fungal spores. I do not know if this fungus reproduces only in the ponderosa pine country (that is, Los Alamos), or if it is by chance simply better preserved.

SPORES

Spores bearing trilete marks were present in two of three samples derived from pre-occupation A-zonal soils and in eight samples dating from the occupation of the site. They are absent from the three modern surface samples. The occurrence of the spores in archaeological contexts probably relates to wind transport from surrounding natural vegetation rather than economic usage because only one or two spores were observed in each sample of 200 pollen grains, and each spore seemed unique in size and shape. Spores bearing trilete marks are characteristic of non-flowering plants (cryptogams) like mosses, lichens, lycopods, and ferns.

Notes

1. All scientific names of plants in this report conform to Kearney and Peebles (1960).

2. Two basic studies indicate that the role of these annuals has changed. The first, in Mesa Verde National Park, Colorado (Erdman 1970), reports vegetation nearing pristine conditions due to its isolation in an area of rough topography. The cool season grass *Poa fendleriana* (muttongrass) dominates the herb layer, but sectors cleared by lightning fires have *Chenopodium pratericola* and *Helianthus annuus* as the common initial annuals in succession (Erdman 1970:18). The second study (Weaver and Albertson 1956) covers the recuperation from drought of native rangelands, some overgrazed and some in good condition, on the Great Plains (Colorado, Kansas, and Nebraska). Unlike the case in Santa Fe, the period of settlement and potential abuse in the Plains study areas was relatively short. It was found that *Chenopodium* grew more abundantly during the first weed stage in wet years than any other annual, although *Helianthus* was also common (Weaver and Albertson 1956:145).

3. The results of the climatic study will be published elsewhere.

4. The confidence interval is calculated on the basis of a binomial distribution. Whenever a population of objects can be classified into two categories—for example, cheno-am or not cheno-am—it is called a binomial distribution. A trial with two possible outcomes, as in this example, is called a Bernoulli trial if two conditions are met. Each new grain must be identified independently of any preceding identification, and the probability of a pollen type occurring in the trial should be

constant over all trials from a sample (Maher 1972:86). In other words, all pollen in the sample must be well mixed and evenly distributed across the surface of the microscope slide. If the assumptions for a Bernoulli trial are met, the resulting distribution is binomial. This distribution then forms the basis for calculating the confidence interval. One need not assume the populations are normal (Li 1964:479).

A confidence interval states the degree to which it is probable that the true mean of a population is included within an estimated range of figures (Fryer 1966:67). Thus a 95 percent confidence interval signifies that there are 95 chances in 100 that the true mean does fall within the interval computed, which is based on a sample from the population. As the size of the sample used in making the calculation increases, the confidence interval becomes shorter—that is, one can predict more and more precisely where the true mean lies. Although the confidence interval can be computed from a formula (Mosimann 1965), a nomogram (Maher 1972), or tables (Fryer 1966), the latter source was almost exclusively employed.

Using the confidence interval makes it easier to recognize significant differences between samples. For example, if the 95 percent confidence intervals of the estimated proportions of cheno-am pollen in two samples do not overlap, one can feel reasonably safe in assuming that the samples are significantly different in their cheno-am frequencies. If the confidence intervals do overlap, one can dismiss the differences as probably representing only minor fluctuations in the frequency.

5. Jannifer Gish (1982) studied the occurrence of pollen clumping in surface samples and refined the use of pollen aggregates as an interpretive tool.

6. Jannifer Gish demonstrated that pit steam roasting of cholla buds created variation in pollen diameters (Greenhouse, Gasser, and Gish 1981). At the Ninth Annual Ethnobiology Meeting in Albuquerque, New Mexico (March 21–22, 1986), a paper presented by Lucile Housley, "The Human Factor in Cholla (*Cactaceae*) Distribution in Northwest New Mexico and Southwest Colorado," reported the results of measuring 16 characters on 5 plants growing near the periphery of the Arroyo Hondo site and comparing them with *O. whipplei* and *O. imbricata*. Her work demonstrated the closeness of the plants to *O. imbricata* while showing some residual influence from *O. whipplei*.

II

Artifacts of Woody Materials From Arroyo Hondo Pueblo

Richard W. Lang

The Arroyo Hondo excavations produced a substantial collection of artifacts made from wood, seeds, bark, leaves, and plant fibers. Most of these remains were preserved in burial pit contexts under moist, acid, and semianaerobic conditions, as previously discussed by Lang (1984). When perishables of this type were preserved in room or kiva contexts, the specimens were either carbonized, protected by an overlying rock slab, or deeply buried in air pockets within the fill. In the following sections are descriptions of, and comments on, major artifact categories.

TWINE

The most common category of artifact made from vegetal materials was twine. At least 58 specimens were represented in the hundreds of fragments present in the sample. Most of the specimens formed the warp and weft foundation cords of feather and fur textiles associated with burials (Lang 1984). Others had been used in the manufacture of basketry items. Clearly, twine making was an important activity at

Arroyo Hondo, and the uses that could be identified fall far short of the actual range.

Fifty-five of 57 specimens were made from hard plant fibers. Four were provisionally identified as bast fiber, 51 as leaf or bast fiber. The latter category compares favorably with yucca (*Yucca* spp.) leaf fiber, but the degree of maceration made any positive identification impossible, given the analytic tools available. Another specimen consisted of finely macerated fibers of unidentified type, and one specimen, which may have been used as a hair tie, was formed of very fine, soft fibers similar to those of cotton (*Gossypium* sp.).

Nineteen specimens of 4-ply twine were present. All were Z-twist and had been spun from 2-ply strands of S-twist twine. In 17 cases the angle of twist was loose—10 degrees or less—and in one case it was a tight 50 degrees. Twists ranged from 1.5 to 4 per cm. Twine diameter ranged from 1 to 4 mm, with as much as 1 mm variation occurring in the diameter of the same twine strand. Average diameter was 2.26 mm.

Thirty-five examples of 2-ply twine were present in the collection, not including the 38 specimens of 2-ply twine used in making the 4-ply material. In 34 cases twist direction could be identified: 20 showed a Z-twist and 14 showed an S-twist. In 25 cases the angle of twist was loose, with 1 to 10 twists per cm. In 3 cases the angle was medium—about 20 degrees—with 2 or 3 twists per cm, and in 5 cases it was a tight 30–40 degrees with 0.75 to 3 twists per cm. The diameter range for loose-twisted twine was 0.25 to 3.25 mm, with an average of 2 mm; diameters of specimens with medium twist ranged from 2.3 to 3 mm, with an average of 3 mm; and diameters of tightly-twisted specimens ranged from 2 to 5 mm, with an average of 3.5 mm. There is a rough correlation between the angle of twist and the diameter of the finished twine. However, the great variation in the range of diameters within the variously angled twines does not fully correlate with the number of twists per centimeter or the diameters of the contributing threads.

UNSPUN STRANDS AND BARK STRIPS

Unspun fiber strands were recovered from two Component II contexts. One knotted sample was associated with a rooftop hearth. The others formed the weft of an open-twined mat used in roof construction. In both cases, the raw material appeared to be yucca fiber.

Strips of bark cut from new deciduous tree growth were recovered from contexts of both components. In three specimens from Component I the strips were about 1 cm wide and appeared to be maple (cf. *Acer* spp.). All had been tied into overhand knots. A room of Component II produced 3-mm-wide strips of unidentified bark that had been braided into 4-ply cord. Precise functions could not be identified. Bark strips were also used in the manufacture of some basketry mats, discussed later.

A mass of matted bast fibers found near the pelvic area of infant burial 12-15-7-5-1 could represent an absorbent diaper pad, but other functions are possible.

BARK SHEETS

The remains of bark sheets were found in association with four burials. All specimens appeared to have been used as floor-covering in the burial pits. Pinyon *(Pinus edulis)*, ponderosa pine *(P. ponderosa)*, and cottonwood (cf. *Populus* spp.) were represented.

FIBER CLOTH

Twelve examples of cloth woven from seed fibers or very fine bast fibers were associated with nine Component I burials. The fibers compared well with cotton—successfully raised at Arroyo Hondo in the summer of 1971. Evidence of weave type and warp and weft diameters could be obtained for nine specimens.

One specimen, probably a sash, was represented only by braided warp tassels with diameters of 2 mm. Warp diameters were 0.5 mm. Seven specimens represented plain weaves which were weft faced in six cases. The weft-faced plain-weave textiles exhibited warps with diameters of 0.25 to 0.35 mm, and wefts of 0.5 to 1.5 mm, averaging 0.27 and 0.87 mm, respectively. Warps and wefts per centimeter of cloth ranged from 7 to 12, averaging 10.7. The remaining plain-weave specimen had warps and wefts measuring 1.5 mm in diameter, and exhibited 8 warps and wefts per cm. Only one twill-weave textile was identified. Warp diameter was 0.3 mm, and weft diameter ranged from 0.5 to 0.6 mm. There were six warps and wefts per centimeter. With the exception of the tasseled item, all of these textiles appeared to represent blankets, and were presumably woven on vertical looms like those evidenced in one Component I room and Kiva 12-C-2 of Component II.

As noted by Kent (1957:491), plain weave is "the simplest of loom processes, [and] was a practical, relatively rapid means of weaving large articles. It was used especially in making blankets, shirts or poncho-like garments, kilts, broad sashes, and breech cloths." Such textiles would have been "woven on a loom rigged with one heddle and a shed rod" (Kent 1957:491). In the case of most of the Arroyo Hondo specimens, the wefts were battened closely together, largely concealing the warps. The twill-weave specimen is the only example of this type of weave so far reported in the northern Rio Grande area of prehistoric times.

Fiber-cloth textiles were not commonly used as burial shrouds. When they were, they most often formed the primary wrapping of the body (six specimens). Four such textiles occurred as secondary wrappings, but none were used as outer wrappings.

BASKETRY

Basketry artifacts were the second most common artifacts in the sample, after twine. This is due to the frequent use of plaited mats as coverings for both burials and burial pit floors. At least 24 mats were associated with 22 burials, two of Component II and the remainder of Component I. In a sample of 39 burials, 12 (31 percent) had plaited-mat outer coverings, 3 (8 percent) had mats which formed the only identified covering, one had a mat used as a secondary covering, and one burial showed use of a mat as a primary covering with other coverings also present.

Twenty-six mats were represented in the sample. The most common variety was a closely-plaited mat made of yucca splints, nineteen of which were identified. Eight of these were made using laterally-trimmed yucca leaves cut to a fairly uniform width. One employed untrimmed leaves of the soapweed yucca *(Yucca glauca)*, and another a combination of trimmed and untrimmed leaves. In the remaining nine specimens, the splints were too fragmentary for definition of this attribute. Splint width ranged from 2.5 to 10 mm, showing as much as 4 mm variation in the same mat. Average splint width was 5.33 mm. Weave could be identified in five examples, with 1 specimen being plain-plaited and four twill-plaited. Self-selvage edges were preserved in one case. Based on the distribution of the fragments in the burial pits, outlines were square or rectangular, widths ranged from about 7 to 40 cm, and lengths extended to at least 1 meter.

One mat with trimmed splints 3 to 7 mm wide and exhibiting self selvage edges was made from narrow-leaf cattail *(Typha angustifolia)* leaves. Another combined yucca and cattail splints measuring about 4 mm wide. The remains of a mat apparently used as a primary burial wrapping seemed to have been made with leaves of corn (cf. *Zea mays*).

Two specimens of plaited mats, one from room fill and one from floor contact, were made using the open lattice-work technique. One was made of bark strips 4 to 5 mm wide; the other from decorticated twigs and grass leaves 3 mm wide and spaced approximately 3 mm apart.

Another category of mat was open-twined. Wood lengths 1 to 9 mm in diameter were bound together using yucca fiber strands and twine wefts. Two examples which had been used in roof contruction were present.

Fragments of three basketry bowls were recovered, one from a Component I store room, and the others from Component I burials. Two were coiled baskets of rod and rod-and-welt foundation with yucca stitching. The third was of the plaited ring type and was made using narrow-leaf cattail splints. These are described in detail under field specimen numbers 12-G-B110-2, 12-15-14-5-3, and 12-21-3-12-3.

WOODEN OBJECTS

A variety of wooden objects were present in the collection, with no single type of artifact forming a major class of specimen. The reader is therefore referred to individual descriptions under the field specimen numbers in the following list of wooden artifacts: (a) two stick bundles, 12-5-9-2W and 12-9-10-IIN; (b) branch and reed corn-drying rack, 12-9-6-IV-1; (c) decorticated twig, 12-G-2-4-14-8; (d) digging stick tip, 12-10-3-IX-9; (e) recurved bow and possible bow, 12-11-3A-2-3 and 12-19-1-II-4; (f) probable ax handle, 12-G-2-4-14-8; (g) probable canteen plug, 12-G-C35-3-3; (h) spoon, 12-18-6-3S-2; (i) fir branch, 12-ST7-3-1-7; (j) lattice-work hoop, 12-G-2-2-1; (k) juniper seed beads, 12-18-8-VII-4; and (l) pendant, 12-18-15-2-5.

SPECIMENS FROM COMPONENT I

Specimen 12-C-A-12-1-9: Twine adhering to the surface of the occipital of burial 12-C-A-12-1, a 16- to 18-year-old male interred in plaza C (Palkovich 1980:102).

Two pieces of twine were arranged parallel to each other and spaced less than 1 mm apart. The twine was associated with bits of human hair and was underlain by hide fragments from the body wrapping (Lang 1984:258). The 2-ply twine strands were made from finely macerated plant fibers with diameters of about 1 mm, showing about 6.5 loose Z-twists per cm. The position of the twine between the back of the skull and the hide layer indicates that it was not used to tie the hide around the body. It could represent a hair tie.

Also present in patches over the 56 cm x 101 cm floor of the burial pit were remains of a "finely woven" plaited mat. Examination of these remnants in situ indicated a form of twill plaiting (see 12-G-B110-2 below), and the use of splints probably made from either yucca (*Yucca* spp.) or cattail (*Typha* spp.). No samples were recovered.

Specimens 12-G-B110-2-5, -6, -7, -8, -9, and -12: Twine from a feather cord blanket, carbonized cordage, a basket coil, and plaited matting associated with burial 12-G-B110-2, a 4- to 5-year-old child interred in plaza G (Palkovich 1980:105, 161).

The 2- and 4-ply leaf or bast fiber twine elements of the feather cord blanket have been described elsewhere (Lang 1984:271–72). The carbonized cord appears to have been contained within the hide wrapping of the body. It was described as a "braid" by the excavator, but had unraveled by the time of examination. It appeared to have been about 7 cm long and was composed of very loosely twisted leaf or bast fiber strands 2 to 3 mm in diameter.

Two plaited mats were present, one beneath and the other on top of the hide- and feather-blanket-wrapped body. Both mats were made of trimmed yucca leaf splints, and were twill plaited, a form of warp and weft arrangement that produces a diagonal pattern. The lower mat was obviously used as a floor covering in the burial pit. The measurable yucca splints were 4 to 5 mm wide, and showed a two-over-two, under-two weave. The surviving measurable fragments of the top mat consisted of splints 7 mm wide. They exhibited a one-over-three, under-three weave, with one shift to a two-over-three weave. The total pattern in the area of this shift could not be determined. One fragment exhibited a diagonal arrangement of weave-shifts to a one-over-four pattern, which must have represented part of an oblique linear design.

The basket fragment was associated with the upper mat, and consisted of a single coil section broken in three pieces. The coil foundation was formed by a single wood rod from which the bark had been removed. It had an ovate cross-section 3 mm by 7 mm. The combined length of the fragments was about 9 cm, and the rod showed a slight curvature. Bits of yucca leaf stitching adhered to the rod. Stitch width was 1.5 to 2 mm, with 13 stitches per inch and no gaps between stitches. Total coil diameter appeared to have been about 1 cm. The evidence indicated close coiling on a whole-rod foundation. The fragment represented a relatively large, circular basket. There were no indications that a whole basket had been present. Both the basket fragment and the burned cord probably represent what Ellis (1968:71) has termed a "token deposit" expected to regain wholeness in the next world.

Specimen 12-G-B110-3-3: Twine from a feather cord blanket and matting fragments representing the body wrapping of burial 12-G-B110-3, a 16- to 18-month-old infant infant interred in plaza G (Palkovich 1980:105).

The 2-ply twine has been described elsewhere (Lang 1984:272). The matting was plaited and made from trimmed yucca leaf splints. It formed the outer wrapping of the body. Two to three layers were present suggesting that the mat had been wrapped at least twice around the body and its feather blanket covering. The length of the burial pit suggests that the mat was about 65 cm wide. Measurable splints were about 10 mm wide. The weave could not be determined. The mat was held in place by a stone slab set on top of it.

Specimen 12-G-B110-4-3: Twine from a feather blanket and matting fragments representing the body wrappings of burial 12-G-B110-4, a 2½- to 3-month-old infant interred in plaza C (Palkovich 1980: 105–6, 160).

The 2-ply, leaf- or bast-fiber blanket twine has been described elsewhere (Lang 1984:272–73). The matting was plaited and made from trimmed yucca leaf splints. It was found both above and below the blanket-wrapped body. A single small mat was indicated, no more than 40 cm wide (the length of the burial pit), wrapped around the body and its feather blanket covering. The mat wrapping was held in place with a small stone slab. Weave characteristics could not be determined.

Specimen 12-G-B111-4-3: Plaited matting fragments covering the pit floor upon which rested burial 12-G-B111-4, a 25- to 28-year-old male interred in plaza G (Palkovich 1980:106, 162). The mat was made of yucca leaf splints. No other information could be obtained from the specimens.

Specimen 12-G-C35-3-3: A partially carbonized wooden object recovered from level 3 of plaza G.

The specimen was made of juniper (*Juniperus* spp.). It was 6.7 cm long, with a maximum width of 2.5 cm and a maximum thickness of 2 cm. One end tapered to a blunted point, the other had been partially sawed through and snapped to produce a flattened end. The short axis cross-section was plano-convex with nearly vertical, slightly rounded sides. The surface was charred with the exception of the flat end. Marginal whittling marks and the condition of the sawed and snapped end indicate that this procedure took place after the item had been burned and involved the removal of a portion of the object present at the time of burning. The cut end had also been flattened by pounding, which compressed the wood fibers. Remnants of a yucca leaf binding of some sort adhered to the surface of both sides at the cut end and 1.5 cm below it, with the fibers oriented across the object's short axis. The yucca strip fragments—similar to those used in plaited matting—were not burned, and must have been attached to the object after it was charred.

The specimen appears to have originally been the tip of a digging stick, and its width agrees with the 2- to 3-cm width of the marks of digging stick tips left in the sides of pits excavated by the Arroyo Hondoans. The charring showed no relationship to the original shaping of the tip, which was accomplished by removing lateral wood slivers from both sides as well as from the convex surface. The charring suggests use of the digging stick as a fire tender, a function well represented among worn-down digging sticks at Tularosa Cave, New Mexico (Hough 1914:65–66).

A third, and apparently final function of the object was represented by its reduction to its present size by cutting and snapping it from the shaft. Following this, the upper, whittled one-third of its length had been wrapped with yucca strips, and the cut end further flattened by pounding. The only function which I can imagine for an object of this sort is that of a stopper for a jar or canteen. Areas of smoothing over the charred surface were probably produced by friction between the wood and the mouth or neck of the container. The yucca wrapping probably served as a seal.

Specimens 12-G-D6-4-1, -1-3, -1-4, and -1-5: Twine associated with the head and feet areas and matting fragments from the covering of burial 12-G-D6-4-1, a 20- to 22-month-old child interred in plaza G (Palkovich 1980:108). Also present was twine forming part of feather- and fur-cord blankets used as body wrappings.

The 2- and 4-ply leaf or bast twine associated with the blankets has been previously described (Lang 1984:274–75). The twine located at the head and feet of the burial appeared to have been used to tie the body wrappings in place. Three categories of leaf or bast fiber twine were noted in the sample: 2-ply, S-spun, 1.5 mm diameter, 4 loose twists per cm; 2-ply, Z-spun, 2 mm diameter, 2.5 loose twists per cm; and 4-ply, Z-spun, 3.25 mm diameter, 2 loose twists per cm.

The plaited matting occurred as a cover over the wrapped body. It was formed of trimmed yucca splints having widths of 2.5 to 3.5 mm, the most common width being 2.5 mm. Spacing between elements was variable, 0 to 1 mm. The mat was twill-plaited, with a one-over-three, under-three weave.

Specimen 12-G-D8-4-3-3: Twine from a feather cord blanket and fragments of a plaited mat surrounding the bones of burial 12-G-D8-4-3, a 10- to 11-month-old infant interred in plaza G (Palkovich 1980:109–110, 160).

The 2-ply leaf or bast fiber twine has been previously described (Lang 1984:275). The plaited mat appeared to have been fully wrapped around the infant, covering other hide and feather blanket wrappings. The mat was made using untrimmed narrow-leaf cattail *(Typha angustifolia)* leaves having widths of 3 to 7 mm. No evidence of the type of weave remained. A few pieces of self-selvage were present and exhibited an oblique engagement of splint elements. The narrow-leaf cattail identification is of special interest, as Kelley (1980:93) reported only the broad-leaf cattail *(T. latifolia)* in the Arroyo Hondo study area.

Specimens 12-G-ST7-3-1-7 and -10: Fragments of twine, plaited matting, and a Douglas fir *(Pseudotsuga taxifolia)* branch associated with burial 12-G-ST-3-2, a 2- to 2¼-year-old child interred in plaza G (Palkovich 1980:110–111, 161).

Associated with the fir branch were four bone tubes and a hematite cylinder (Beach and Causey 1982). Excavation notes suggest that the body had been initially wrapped in a hide, but no samples were collected for verification.

The mat sample was badly disintegrated, but excavation notes suggest simple plaiting. The splints, made of trimmed yucca leaves, ranged in width from 5 to 9 mm. The mat appeared to have been rolled about the body and had a width of approximately 70 cm.

A small amount of leaf or bast fiber twine was associated with the mat and branch. Three categories were represented: 2-ply, Z-spun, 4 loose-angled twists per centimeter, with a diameter of 1.75 mm; 2-ply, Z-spun, 2.75 loose-angled twists per centimeter, with a diameter of 1 mm; and 4-ply, Z-spun, 2 loose-angled twists per cm, and a diameter of 2 mm. The 4-ply twine had been made using 2-ply, S-spun twine with 3 loose-angled twists per cm, and a diameter of 1 mm. One piece of the thicker 2-ply, Z-twist twine showed knotting. The function of the twine could not be determined. It may have been used to hold the mat in place around the body, or it may represent warp and weft material from a cord textile.

The fir branch included a bough end complete with needles. It had been broken into two sections, the bough section being about 28 cm long and 5 mm thick near its unbroken end. The remainder was about 25 cm long and 11 mm thick. The two pieces lay side by side, partially overlying the right arm and ribs of the skeleton. The branch of the bough end had been passed through four decorative bone tubes. Three of the tubes aligned directly with the bough end, while the fourth had been slightly displaced. Parallel to the tubes was a hematite cylinder, which appeared to have been attached below them on the branch just above the point at which it had been broken in two. No fully comparable item, either archaeological or ethnological, is known to me. Handheld, undecorticated evergreen boughs are a common dancer's accoutrement in the Rio Grande pueblos. It is possible that the specimen represents an elaborate form of this sort of dance wand. A prayerstick is another good possibility. The swollen condition of the terminal leaf buds of the fir branch indicate that it was cut in the spring.

Specimen 12-G-2-3-35-1: Matting covering the skeleton of burial 12-G-2-3-35, a 39- to 43-year-old woman interred in plaza G (Palkovich 1980:115, 163).

A single, folded, twill-plaited mat of trimmed and untrimmed yucca leaf splints was indicated. Splint width was 3.75 to 7 mm. One piece of corner selvage was present and had a thickness of 2.25 mm. The corner was turned at an angle of about 120 degrees. The specimen represented a self-selvage in which the terminal elements were folded back into the fabric of the mat for replaiting at a 90-degree angle. No further observations on the weave could be made.

Specimens 12-G-2-2-1, -2, and -3: Remains of lattice-work basketry located over the cranium, mandible, and right femur of burial 12-G-2-3-21-2, a 14- to 15-year-old adolescent buried behind the retaining wall of a bench-like feature near the plaza G entryway (Lang 1984:276; Palkovich 1980:112–13, 162). Also a plaited mat upon which the body was lying.

Fragments of the poorly preserved mat suggested twill-plaited construction, with yucca as the raw material. No other observations were possible.

The basketry item had been broken into two sections and deposited over the head and legs of the adolescent. Despite fragmentation and decay of the object, examination of the surviving elements, both in the field and afterwards, indicated a hoop-framed, open-weave, lattice-work artifact made of willow (*Salix* spp.) branches and twigs, and 1-ply, unspun, leaf or bast fiber strands.

Two similar items have been reported by Adovasio (1977:154–55) from the ruin of Antelope House at Canyon de Chelly, Arizona. Other comparable items referred to as gaming wheels, hoops, or targets have been reported for the historic Tiwa (Isleta), Keres (Laguna), Zuni, and Hopi (Culin 1907:420–27; Mason 1904:507–8). Particulars of raw materials, construction, and form vary, but two traits—an open-weave and a hoop frame—are constants. They differ in certain characteristics from the similar snowshoes reported by Fox (1979) of the Tiwa of Taos.

In the case of the Arroyo Hondo specimen an undecorticated willow rod hoop with a diameter in excess of 14 cm was suggested by a curved rod fragment in the sample. Rod diameter was 7 mm, within the diameter range recorded by Adovasio for the Antelope House specimens. The form of the lattice-work center was undetermined, but it was obviously made of lengths of undecorticated willow about 2 to 4 mm in diameter secured to each other and the hoop by 0.5-mm-diameter strands of leaf or bast fiber. Portions of the crisscrossed lattice arrangement of the willow branches were evident at the time of excavation, but no other attributes were discerned. In the sample, the yucca fiber strands occurred as partially attached wrapping stitches and loose fragments.

Three V-shaped elements of bent willow with diameters of 4 to 5 mm were present. All were broken, but appeared to have been formed with one arm of the V shorter than the other. The arms of the two best-preserved examples measure about 3.8 cm x 6.1 cm and 3 cm x 3.8 cm. One of the lattice-work hoops illustrated by Adovasio has a strikingly similar element made of yucca attached to the interior of the foundation hoop at the terminals of the lop-sided V. This element was lying over one face of the lattice-work, unattached. Adovasio (1977:154) noted that "while only one such structure is extant, there may have been a series of them spaced along the hoop." As mentioned above, at least three of these V-shaped elements were present on the Arroyo Hondo hoop.

In addition to the willow rod and yucca materials, willow leaves were abundant in the sample, and it was obvious that it was constructed without removing the leaves from the branches. Many were still attached at the time of excavation.

Specimen 12-G-2-3-159-13: Twine from a feather cord blanket wrapping and fragments of a mat which lined the pit floor of burial 12-G-2-3-159, a 2- to 2½-year-old child buried in plaza G (Palkovich 1980:116–17, 161).

The 2- and 4-ply fiber twine of the blanket has been previously described (Lang 1984:276). The plaited mat was made of yucca leaf splints, and was too deteriorated to provide any additional information.

Specimens 12-G-2-4-14-8, -9, -11, and -13: Twine, matting, bark, a twig, and a probable ax handle associated with burial 12-G-2-4-14, a 35- to 45-year-old man interred in plaza G (Palkovich 1980:118–19, 163).

The 2-ply leaf or bast fiber twine has been previously described (Lang 1984:277). The twine formed part of a feather cord garment or blanket.

The mat was rotted, but its remains showed a clear and continuous distribution over the floor of the burial pit, extending up the walls of the pit. The distribution of the mat remains suggested a rectangular shape, a length of about 1 meter, and a width of more than 50 cm. The type of plaiting could not be determined. The splints appeared to have been formed of yucca leaves.

A twig-like piece of wood, possibly willow, was recovered from the area of the hands and knees. It had been positioned either on top of or inside the feather cord body covering. It was decorticated, and had a diameter of 6 mm. Function was undetermined—possibly the specimen represents a prayer stick.

Fragments of ponderosa pine bark were present over and in the general area of the left humerus. The bark did not appear to represent an additional body covering. Most probably it represented the remains of a pit floor covering.

A painted ax head located on the pit margin near the front of the skull exhibited the remains of juniper bark lashings. What appeared to be a broken wooden ax handle, originally about 50 cm long, was located 10 cm northwest of the ax head, in front of the skeleton's rib cage and beneath the hide covering.

Specimen 12-G-2-4-33-6: Bark fragments present on the pit floor beneath the right femur and tibia of burial 12-G-2-4-34, the well-preserved skeleton of an adult. The material was previously reported as "leather-like," and as a "hide blanket" (Palkovich 1980:119, 163).

The bark appeared to be pinyon and it may represent the remains of a bark pit floor covering.

Specimens 12-G-2-4-62-8 and -9: Grasslike fragments, twine, and a tasseled portion of a textile associated with, or forming, the innermost body wrappings of burial 12-G-2-4-63, a 5- to 6-year-old child interred in plaza G (Palkovich 1980:120, 161).

The grasslike material surrounded the skeleton and clearly formed the innermost wrapping or covering of the body. The fragmentary specimens appeared to represent the remains of matting splints. The excavator described the remains as an "enclosing . . . fibrous matting of uncertain nature." A soft, flexible mat wrapped about the body is most likely, but the sample provided no certain indication that a mat was represented. The raw material appeared to have been corn leaves.

The cloth remains were present between the "matting" and the hides which formed the outer body wrappings (Lang 1984:277–78). The sample consisted of at least four braided tassels cemented together in a close parallel arrangement, one braid deep. All were fragmentary, with the longest braid having an incomplete length of 5 cm. The fibers were of bast or seed origin, and extremely fine. The braids were 5- or 6-ply. Twists were tightly angled—about 40 degrees, with 3 twists per cm. Braid diameter was a delicate 2.5 to 3 mm. Contributing fiber threads were finely spun and had diameters of about 0.5 mm. All of the braids appeared to represent a loose arrangement of warp elements. They were of much finer quality in both thread and braid diameter than the similar warps of certain Anasazi tumplines and bands (Judd 1954:171; Morris 1980:106, 108), and probably represent the fringe of a belt or other garment. Either decay or sampling method may have been responsible for the absence of other parts of this item.

Bits of 2-ply, S-spun twine, less fine than those of the braids and formed of fibers that were probably soft bast, could represent unattached weft fragments; however, other functions were possible. The twine showed 2.5 loose-angled twists per cm and had a diameter of about 2 mm.

Specimen 12-G-5-3-1: Yucca and twine fragments overlying a small area of the dorsal torso of "burial" 12-G-5-3, a 45- to 49-year-old male sprawled on the floor of Kiva 12-G-5.

The specimen included a section of decayed, plaited, yucca-splint material with underlying bits of 2-ply, S-spun, vegetal fiber twine, about 1 mm in diameter. The twine was loosely twisted, and the fibers were of medium fineness, probably bast. It could not be determined whether this material represented a body covering or was simply an element of the trashy lower fill of the kiva.

Specimen 12-K-3-III-5: Minute fragments of a badly decomposed textile positioned between the femur and the hide wrappings of burial 12-K-3-IIIA#1, a 1½- to 2-month-old infant interred in plaza K (Lang 1984:278; Palkovich 1980:126–27).

Specimen condition allowed few comments. Apparently, the textile formed either a garment or the innermost body wrapping of the burial. Bits of textile adhered to fragments of the hide wrapping. The raw material was a finely spun bast or seed fiber. Weave and other attributes could not be determined reliably.

Specimen 12-K-3-IV, pit J: Fabrics forming the inner body wrappings of burial 12-K-3-IV J, a 7- to 8-month-old infant interred in plaza K. See Lang (1984:278–79) and Palkovich (1980:131) for additional information.

Among the layered fragments of plain- and twill-weave cloth, four individual textile wrappings appeared to be represented. All were blackened and showed no indication of original color. They were made from strands of very fine bast or seed fibers that appeared to be identical in all four cases, although warp and weft thread thickness varied between textiles. The thread was finely spun. Three of the fabrics were weft-faced plain weave in which the wefts had been battened closely together, largely obscuring the finer warp thread.

The uppermost textile, located directly beneath the hide wrapping, had warps about 0.35 mm in diameter and wefts about 1 mm in diameter. The specimens exhibited 10 warps and wefts per cm (23 per inch).

The textile located just below the uppermost had warps of about 0.25 mm diameter, wefts of about 0.6 mm diameter, and 11 warps and wefts per cm (25.5 per inch). Up to six layers of this fabric were represented in some of the cemented chunks of textile, probably the result of folding rather than wrapping.

The third plain-weave textile probably formed the innermost wrapping of the body, as thin sheets of human bone adhered to some pieces of the cloth. Warp and weft thread diameters were about 0.25 mm and 0.75 mm, respectively, with 10 warps and wefts per cm (25 per inch).

The fourth textile was represented by one small, folded fragment. It was a twill-weave, in which the wefts of a two-over, one-under pattern formed diagonal ribs which were accentuated by the greater thickness of the weft threads. Weft thread diameters were about 0.5 to 0.6 mm, and those of the warp, about 0.3 mm. There were 6 warps and wefts per centimeter (15 per inch). This fragment was cemented to a piece of the plain-weave textile forming the innermost wrapping. Therefore, the twill fabric appeared to have occupied a place in the body wrappings between the second and third plain-weave wrappings.

All four fabrics were probably woven on a vertical loom, the presence of which was indicated by loom anchor holes in the floors of a second-story room of roomblock 9 (Component I) and Kiva 12-C-2 (Component II). The available data suggests that all of the plain-weave textiles were blankets.

While no selvage fragments were identified in the sample, I have assumed that the thinner threads of each textile represented warps. Warps are under tension from the loom bars, and the thinner threads, which represent finer spinning, would have been stronger than the thicker ones that I identified as wefts. The thinness of the "warp" threads may be partly due to stretching on the loom (Kate Peck Kent, personal communication). The facing of the plain-weave textiles with the thicker "wefts" would agree with the results of a weft-battening process.

Specimen 12-K-6-II-3: Twine and a possible textile associated with the mandible of burial 12-K-6-II D, a 30- to 36-year-old male interred in the deposits overlying plaza K (Lang 1984:279; Palkovich 1980:128).

The textile-like material, underlying a hide fragment, was very decayed. Its condition precluded positive identification, but the texture was similar to that of the loom-woven fabrics of fine fiber described above.

A few unraveled fragments of leaf or bast fiber twine were also present. The twine was 2-ply, Z-spun, with about 2.25 loose-angled twists per cm. Diameter was about 2 mm.

Specimen 12-K-12-IV-1: The remains of a feather cord textile and a plaited mat surrounding the bones of burial 12-K-12-IV E (Lang 1984: 279; Palkovich 1980:129, 160).

The plaited mat formed the outer wrapping of the body. It was mostly disintegrated. The splints were of yucca leaves and had widths of 3.5 to 5 mm.

Specimen 12-K-12-IV-3: Plaited mat and cloth body coverings of burial 12-K-12-IV F, a 1¼- to 1½-year-old infant interred in plaza K (Lang 1984:279; Palkovich 1980:129, 161).

The cloth was weft-faced plain weave showing 14 warps and wefts per centimeter (35 per inch). Warp thread diameters were about 0.25 mm, and weft thread diameters, about 0.5 mm. The threads were made of very fine bast or seed fiber. The specimens were black and folded. They probably represented a blanket wrapping which directly covered the body of the infant.

The plaited mat served as the final wrapping of the body, separated from the cloth by hide and feather-cord textile wrappings. The splint elements were trimmed yucca leaves. Excavation notes identified the weave as simple plaiting, one-over-one, under-one, with one element per set.

Specimen 12-K-15-IV-3: Fragments of a plaited mat which formed the outer wrapping of burial 12-K-15-IV G, and twine from a feather-cord textile wrapping (Lang 1984:279; Palkovich 1980:129–30, 160).

The plaited mat was formed of trimmed yucca leaf splints about 4.75 mm wide. It appeared to have been twill plaited.

Specimen 12-5-5-V-1: A piece of plaited selvage from a basketry item recovered from the lower fall deposit of the first-story roof/second-story floor of room 12-5-5. Depth below surface was about 1.9 meters.

The sample, when examined, consisted of narrow strips of thin bark, 2 to 3 mm wide and up to 4 cm long. The bark was curled at the margins, but was originally uncurled and 4 to 5 mm wide. It had been removed from a branch by incising along a median of the branch's long axis, and then peeling. A shrub, possibly squawbush *(?Rhus trilobata)*, was the source of the bark.

The field description and drawing of the item in situ indicated open lattice-work plaiting. The item appears to have been a mat. The plaiting was a simple over-one, under-one pattern and one element per set. The seven elements present represented four strips of bark, one element formed by the strip being bent to double back at the selvage edge to form the adjacent parallel element. The spacing within the latticework was not indicated in the field sketch.

Specimen 12-5-9-2W: Twine, rotted pieces of small-diameter sticks, and a bark strip knot, all associated with a fallen hearth in the fill of room 12-6-9. The hearth derived from the collapse of the roof of contiguous room 12-6-14. The specimens were located about 1 meter below the surface.

The twine, made from leaf or bast fibers, was 2-ply S-spun and showed two loose-angled twists per cm. Diameter was 1 to 1.25 mm. It formed the binding of a bundle of sticks, presumably part of the roofing material of the second-story room.

The knot was overhand and was made from a single strip of thin, new-growth bark, with a width of about 1 cm. The bark was stripped from a branch or sucker using the method described under specimen number 12-5-5-V-1. The partially carbonized bark appeared to be that of a maple.

Specimen number 12-5-14-4-1: A knot associated with the second-story floor fall of room 12-6-14. Depth below surface was about 1.55 meters. The specimen was virtually identical to the knot described as specimen 12-5-9-2W, but was not carbonized.

Specimen 12-10-3-IX-9: Wooden artifact from floor contact of storage room 12-10-3, about 1.9 meters below surface.

The item appeared to be the broken tip of a digging stick made of juniper wood. The unbroken end was pointed. Both ends were superficially carbonized. Length was 11.3 cm, width 2.2 cm, and thickness 1.1 cm. The cross-section was roughly plano-convex.

Specimens 12-11-3A-2-3 and -4: A small bow located along the right side and over the right arm of burial 12-11-3A-2-2, a 7- to 8-year-old child interred in plaza C (Palkovich 1980:132–33). It was broken in two, with the pieces laid side by side. Also present beneath the bow and skeleton were two cord textiles with twine warp foundations and wefts, and two plaited mats.

The recurved bow was made of juniper that had been uniformly scraped and smoothed. The inward curve in the grip area was slight. Cross-section over most of the bow's length was biconvex with almost flat, slightly rounded margins. Near the ends, the cross-section becomes nearly plano-convex, the inner face of the bow having been thinned and planed near the terminals. Maximum width (2.9 cm) and thickness (1.1 cm) were in the grip area, at the center point of the bow's long axis. From there, the bow tapered toward its ends. The extreme ends were missing, but width and thickness at the existing ends were 9 mm and 6 mm, respectively. The bow fragments collectively measured about 71 cm. There appeared to be no more than a few centimeters missing. If the ends were notched for cord attachment, none could be discerned when the badly rotted ends were examined during excavation. No bow string was present, but if made of sinew or other proteinaceous material, it would not have been preserved, since protein materials were almost completely destroyed in the case of this interment and its grave goods. The bow was very similar to a larger self-type bow of the recurved variety from Jemez Pueblo in the collection of the Laboratory of Anthropology, Museum of New Mexico (catalog number 865/12).

Underlying the skeleton and bow were the remains of a feather cord textile, a simple plaited mat, a fur cord textile, and a twill-plaited mat, in that order. Both mats showed a close-spaced arrangement of trimmed yucca leaf splints 6 to 7 mm in width. The upper plaited mat showed the characteristic over-one, under-one pattern, with one element per set. The twill-plaited specimen exhibited an over-two, under-two pattern and simple, 90-degree self-selvages. The upper mat was either overlapped or doubled over beneath the body and its feather-cord textile wrapping. Both mats appeared to have been wrappings, the outermost being formed by the twill-plaited mat.

Specimen 12-5-11-5-14: Cord, twine, and a bark-strip knot found together, all associated with the collapsed second-story floor of room 12-5-11, about 2 meters below the surface.

The twine and cordage was 2-ply, Z-twist, and relatively fine-fibered, possibly of bast. Three diameters were present, all showing tight-angled twists of 30 to 40 degrees: the first was 5 mm in diameter, 0.75 to 1.5 twists per cm; the second was 3.5 mm in diameter with 1.25 twists per cm; and the third was 3 mm in diameter with 2.5 twists per cm. The bark appeared to be maple, identical to that of the knots from room 12-6-14 (see specimens 12-5-9-2W and 12-5-14-4-1).

Specimen 12-15-7-5-6: Matted fibers and small fragments of a plaited mat associated with the pelvic region of burial 12-15-7-5-1, a 9- to 9½-month-old infant buried beneath the floor of storage room 12-5-7 (Lang 1984:281; Palkovich 1980:134). These items, along with a feather textile, form grave goods in addition to those noted by Palkovich, and replace her "hide" identification.

The matted fibers were about 3 mm thick. Both medium-coarse and fine bast fibers, primarily the latter, were represented. The location and character of the material suggested the possibility of a diaper pad. The plaited mat, made with yucca splints, appeared to have formed the outer wrapping of the burial bundle.

Specimen 12-15-14-5-3 (correct number 12-5-14-5-3): A basketry bowl found on the floor of lower-story storage room 12-6-14, about 2 meters below the surface.

This small, flat-bottomed coiled basket with relatively vertical walls was found resting mouth-down on the floor near the west end of the room. Diameter was about 20 cm, height about 16 cm. It was close-coiled on a two-rod-and-welt foundation. Welts and rods were completely rotted, but the resulting cavities provided a basis for measurement. Welt cavities averaged about 1 mm x 4 mm, and rod cavities ranged between 2 and 2.25 mm in diameter. The foundation was of the bunched type. Stitching appeared to be wrapped and non-interlocking. Mean coil width on the basket's surface was 3.8 mm, with a range of about 3 to 5 mm. Wall thickness was 6.5 mm and base thickness, 5 to 6 mm. The range in coils per cm was 2 to 3, with a mean of 2.6. The mean and range of stitch width was 1.5 and 1.25–2 mm, respectively. Stitches ranged from 4.5 to 5 per cm, with a mean of 4.75. The range in gaps between stitches was 0 to 1 mm, and the mean was about 0.25 mm. The raw materials could not be identified.

Specimen 12-16-29-5-3: The remains of a mat that formed the outer body wrapping of burial 12-16-29-5-1, a 44- to 54-year-old woman interred in plaza C (Lang 1984:281; Palkovich 1980:135). The mat was indicated only by fragments of yucca leaf splints.

Specimen 12-16-36-4-7: Cloth found above and below the flexed legs of burial 12-16-36-4, a 39- to 44-year-old male buried beneath the floor of room 12-16-36 (Palkovich 1980:136).

The position of the cloth suggested a blanket, mostly decayed. Up to two layers were present, separated from each other by fragments of a thin hide (Lang 1984:281). The blanket appeared to have formed the second layer of body wrapping, with hides over and underneath. The fibers were of the very fine bast or seed type. It appeared to have been a weft-faced plain weave in which the warp threads were much more finely spun than the wefts. The weft picks measured about 1 to 1.5 mm across, with 7 wefts per cm (about 16 per inch).

Specimen 12-18-6-3S-2 and -4: Twine, matting fragments, and a wooden spoon present on the floor of the pit of burial 12-18-6-3S-2, a 4- to 5-year-old child buried beneath the floor of storage room 12-18-6 (Palkovich 1980:138).

The twine was associated with feather fragments and appeared to represent a feather cord textile which formed the primary body wrapping (see Lang 1984:282).

The plaited mat fragments represented both the body and self-selvage of the specimen. The splints were of untrimmed soapweed yucca leaves about 6 mm wide. The mat fragments occurred, as did all of the other materials, on the pit floor only, and may have served as either the pit floor covering or the outer body wrapping.

The spoon lay above the textile fragments, seeming to have been wrapped with the body. It was essentially complete when excavated, although exhibiting insect galleries, humic blackening, and some superficial decay on surfaces not in contact with the other pit floor materials. The wood appeared to be pine (cf. *Pinus* spp.). The handle formed 11 cm of a total length of 18 cm. A maximum width of about 5 cm occurred at the bowl, just below the handle juncture. The handle contracted toward both ends from a maximum width of about 2 cm near its axial mid-point. Width at the handle-bowl juncture was about 1.9 cm, and width at the end of the handle was 1 cm. Maximum thickness of the handle and near-handle bowl was about 1.6 cm, thinning to about 8 mm at the tip of the spoon. In cross-section, the underside of the handle was flat, and the margins and upper surface were rounded. The bowl cross-sections were essentially concave-convex. Bowl walls were 3.7 to 7 mm thick, and the base of the bowl was 3 to 4 mm thick. The end of the handle was bifurcated by a notch 1 to 1.75 mm wide and originally about 2 mm long. The function of the notch is questionable, but it could have been used for attachment of a handle extender.

Specimens 12-18-8-VII-4, -5, and -6: Twine from a feather-cord textile, bark, and juniper seed beads associated with burial 12-18-8-VII-1, a 7½- to 8-month-old infant buried in room 12-18-8 (Palkovich 1980:141).

For comments on the twine, see Lang (1984:282). The juniper beads numbered 177 and formed part of a necklace which included two discoidal jet beads, two cylindrical jet beads, one discoidal turquoise bead, a triangular shell pendant, and a fragment of an ovoid shell pendant. The juniper seeds had diameters of 3.75 to 5 mm and widths of 2.25 to 2.5 mm. Holes were 2 to 2.5 mm in diameter. Both ends of the seeds had been ground flat.

The bark fragments appeared to represent sheets stripped from a young cottonwood tree and used to line the pit floor.

Specimen 12-18-8-4S: Cloth and plaited mat fragments representing part of the body wrappings of burial 12-18-8-4S-8, a 10- to 11-month-old infant buried beneath the floor of storage room 12-18-8 (Lang 1984:283; Palkovich 1980:140).

The cloth remains represented the inner wrapping of the burial bundle. While minute fragments clearly showed the tight weave of a textile, their condition defied further description. The raw material was a very fine bast or seed fiber.

The mat was represented by fragments of yucca and cattail splints. Plaiting was obvious, but the type could not be determined. At least some of the cattail splints were untrimmed, about 4 mm wide, and were representative of the narrow-leaf species. The mat formed the outer wrapping of the burial materials, separated from the cloth by a hide wrapping.

Specimen 12-18-15-2-5: A wooden pendant recovered from the trash fill of room 12-18-5, about 1 meter below the surface. The pendant appeared to have been dumped into the room during the clearing of adjacent burned rooms of roomblock 18, and was accompanied by a quantity of carbonized roofing material. The item had been heavily burned.

The pendant was incomplete; one lateral margin and parts of both ends had been broken off. However, the surfaces of the breaks exhibited a patina, so the piece must have seen some use after being broken. The form was subrectangular with flat margins. The faces were plain and essentially flat. The long-axis cross-section was triangular, thinning from top to bottom. The top had been drilled from one face and one corner of the margin to form a single hole for stringing. Both were drilled at oblique angles. The drill holes measured 5.5 to 6.5 mm at the mouths and had conical cross-sections, suggesting the use of a tapered, chipped-stone drill head. A pit produced by a drilling start is located directly above the completed hole in the face, at the junction of the face and upper margin. The pit had a diameter of about 1.25 mm. The wood was hard, and appeared to be juniper. Manufacturing marks indicate that the specimen was primarily formed by scraping, followed by grinding and polishing to achieve a reasonably smooth surface. Total measurements were 1.5 cm wide by 2.5 cm long by 2.25 to 7 mm thick.

Specimen 12-19-1-II-4: Wood fragments identified in the field as a possible bow associated with burial 12-19-1-IV-1, a 22- to 24-year-old male buried in a subfloor cist of storage room 12-19-1 (Palkovich 1980:143–44).

The juniper wood fragments showed curvature along the long axis and rounded cross-sections, but their poor condition allowed neither measurement nor absolute identification of function. A bow is entirely possible.

Specimens 12-21-3-12-3, -5, and -6: A corncob fragment and fragments of a cloth blanket, a plaited mat, and a plaited basket associated with burial 12-21-3-12-2, an 8- to 9-month-old infant buried beneath the floor of storage room 12-21-3 (Palkovich 1980:145).

The corncob was represented by microscopic pieces. They were not noted during excavation, but their direct association with fragments of body wrappings suggest that the corncob was part of the grave goods.

The cloth was represented by fragments showing up to two layers, and some folding. Its distribution in the pit suggested a blanket forming the primary body wrapping. It had been covered by a second wrapping of hide. It was a weft-faced plain weave exhibiting 12 warps and wefts per cm (30 per inch). Weft threads were 0.75 mm wide, and warps about

0.25 mm wide. The fiber was a very fine bast or seed type. The cloth fragments were present both above and beneath the skeleton.

Plaited basketry was noted over the foot-pelvic area and over and under the skull. Represented in the fragments were splints of both yucca and cattail, and a slightly curved, decorticated twig with bits of cattail splint self-selvage adhering to it. The twig had a diameter of 4 mm and represented the rod rim foundation of a small, plaited ring basket formed of cattail splints. Both the excavation notes and the occurance of two raw material types in the splint fragments suggested that two items were represented, one the ring basket, and the other a mat which served as the outer body wrapping. The position of the basket could not be determined.

SPECIMENS FROM COMPONENT II

Specimen number 12-C-A-6-1-7: Fragments of twine and bark underlying the skeleton and hide wrapping of burial 12-C-A-6-1-1, a 20- to 22-month old infant interred in a borrow pit of plaza C (Lang 1984:284; Palkovich 1980:148, 164).

The disintegrated twine adhered to the underside of a piece of hide and may have represented either cords used to hold the hide wrapping in place or elements of a feather- or fur-cord textile. It was made from strands of leaf or bast fiber. The bark was pinyon and was located between the hide and the burial pit floor. It may have been used to cover the pit floor before placement of the body.

Specimen 12-C-A-8-1-4: Twine from fur- and feather-cord textiles used to wrap the body of burial 12-C-A-8-1, and 5½- to 6-year-old child interred in placa C. Also a piece of cloth from a fabric positioned between the cord textiles. For additional descriptions of this burial and its grave goods, see Lang (1984:284) and Palkovich (1980:148, 164).

The cloth, like virtually all materials from inhumations, was blackened. Only a very small, poorly-preserved fragment survived. The threads of both warp and weft had diameters of about 1.5 mm and were formed of spun bast or seed fibers of very fine texture. The cloth was plainweave, with an over-one, under-one engagement of warp and weft. There were 8 warps and wefts per cm (20 per inch). The remains provided no indication of the type of item represented or of its original size. Such cloth would have been loom woven.

Specimen 12-9-6-3: Looped and twisted fragments of unspun yucca fiber strands associated with the collapsed, burned roof of room 12-9-6. Specimens were located about 90 cm below the surface.

The specimens were both unburned and carbonized. Cross-sections measured 0.6 mm by 1.25–2 mm in diameter. The strand fragments were associated with pieces of small-diameter wood, larger latias, and planks which formed part of the roofing. The semicircles formed by the loops had interior measurements of about 5 to 9 mm across, roughly within the diameter range of the small wood fragments. Apparently, the strands represent wefts in a type of open-twined matting in which the wood lengths constituted the warps. The use of mats of this type as roofing material at Arroyo Hondo is supported by a similar specimen from room 12-9-10 and impressions remaining in adobe roof fragments.

Specimen 12-9-6-IV-1: Partially carbonized remains of a racklike object from floor contact of burned room 12-9-6, about 1 meter below the surface.

The specimen consisted of twigs, branches, and stems of willow, pinyon, and reed (*Phragmites* spp.) arranged in layers over the floor of the room, and covering most of a floor area measuring about 2.25 by 3 meters. Three layers of this material were noted, primarily composed of undecorticated willow lengths showing branches and branchlets, but no leaves. The willow twigs had been cleanly cut at an angle of about 70 degrees. The longest measurable twig was about 91 cm. In contrast to the willow twigs, the undecorticated pinyon branches had been roughly broken off the tree. The longest measurable branch was 60 cm. Specimen diameters were 2 to 8 mm (willow), about 1 cm (pinyon), and 6.5 to 8 mm (reed).

The main branches and stems of the layers were laid parallel to each other; spaced 1 to 3 cm apart, and oriented across the short axis of the room. The lowest layer rested on the floor. Spacers formed of 3 to 5 willow and pinyon lengths were then arranged over this layer, parallel and adjacent to the long-axis walls, and perpendicular to the branches beneath them. Husked corn ears were then placed on the branch layer, oriented in the same direction as the boughs on which they lay. The corn ears were then covered with a second layer of twigs and branches. More corn ears, and presumably spacers which were not preserved, were placed on this layer, but the ears were now generally oriented in the same direction as the spacers. These were capped by another layer of branches, etc. Finally, more ears, oriented in the same direction as the elements of the layer beneath them, were laid on the upper rack. Presumably, this racking method represents a means by which the ears were aerated in storage.

Specimen 12-9-6-4-1: A partially carbonized fragment of open latticework basketry similar to the item described under specimen 12-5-5-V-1. Floor contact, room 12-9-6, beneath the layered rack described above.

The specimen was obviously of plaited construction, but no evidence of the weave type remains. Measurable splints were 3 mm wide. The elements were formed of decorticated twigs (?*Salix* spp.), interwoven with what appeared to be leaves of one of the larger grasses (cf. Graminea). The splints appeared to have been spaced about 3 mm apart. The remains suggested a mat-like object.

Specimen 12-9-10-IIN: Twine and small-diameter sticklike fragments associated with the burned, collapsed roof of room 12-9-10, located about 70 cm below the surface.

The twine.was carbonized and consisted of small, straight fragments and loop sections. All specimens were 2-ply, Z-twist, and made from leaf or bast fibers. Two categories were present: tight-twist at an angle of about 40 degrees, 3 twists per cm, 2 mm in diameter; and medium-twist at an angle of about 20 degrees, two twists per cm, 2.3 mm in diameter. One piece of the second category was straight and exhibited three small, straight "sticks" laid side by side, adhering to one face of the twine. This fragment is one of several "stick bundles" noted during roof-fall excavation. The bundles were short—about 20 cm long—and tied at both ends with twine. Oriented across the room's short axis, along with poles, planks, and willow and cottonwood branches, they appeared to have formed an insulating layer and to have served as chinking. A similar bundle was found in the roof-fall of room 12-6-14 of Component I (see specimen number 12-5-9-2W).

The looped twine fragment of the same type defined a semicircle with an interior diameter of about 5 mm. It was possibly a weft fragment from a mat of willow and/or cottonwood branches, forming the roofing layer directly beneath the adobe roof surface. Similar fragments of twine from room 12-9-6 have also been designated as representing wefts from open-twine roofing mats (see specimen 12-9-6-3).

Specimen 12-16-20-4-17: Knotted, unspun fiber strands associated with ash from the fallen roof-top hearth of room 12-16-20.

The form of the knot could not be determined in the field, and the specimen was unraveled at the time of examination. The material was carbonized and represented a hard leaf fiber, probably yucca.

References

ABERLE, S. B. D.
1931 "Frequencies of Pregnancies and Birth Intervals Among Pueblo Indians," *American Journal of Physical Anthropology* 16:63–80.

ADAMS, KAREN R.
1980 *Pollen, Parched Seeds, and Prehistory: A Pilot Investigation of Prehistoric Plant Remains from Salmon Ruin, a Chacoan Pueblo in Northwestern New Mexico*, Eastern New Mexico University Contributions in Anthropology, vol. 9.

ADOVASIO, J. M.
1977 *Basketry Technology: A Guide to Identification and Analysis* (Chicago: Aldine Publishing Co.).

ALDRICH, SAMUEL R.
1970 "Corn Culture," in *Corn: Culture, Processing, Products*, ed. G. E. Inglett (Westport, CT: Avi Publishing).

ALEXANDER, HUBERT G., AND PAUL REITER
1935 "Report on the Excavation of Jemez Cave, New Mexico," Monographs of the School of American Research, no. 15 (Albuquerque: University of New Mexico Press).

ANGEL, J. LAWRENCE
1971 "Disease and Culture in the Ancient East Mediterranean," in *Anthropological Congress Dedicated to Ales Hrdlicka*, ed. Vladimir V. Novotny.

ARROYAVE, GUILLERMO
1975 "Amino Acid Requirements and Age," in *Protein-Calorie Malnutrition*, ed. Robert E. Olson (New York: Academic Press).

ASCH, NANCY B., AND DAVID L. ASCH
1978 "The Economic Potential of *Iva Annua* and its Prehistoric Importance in the Lower Illinois Valley," in *The Nature and Status of Ethnobotany*, ed. Richard I. Ford, Anthropological Paper no. 67, Museum of Anthropology, University of Michigan.

ASTRAND, P-O.
1979 "Nutritional and Physical Performance," in *Nutrition and the World Food Problem*, ed. Miloslav Rechcigl, Jr. (Basel: S. Karger).

BAILEY, FLORA L.
1940 "Navaho Foods and Cooking Methods," *American Anthropologist* 42: 270–90.

BAILEY, VERNON
1931 *Mammals of New Mexico*, United States Department of Agriculture Bureau of Biological Survey, North American Fauna no. 53.

BARNEY, MILO, AND NEIL C. FRISCHKNECHT
1974 "Vegetation Changes Following Fires in the Pinyon-Juniper Type of West Central Utah," *Journal of Range Management* 27(2):91–96.

BARCLAY, GEORGE W.
1958 *Techniques of Population Analysis* (New York: John Wiley and Sons, Inc.).

BAXTER, CLAY
1977 "A Comparison Between Grazed and Ungrazed Juniper Woodland," in *Ecology, Uses, and Management of Pinyon-Juniper Woodlands*, eds. E. F. Aldon and T. J. Loring, U.S. Dept. of Agriculture Forest Service General Technical Report RM-39 (Fort Collins, CO: Rocky Mountain Forest and Range Experiment Station).

BEACH, MARSHALL A. AND CHRISTOPHER S. CAUSEY
1984 "Bone Artifacts from Arroyo Hondo Pueblo," in *The Faunal Remains from Arroyo Hondo Pueblo, New Mexico*, Richard W. Lang and Arthur H. Harris, Arroyo Hondo Archaeological Series, vol. 5 (Santa Fe: School of American Research Press).

BEAGLEHOLE, ERNEST
1936 *Hopi Hunting and Hunting Ritual*, Yale University Publications in Anthropology no. 4.

BEAGLEHOLE, PEARL
1937 "Foods and Their Preparation," in *Notes on Hopi Economic Life*, ed. E. Beaglehole, Yale University Publications in Anthropology 15:60–71.

BEAL, JOHN D., AND WINIFRED CREAMER
1986 *The Architecture of Arroyo Hondo Pueblo*, Arroyo Hondo Archaeological Series, vol. 7 (Santa Fe: School of American Research Press).

BEAN, LOWELL, AND K. SAUBEL
1972 *Temalpakh* (Banning, CA: Malki Museum Press).

BEHAR, MOISES
1968 "Prevalence of Malnutrition Among Pre-School Children of Developing Countries," in *Malnutrition, Learning, and Behavior*, eds. Nevin S. Scrimshaw and John F. Gordon (Cambridge, MA: MIT Press).

BERLIN, G. LENNIS, J. R. AMBLER, R. H. HEVLY, AND G. G. SCHABER
1977 "Identification of a Sinagua Agricultural Field by Aerial Thermography, Soil Chemistry, Pollen/Plant Analysis, and Archaeology," *American Antiquity* 42(4):588–600.

BOHRER, VORSILA L.
1962 "Nature and Interpretation of Ethnobotanical Materials from Tonto National Monument, 1957," in *Archaeological Studies at Tonto National*

Monument, Arizona, by Charlie R. Steen, L. M. Pierson, V. L. Bohrer, and K. P. Kent, Southwestern Monuments Association Technical Series, vol. 2.

1968 "Paleoecology of an Archaeological Site near Snowflake, Arizona" (Ph.D. diss., University of Arizona).

1970 "Ethnobotanical Aspects of Snaketown, A Hohokam Village in Southern Arizona," *American Antiquity* 35(4):413–30.

1972 "Paleoecology of the Hay Hollow Site, Arizona," Fieldiana: Anthropology 63(1):1–30.

1973 "Ethnobotany of Point of Pines Ruins," *Economic Botany* 27(4):423–37.

1975a "The Prehistoric and Historic Role of the Cool-Season Grasses in the Southwest," *Economic Botany* 29:199–207.

1975b "The Role of Seasonality in the Annual Harvest of Native Food Plants in the Puerco Valley, Northwest of Albuquerque, New Mexico," *New Mexico Academy of Science Bulletin* 15(2):3.

1979 "Pollen Studies at the Arroyo Hondo Site (LA 12) Near Santa Fe, New Mexico," unpublished ms. (Santa Fe: School of American Research).

1980 "Part 7, Salmon Ruin Ethnobotanical Report," in "Investigations of the Salmon Site: the Structure of Chacoan Society in the Northern Southwest, Final Report to Funding Agencies," vol. 3, eds. Cynthia Irwin-Williams and Philip H. Shelley.

1982 "Plant Remains from Rooms at Grasshopper Pueblo" in *Multidisciplinary Research at Grasshopper Pueblo Arizona*, eds. William A. Longacre, Sally J. Holbrook, and Michael W. Graves, Anthropological Papers of the University of Arizona 40:97–105.

BOHRER, VORSILA L., AND KAREN R. ADAMS

1977 *Ethnobotanical Techniques and Approaches at Salmon Ruin, New Mexico*, Eastern New Mexico University Contributions in Anthropology, vol. 8, no. 1.

BONGAARTS, JOHN

1980 "Does Malnutrition Affect Fecundity? A Summary of Evidence," *Science* 208:564–69.

BRAIDWOOD, ROBERT, AND C. A. REED

1957 "The Achievment and Early Consequences of Food-Producing: A Consideration of the Archaeological and Natural-Historical Evidence," *Cold Spring Harbor Symposia in Quantitative Biology* 22:19–31.

BRESSANI, R., A. T. VALIENTE, AND C. TEJADA

1962 "All-Vegetable Protein Mixtures for Human Feeding, VI, The Value of a Combination of Lime-Treated Corn and Cooked Black Beans," *Journal of Food Science* 27:394.

BRONSON, FRANKLIN H., AND OTTO W. TIEMEIER

1959 "The Relationship of Precipitation and Black-Tailed Jackrabbit Populations in Kansas," *Ecology* 40:194–98.

BRYANT, VAUGHN M.

1974 "Prehistoric Diet in Southwest Texas: the Coprolite Evidence," *American Antiquity* 39(3):407–20.

BUECHNER, HELMUT K.
1950a "Life History, Ecology, and Range Use of the Pronghorn Antelope in Trans-Pecos Texas," *The American Midland Naturalist* 43:257–354.
1950b "Range Ecology of the Pronghorn Antelope on the Wichita Mountains Wildlife Refuge," *Transactions of the Fifteenth North American Wildlife Conference.*
CASSIDY, CLAIRE MONOD
1972 "A Comparison of Nutrition and Health in Preagricultural and Agricultural Amerindian Skeletal Populations" (Ph.D. diss., University of Wisconsin).
CASTETTER, EDWARD F.
1935 "Uncultivated Native Plants Used as Sources of Food," University of New Mexico Bulletin, Biological Series 4:1–62.
CASTETTER, EDWARD F., AND WILLIS H. BELL
1942 *Pima and Papago Indian Agriculture* (Albuquerque: University of New Mexico Press).
CASTETTER, EDWARD F., AND M. E. OPLER
1936 *The Ethnobiology of the Chiricahua and Mescalero Apache,* University of New Mexico Bulletin, Biological Series, vol. 14, no. 5.
CASTETTER, EDWARD F., AND RUTH UNDERHILL
1935 *The Ethnobiology of the Papago Indians,* University of New Mexico Bulletin no. 275, Biological Series 4:1–84.
CHILDE, V. GORDON
1941 *Man Makes Himself,* second edition (London: Watts).
CLARK, ANN NOLAN
1972 *In My Mother's House,* 1941, Viking Seafarer edition (New York: Viking Press).
COLSON, ELIZABETH
1979 "In Good Years and Bad: Food Strategies of Self-Reliant Societies," *Journal of Anthropological Research* 35:18–29.
COOK, DELLA C.
1971 "Patterns of Nutritional Stress in some Illinois Woodland Populations" (M.A. thesis, University of Chicago).
COOK, SARAH LOUISE
1930 "The Ethnobotany of the Jemez Indians" (M.A. thesis, University of New Mexico).
CULIN, STEWART
1907 "Games of the North American Indians," in *24th Annual Report of the Bureau of Ethnology* (Washington, D.C.: Smithsonian Institution).
CURTIN, LEONORA S. M.
1949 *By the Prophet of the Earth* (Santa Fe, NM: San Vincente Foundation, Inc.).
1965 *Healing Herbs of the Upper Rio Grande* (Los Angeles: Southwest Museum).
CURTIS, EDWARD S.
1970 *The North American Indian,* 1926, vol. 17 (New York: Johnson Reprint Corp.).

CUSHING, F. H.
1920 *Zuni Breadstuffs*, Indian Notes and Monographs, vol. 8, Museum of the American Indian, Heye Foundation.

CUTLER, HUGH C.
1952 "A Preliminary Survey of Plant Remains," in *Mogollon Cultural Continuity and Change: The Stratigraphic Analysis of Tularosa and Cordova Caves*, by Paul S. Martin et al., Fieldiana: Anthropology, 40:461–80.
1966 "Corn, Cucurbits and Cotton from Glen Canyon," Glen Canyon Series no. 30, University of Utah Anthropological Papers no. 80.

CUTLER, HUGH C., AND T. W. WHITAKER
1961 "History and Distribution on the Cultivated Cucurbits in the Americas," *American Antiquity* 26(4):469–85.

DASMANN, RAYMOND F.
1964 *Wildlife Biology* (New York: John Wiley).

DAVIDSON, SIR STANLEY, AND R. PASSMORE
1969 *Human Nutrition and Dietetics* (Edinburgh: E. & S. Livingstone).

DAYTON, WILLIAM
1931 "Important Western Browse Plants," U.S. Department of Agriculture Miscellaneous Publication no. 101.

DICK, HERBERT W.
1965 *Bat Cave*, Monograph of the School of American Research, no. 27 (Albuquerque: University of New Mexico Press).

DICKSON, D. BRUCE, JR.
1980 *Prehistoric Settlement Patterns: The Arroyo Hondo, New Mexico, Site Survey*, Arroyo Hondo Archaeological Series, vol. 2 (Santa Fe: School of American Research Press).

DONALDSON, THOMAS
1893 *Extra Census Bulletin, Moqui Pueblo Indians of Arizona and Pueblo Indians of New Mexico* (Washington, D.C.: U.S. Census Printing Office).

EGGAN, FRED
1950 *Social Organization of the Western Pueblos* (Chicago: University of Chicago Press).
1972 "Summary," in *New Perspectives on the Pueblos*, ed. Alfonso Ortiz (Albuquerque: University of New Mexico Press).

ELLIS, FLORENCE H.
1968 "An Interpretation of Prehistoric Death Customs in Terms of Modern Southwestern Parallels," in *Collected Papers in Honor of Lyndon Lane Hargrave*, Papers of the Archaeological Society of New Mexico, no. 1 (Santa Fe: Museum of New Mexico Press).

EL-NAJJAR, MAHMOUD, D. RYAN, C. TURNER, AND B. LOZOFF
1976 "The Etiology of Porotic Hyperostosis Among the Prehistoric and Historic Anasazi Indians of the Southwestern United States," *American Journal of Physical Anthropology* 44:477–88.

ESPAÑOLA HOSPITAL AUXILIARY
1975 *Española Valley Cookbook* (Española, NM: Espanola Hospital Auxiliary).

ERDMAN, JAMES A.
1970 "Pinyon-Juniper Succession after Natural Fires on Residual Soils of Mesa Verde, Colorado," *Brigham Young University Science Bulletin*, Biological Series 11(2):1–26.
FAEGRI, KNUT, AND J. IVERSON
1975 *Textbook of Pollen Analysis* (New York: Hafner Press).
FEWKES, J. W.
1896 "Contributions to Ethnobotany," *American Anthropologist* 9:14–21.
FOOD AND AGRICULTURE ORGANIZATION (FAO)
1970 *Amino-Acid Content of Foods and Biological Data on Protein*, Food and Agriculture Organization Nutritional Studies no. 24.
FOOD AND AGRICULTURE ORGANIZATION AND WORLD HEALTH ORGANIZATION (FAO/WHO)
1973 *Energy and Protein Requirements*, Report of a Joint FAO/WHO ad hoc Expert Committee, Food and Agriculture Organization Nutrition Meeting Report Series no. 52, World Health Organization Technical Report Series no. 522.
FORD, RICHARD I.
1968a "An Ecological Analysis Involving the Population of San Juan Pueblo, New Mexico" (Ph.D. diss., University of Michigan).
1968b "Floral Remains," in *The Cochiti Dam Archaeological Salvage Project, Part 1: Report on the 1963 Season*, ed. Charles H. Lange, Museum of New Mexico Research Records no. 6.
1972 "An Ecological Perspective on the Eastern Pueblos," in *New Perspectives on the Pueblos*, ed. Alfonso Ortiz (Albuquerque: University of New Mexico Press).
FOX, J. ROBIN
1967 *The Keresan Bridge*, The London School of Economics Monographs in Social Anthropology, no. 35. (London: The Athlone Press).
1972 "Some Unresolved Problems of Pueblo Social Organization" in *New Perspectives on the Pueblos*, ed. Alfonso Ortiz (Albuquerque: University of New Mexico Press).
FRANCISCAN FATHERS
1910 *An Ethnologic Dictionary of the Navaho Language* (St. Michaels, Arizona: Franciscan Fathers).
FRYER, HOLLY C.
1966 *Concepts and Methods of Experimental Statistics* (Boston: Allyn and Bacon, Inc.).
GARDNER, PETER M.
1969 "Paliyan Social Structure," in *Contributions to Anthropology: Band Societies*, ed. David Damas, National Museums of Canada Bulletin 228, Anthropological Series no. 84.
GARN, STANLEY M.
1966 "Malnutrition and Skeletal Development in the Pre-School Child," in *Pre-School Child Malnutrition: Primary Deterrent to Human Progess, An International Conference on Prevention of Malnutrition in the Pre-School Child,*

National Academy of Sciences–National Research Council Publication 1282.

GASSER, ROBERT

1978 "Cibola-Anasazi Diet: The Evidence from the Coronado Project," paper presented at the 43rd Annual Meeting of the Society for American Archaeology, Arizona.

GAULIN, STEVEN J. C., AND MELVIN KONNER

1977 "On the Natural Diet of Primates Including Humans," in *Nutrition and the Brain*, vol. 1, eds. R. J. Wurtman and J. J. Wurtman (New York: Raven Press).

GISH, JANNIFER W.

1982 "Pollen Results," ch. 3 in *The Specialists Volume: Biocultural Analyses*, compiled by Robert E. Gasser, Museum of Northern Arizona Research Papers 23, Coronado Series 4 (Flagstaff).

GLASSOW, MICHAEL A.

1980 *Prehistoric Agricultural Development in the Northern Southwest: A Study in Changing Patterns of Land Use* (Socorro, NM: Ballena Press).

GOLDFRANK, ESTHER R.

1927 "The Social and Ceremonial Organization of Cochiti," *Memoirs of the American Anthropological Association* no. 33.

1954 "Notes on Deer Hunting Practices at Laguna Pueblo, New Mexico," *Texas Journal of Science* 6(4):407–21.

GOPALAN, C.

1975 "Protein versus Calories in the Treatment of Protein-Calorie Malnutrition: Metabolic and Population Studies in India," in *Protein-Calorie Malnutrition*, ed. Robert E. Olson (New York: Academic Press).

GRAHAM, GEORGE G.

1967 "Effect of Infantile Malnutrition on Growth," Federation of American Societies for Experimental Biology, *Federation Proceedings* 26:139–43.

GRAY, ASA

1849 "Plantae Fendlerianae Novi-Mexicanae," *Memoirs of the American Academy I.*

GREENHOUSE, RUTH, R. E. GASSER, AND J. W. GISH

1981 "Cholla Bud Roasting Pits: An Ethnoarchaeological Example," *The Kiva* 46(4):227–42.

HACK, JOHN T.

1942 *The Changing Physical Environment of the Hopi Indians of Arizona*, Papers of the Peabody Museum of American Archaeology and Ethnology, Harvard University 31(1).

HALL, E. R., AND K. R. KELSON

1959 *The Mammals of North America* (New York: Ronald Press).

HANSEN, H. P.

1947 "Post Glacial Vegetation of the Northern Great Basin," *American Journal of Botany* 34:164–71.

HARRINGTON, H. D.
1967 *Edible Native Plants of the Rocky Mountains* (Albuquerque: University of New Mexico Press).
HARRINGTON, J. F., AND P. A. MINGES
1954 "Vegetable Seed Germination," University of California Agricultural Extension Service Mimeograph.
HARRIS, ARTHUR H., JAMES SCHOENWETTER, AND A. H. WARREN
1967 *An Archaeological Survey of the Chuska Valley and Chaco Plateau, New Mexico, Part 1: Natural Science Studies*, Museum of New Mexico Research Records no. 4.
HENDRICKSON, G. O.
1943 "Mearns' Cottontail: Investigations in Iowa," *Ames Forester* 21:59–74.
HENDERSON, JUNIUS, AND JOHN P. HARRINGTON
1914 "Ethnozoology of the Tewa Indians," *Bureau of American Ethnology Bulletin* 56.
HENDRY, G. W.
1921 "Bean Culture in California," *University of California Agricultural Experiment Station Bulletin* 294.
HERBEL, CARLTON H., FRED N. ARES, AND ROBERT A. WRIGHT
1972 "Drought Effects on a Semidesert Grassland Range," *Ecology* 53:1084–93.
HEVLY, RICHARD H.
1964 "Pollen Analysis of Quarternary Archaeological and Lacustrine Sediments from the Colorado Plateau" (Ph.D. diss., University of Arizona).
HIGGS, E. S.
1975 "Appendix A: Site Catchment Analysis: A Concise Guide to Field Methods," in *Paleoeconomy*, ed. E. S. Higgs (Cambridge: Cambridge University Press).
HIGGS, E. S., AND C. VITA-FINZI
1972 "Prehistoric Economies: A Territorial Approach," in *Papers in Economic Prehistory*, ed. E. S. Higgs (Cambridge: Cambridge University Press).
HILL, JAMES N., AND RICHARD H. HEVLY
1968 "Pollen at Broken K Pueblo: Some New Interpretations," *American Antiquity* 33(2):200–10.
HOROWITZ, W., ED.
1965 *Official Methods of Analysis*, Tenth Edition (Washington: Association of Official Agricultural Chemists).
HOUGH, WALTER
1898 "Environmental Interpretations in Arizona," *American Anthropologist* 11:133–55.
1914 *Culture of the Ancient Pueblos of the Upper Gila River Region, New Mexico and Arizona,"* Smithsonian Institution, Bulletin 87 (Washington D.C.: Smithsonian Institution).
HOUSLEY, LUCILE K.
1974 "*Opuntia imbricata* Distribution on Old Jemez Indian Habitation Sites" (M.A. thesis, Pomona College, Claremont, CA).

HRDLICKA, ALES

1908 "Physiological and Medical Observations among the Indians of the Southwestern United States and Northern New Mexico," *Bureau of American Ethnology Bulletin* no. 34.

HUGHES, PHYLLIS, ED.

1972 *Pueblo Indian Cookbook* (Santa Fe: Museum of New Mexico Press).

HUMAN SYSTEMS RESEARCH

1973 "A Preliminary Experiment With Chapalote Corn in the Tularosa Basin, New Mexico," *Technical Manual, 1973 Survey of the Tularosa Basin.*

JELLIFFE, D. B.

1968 *Handbook on Child Nutrition in Developing Countries*, U.S. Dept. of Health, Education, and Welfare, Washington D.C.

JONES, P. R. M., AND R. F. A. DEAN

1956 "The Effects of Kwashiorkor on the Development of Bones of the Hand," *Journal of Tropical Pediatrics* 2:51–68.

JONES, VOLNEY H.

1931 "The Ethnobotany of the Isleta Indians" (M.A. thesis, University of New Mexico).

1935 "Ethnobotanical Laboratory Report no. 72," unpublished ms. on file at the Ethnobotanical Laboratory, Museum of Anthropology, University of Michigan.

1936 "Ethnobotanical Laboratory Report no. 86A," unpublished ms. on file at the Ethnobotanical Laboratory, Museum of Anthropology, University of Michigan.

1938 "An Ancient Food Plant of the Southwest and Plateau Regions," *El Palacio* 14:41–53.

1965 "Ethnobotanical Laboratory Report no. 459," unpublished ms. on file at the Ethnobotanical Laboratory, Museum of Anthropology, University of Michigan.

JUDD, NEIL M.

1954 "The Material Culture of Pueblo Bonito," *Smithsonian Miscellaneous Collections*, vol. 124.

KAPLAN, LAWRENCE

1956 "The Cultivated Beans of the Prehistoric Southwest," *Annals of the Missouri Botanical Gardens* 43:189–251.

1963 "Archaeoethnobotany of Cordova Cave, New Mexico," *Economic Botany* 17(4):350–60.

KAPP, RONALD O.

1969 *How to Know Pollen and Spores* (Dubuque, IO: Wm. C. Brown Co.).

KEARNEY, THOMAS H., AND ROBERT H. PEEBLES

1960 *Arizona Flora* (Berkeley: University of California Press).

KEARNEY, THOMAS H., ROBERT H. PEEBLES, AND COLLABORATORS

1973 *Arizona Flora*, Second edition, with supplement by John T. Howell et al. (Berkeley: University of California Press).

KELLEY, NATHAN EDMUND
1973 "The Ecology of the Arroyo Hondo Pueblo Site" (M.S. thesis, University of New Mexico).
1980 *The Contemporary Ecology of Arroyo Hondo, New Mexico,* Arroyo Hondo Archaeological Series, vol. 1 (Santa Fe: School of American Research Press).
KEPPEL, FRANCIS
1968 "Food for Thought," in *Malnutrition, Learning, and Behavior,* eds. Nevin S. Scrimshaw and John E. Gordon (Cambridge, MA: MIT Press).
KENT, KATE PECK
1957 "The Cultivation and Weaving of Cotton in the Prehistoric Southwestern United States," *Transactions of the American Philosophical Society,* vol. 47, part 3.
KEYS, ANCEL, J. BROZER, A. HENSCHEL, O. MICHELSON, AND H. L. TAYLOR
1950 *The Biology of Human Starvation* (Minneapolis: University of Minnesota Press).
KIDDER, A. V.
1958 *Pecos, New Mexico: Archaeological Notes,* Papers of the Peabody Foundation, vol. 5.
KLEIN, DAVID R.
1970 "Food Selection by North American Deer and Their Response to Over Utilization of Preferred Plant Species," in *Animal Populations in Relation to their Food Resources,* ed. Adam Watson, British Ecological Society Symposium no. 10 (Oxford: Blackwell).
KLEINER, EDGAR F., AND K. T. HARPER
1972 "Environment and Community Organization in Grasslands in Canyonlands National Park," *Ecology* 53(2):299–309.
KRENETSKY, JOHN C.
1964 "Phytosociological Study of the Picuris Grant and Ethnobotanical Study of the Picuris Indians" (M.S. thesis, University of New Mexico).
KROEBER, A. L.
1917 *Zuni Kin and Clan,* Anthropological Papers of the American Museum of Natural History, vol. 18, pt. 2, New York.
KURTZ, EDWIN B., JR.
1948 "Pollen Grain Characters of Certain Cactaceae," *Bulletin of the Torrey Botanical Club* 74(5):516–22.
LANG, RICHARD W.
1975a "The Ceramics of Arroyo Hondo Pueblo," unpublished ms. (Santa Fe: School of American Research).
LANG, RICHARD W., AND ARTHUR H. HARRIS
1984 *The Faunal Remains from Arroyo Hondo Pueblo, New Mexico: A Study in Short-Term Subsistence Change,* Arroyo Hondo Archaeological Series, vol. 5 (Santa Fe: School of American Research Press).
LANGE, CHARLES H.
1959 *Cochiti: A New Mexico Pueblo, Past and Present* (Carbondale: Southern Illinois University Press). Reprinted 1968, Arcturus Books.

LEE, RICHARD B.
1968 "What Hunters do for a Living, or How to Make Out on Scarce Resources," in *Man the Hunter*, eds. R. Lee and I. DeVore (Chicago: Aldine Press).
1969 "!Kung Bushmen Subsistence: An Input-Output Analysis," *Contributions to Anthropology, Ecological Essays*, National Museum, Ottowa, Canada.

LEUNG, WOOT-TSUEN WU, AND MARINA FLORES
1961 *Food Composition Tables for Use in Latin America*, Institute for Nutrition in Central America and Panama and the International Committee on Nutrition for National Defense.

LI, JEROME C. R.
1964 *Statistical Inference I* (Ann Arbor, MI: Edwards Bros., Inc.).

LIGON, J. STOKLEY
1946 "History and Management of Merriam's Wild Turkey," *University of New Mexico Publications in Biology*, no. 1.

LILLEVIK, HANS
1970 "The Determination of Total Organic Nitrogen, Second edition," in *Methods in Food Analysis*, ed. Maynard A. Joslyn (New York: Academic Press).

MAHER, LOUIS J.
1972 "Nomograms for Computing 0.95 Confidence Limits of Pollen Data," *Review of Palaeobotany and Palynology* 13(2):85–93.

MANOCHA, SOHAN L.
1972 *Malnutrition and Retarded Human Development* (Springfield, IL: Charles C. Thomas).

MARCY, R. B.
1850 "Report of Captain R. B. Marcy 1850," Reports of the Secretary of War, 31st Congress, 1st Session, Senate Executive Document 64:169–233.

MARTIN, PAUL S., AND W. BYERS
1965 "Pollen and Archaeology at Wetherill Mesa," *American Antiquity* 31(2): 122–35.

MARTIN, PAUL S., AND C. M. DREW
1970 "Additional Scanning Electron Photomicrographs of Southwestern Pollen Grains," *Journal of the Arizona Academy of Science* 6(2):140–61.

MARTIN, PAUL S., AND FLOYD W. SHARROCK
1964 "Pollen Analysis of Prehistoric Human Feces: A New Approach to Ethnobotany," *American Antiquity* 30(2):168–80.

MARTORELL, REYNALDO, AARON LECHTIG, CHARLES YARBROUGH, HERNAN DELGADO, AND ROBERT E. KLEIN
1978 "Small Stature of Developing Nations," in *Progress in Human Nutrition*, vol. 2, eds. Sheldon Margen and Richard A. Ogar (Westport, CT: Avi Publishing).

MASON, OTIS TUFTON
1904 "Aboriginal American Basketry," in *U.S. National Museum Annual Report for 1902* (Washington, D.C.).

MATA, LEONARDO J., JUAN J. URRUTIA, AND BERTHA GARCIA
1967 "Effect of Infection and Diet on Child Growth: Experience in a Guatemalan Village," in *Nutrition and Infection*, eds. G. E. W. Wolstenholme

and Maeve O'Conner, Ciba Foundation Study Group no. 31 (Boston: Little Brown).

MATHER, KIRTLEY F., AND SHIRLEY L. MASON

1964 *A Source Book in Geology* (New York: Hafner Publishing Co.).

MEHRINGER, P. J.

1967 "Pollen Analysis of the Tule Springs Areas, Nevada," in *Pleistocene Studies in Southern Nevada*, eds. M. Wormington and D. Ellis, Nevada State Museum Anthropological Papers, no. 13, pt. 3.

MERRILL, A. L., AND B. K. WATT

1955 *Energy Value of Food: Basis and Derivation*, United States Department of Agriculture Handbook no. 74.

MINNIS, PAUL E.

1981 "Economic and Organizational Response to Food Stress by Non-Stratified Societies: An Example from Prehistoric New Mexico" (Ph.D. diss., University of Michigan).

MORRIS, ELIZABETH ANN

1980 *Basketmaker Caves in the Prayer Rock District, Northeastern Arizona*, Anthropological Papers, no. 35 (Tucson: University of Arizona Press).

MOSIMANN, JAMES E.

1965 "Statistical Methods for the Pollen Analyst: Multinomial and Negative Multinomial Techniques," in *Handbook of Paleontological Techniques*, eds. Bernard Kummel and D. Raup (San Francisco: W. H. Freeman and Co.).

NEQUATEWA, EDMOND

1943 "Some Hopi Recipes for the Preparation of Wild Food Plants," *Plateau* 16:18–20.

OPLER, MORRIS E.

1941 *An Apache Life-Way: The Economic, Social and Religious Life of the Chiricahua Indians* (Chicago: University of Chicago Press).

ORTIZ, ALFONSO

1969 *The Tewa World* (Chicago: University of Chicago Press).

PALKOVICH, ANN M.

1978 "A Model of the Dimensions of Mortality and its Application to Paleodemography" (Ph.D. diss., Northwestern University).

1980 *Pueblo Population and Society: The Arroyo Hondo Skeletal and Mortuary Remains*, Arroyo Hondo Archaeological Series, vol. 3 (Santa Fe: School of American Research Press).

PARSONS, ELSIE C.

1922 "Shohmopovi in 1920," in "Contributions to Hopi History," by F. H. Cushing, J. W. Fewkes, and E. C. Parsons, *American Anthropologist* 24:253–98.

1932 *Isleta, New Mexico*, 47th Annual Report of the Bureau of American Ethnology.

1939 *Pueblo Indian Religion* (Chicago: University of Chicago Press).

PATWARDHAN, V. N.

1964 "Protein-Calorie Deficiency Disease: Public Health Aspects," *Proceedings of the Sixth International Congress of Nutrition* (Edinburgh: E. & S. Livingstone).

PHELPS, ALAN L.
1968 "A Recovery of Purslane Seeds in an Archaeological Context," *The Artifact* 6(4):1–8.
PHILLIPS, F. J.
1909 "A Study of Pinyon Pine," *Botanical Gazette* 48(3):216–23.
PIEPER, REX D., JAMES R. MONTOYA, AND V. LYNN GRACE
1971 "Site Characteristics on Pinyon-Juniper and Blue Grama Ranges in South-Central New Mexico," New Mexico State University Agricultural Experiment Station Bulletin no. 573.
POTTER, LOREN, AND J. C. KRENETSKY
1967 "Plant Succession with Released Grazing on New Mexico Rangelands," *Journal of Range Management* 20:145–51.
PROCTOR, MICHAEL, AND PETER YEO
1972 *The Pollination of Flowers* (New York: Taplinger Publishing Co.).
RASMUSSEN, D. IRWIN
1941 "Biotic Communities of Kaibab Plateau, Arizona," *Ecological Monographs* 11:231–75.
ROBBINS, W. W., J. P. HARRINGTON, AND BARBARA FREIRE-MARRECO
1916 *Ethnobotany of the Tewa Indians*, Bureau of American Ethnology Bulletin no. 55.
ROSE, MARTIN R., JEFFREY S. DEAN, AND WILLIAM J. ROBINSON
1981 *The Past Climate of Arroyo Hondo, New Mexico, Reconstructed from Tree Rings*, Arroyo Hondo Archaeological Series, vol. 4 (Santa Fe, New Mexico: School of American Research Press).
RUSSELL, T. PAUL
1964 *Antelope of New Mexico*, New Mexico Department of Game and Fish, Bulletin no. 12.
SAHLINS, MARSHALL
1972 *Stone Age Economics* (Chicago: Aldine Press).
SCHMUTZ, ERVIN M., C. C. MICHAELS, AND B. I. JUDD
1967 "Boysag Point: A Relict Area on the North Rim of Grand Canyon in Arizona," *Journal of Range Management* 20(6):363–69.
SCHOENWETTER, JAMES
1962 "The Pollen Analysis of Eighteen Archaeological Sites in Arizona and New Mexico," in *Chapters in the Prehistory of Eastern Arizona I*, by Paul S. Martin et al., Fieldiana: Anthropology, vol. 53.
1964 "The Palynological Research," in *Alluvial and Palynological Reconstruction of Environments, Navajo Reservoir District*, by James Schoenwetter and Frank W. Eddy, Museum of New Mexico Papers in Anthropology no. 13 (Santa Fe: Museum of New Mexico Press).
1974 "Pollen Records of Guila Naquitz Cave," *American Antiquity* 39(2):292–303.
SCHORGER, A. W.
1966 *The Wild Turkey: Its History and Domestication* (Norman: University of Oklahoma Press).
SCHRIRE, C.
1972 "Ethno-archaeological Models and Subsistence Behavior in Arnhem Land,"

in *Models in Archaeology*, ed. David Clarke (London: Methuen and Co.).
SCHWARTZ, DOUGLAS W.
1971 *Background Report on the Archaeology of the Site at Arroyo Hondo: First Arroyo Hondo Field Report* (Santa Fe: School of American Research).
1972 *Archaeological Investigations at the Arroyo Hondo Site: Second Field Report—1971 (Santa Fe: School of American Research).*
1980 *"Foreward: The Arroyo Hondo Project," in Pueblo Population and Society: The Arroyo Hondo Skeletal and Mortuary Remains*, by Ann M. Palkovich, Arroyo Hondo Archaeological Series, vol. 3 (Santa Fe: School of American Research Press).
SCHWARTZ, DOUGLAS W., AND R. W. LANG
1973 *Archaeological Investigations at the Arroyo Hondo Site: Third Field Report—1972* (Santa Fe: School of American Research).
SCRIMSHAW, NEVIN
1975 "Discussion: Comments on Arroyave Paper," in *Protein-Calorie Malnutrition*, ed. Robert E. Olson (New York: Academic Press).
SCRIMSHAW, NEVIN S., CARL E. TAYLOR, AND JOHN E. GORDON
1968 *Interactions of Nutrition and Infection*, World Health Organization.
SEGRAVES, B. ABBOTT
1977 "The Malthusian Proposition and Nutritional Stress: Differing Implications for Man and for Society," in *Malnutrition, Behavior and Social Organization*, ed. Lawrence S. Greene (New York: Academic Press).
SILBERBAUER, GEORGE B.
1972 "The G/wi Bushmen," in *Hunters and Gatherers Today*, ed. M. G. Bicchieri (New York: Holt, Rhinehart and Winston).
SIMMONDS, N. W.
1965 "Grain Chenopods of the Tropical American Highlands," in *Economic Botany* 19(3):223–35.
SMITH, JARED G.
1896 "Fodder and Forage Plants, Exclusive of the Grasses," U.S. Department of Agriculture, Division of Agrostology, Bulletin no. 2.
STACY, HAROLD G.
1969 "Ecological Distribution of Small Mammals of Santa Fe County" (M.S. thesis, New Mexico Highlands University).
STEGGERDA, MORRIS, AND RUTH B. ECKARDT
1941 "Navaho Foods and Their Preparation," *Journal of the American Dietetic Association* 17:217–25.
STEVENS, RICHARD, BRUCE C. GIUNTA, AND A. PERRY PLUMMER
1975 "Some Aspects in the Biological Control of Juniper and Pinyon," in *The Pinyon-Juniper Ecosystem: A Symposium* (Logan: Utah State University College of Natural Resources and Utah Agricultural Experiment Station).
STEVENSON, MATILDA COX
1894 *The Sia*, 11th Annual Report of the Bureau of American Ethnology, 1889–90.
1915 "Ethnobotany of the Zuni Indians," 30th Annual Report of the Bureau of American Ethnology (Washington, D.C.: U.S. Government Printing Office).

STEWARD, JULIAN H.
1933 *Ethnology of the Owens Valley Paiute*, University of California Publications in American Archaeology and Ethnology 133(3):233–50.

STIGER, MARK A.
1977 "Anasazi Diet: The Coprolite Evidence" (M.A. thesis, University of Colorado).

STUBBS, STANLEY A., AND W. S. STALLINGS
1953 *The Excavation of Pindi Pueblo, New Mexico*, Monographs of the School of American Research, no. 18 (Santa Fe: Museum of New Mexico Press).

SWANK, GEORGE R.
1932 "The Ethnobotany of the Acoma and Laguna Indians" (M.A. thesis, University of New Mexico).

SWEENEY, EDWARD A., ARTHUR J. SAFFIR, AND ROMEO DE LEON
1971 "Linear Hypoplasia of Deciduous Incisor Teeth in Malnourished Children," *American Journal of Clinical Nutrition* 24:29–31.

THOMSON, A. M., AND F. E. HYTTEN
1979 "Nutrition During Pregnancy," in *Nutrition and the World Food Problem*, ed. Miloslave Rechcigl, Jr. (Basel: S. Karger).

TIERNEY, FRANK
1978 "Urban Population of an Endangered Cactus," *New Mexico Journal of Science* 18(2):43–50.

TROTTER, M., AND G. GLESER
1958 "A Re-evaluation of Estimation of Stature Based on Measurements of Stature Taken During Life and of Long Bones After Death," *American Journal of Physical Anthropology* 16:79–124.

TSUKADA, MATSUO
1964 "Pollen Morphology and Identification, II, Cactaceae," *Pollen et Spores* 6(1):45–84.

TUAN, YI-FU, CYRIL E. EVERARD, JEROLD WIDDISON, AND IVEN BENNETT
1973 *The Climate of New Mexico* (Santa Fe: New Mexico State Planning Office).

VELARDE, PABLITA
1960 *Old Father* (Globe, AZ: Dale S. King).

VESTAL, PAUL A.
1940 "Notes on a Collection of Plants from the Hopi Indian Region of Arizona made by J. G. Owens in 1891," Harvard University *Botanical Museum Leaflets* 8(8):153–68.
1952 "Ethnobotany of the Ramah Navaho," Papers of the Peabody Museum of American Archaeology and Ethnology, Harvard University 40(4).

VITA-FINZI, C., AND E. S. HIGGS
1970 "Prehistoric Economy in the Mount Carmel Area: Site Catchment Analysis," *Proceedings of the Prehistoric Society* 36:1–37.

VITERI, FERNANDO, MOISES BEHAR, GUILLERMO ARROYAVE, AND NEVIN SCRIMSHAW
1964 "Clinical Aspects of Protein Malnutrition," in *Mammalian Protein Metabolism*, vol. 2, eds. H. N. Munro and J. B. Allison (New York: Academic Press).

VORHIES, C. T., AND W. P. TAYLOR
1933 *The Life Histories and Ecology of the Jack Rabbits, Lepus alleni and Lepus californicus spp., in Relation to Grazing in Arizona*, University of Arizona Agricultural Experiment Station, Technical Bulletin no. 49.

VUILLEUMIER, BERYL S.
1967 "The Origin and Evolutionary Development of Heterostyly in the Angiosperms," *Evolution* 21:210–26.

WATKINS, DONALD M.
1979 "Nutrition, Health, and Aging," in *Nutrition and the World Food Problem*, ed. Miloslav Rechcigl, Jr. (Basel: S. Karger).

WEAVER, J. E., AND F. W. ALBERTSON
1956 *Grasslands of the Great Plains* (Lincoln, NE: Johnsen Publishing Co.).

WEISS, KENNETH M.
1973 *Demographic Models for Anthropology*, Society for American Archaeology Memoir no. 27.

WEST, NEIL E., K. REA, AND R. TAUSCH
1975 "Basic Synecological Relationships in Juniper-Pinyon Woodlands," in *The Pinyon-Juniper Ecosystem: A Symposium* (Logan: Utah State University College of Natural Resources and Utah Agricultural Experiment Station).

WETTERSTROM, WILMA E.
1976 "The Effects of Nutrition on Population Size at Pueblo Arroyo Hondo, New Mexico" (Ph.D. diss., University of Michigan).

WHITAKER, THOMAS W., AND GLEN N. DAVIS
1962 *Cucurbits: Botany, Cultivation and Utilization* (New York: Interscience Publishers).

WHITE, LESLIE A.
1932 *The Acoma Indians*, 47th Annual Report of the Bureau of American Ethnology.
1943 *New Material from Acoma*, Bureau of American Ethnology Anthropological Papers no. 32, Bulletin no. 136.
1962 *The Pueblo of Zia, New Mexico*, Bureau of American Ethnology Bulletin no. 184.

WHITING, A. F.
1939 *Ethnobotany of the Hopi*, Museum of Northern Arizona Bulletin no. 15.

WILLIAMS-DEAN, GLENNA, AND VAUGHN M. BRYANT, JR.
1975 "Pollen Analysis of Human Coprolites from Antelope House," *The Kiva* 41(1):97–111.

WING, ELIZABETH, AND ANTOINETTE B. BROWN
1979 *Paleonutrition: Method and Theory in Prehistoric Foodways* (New York: Academic Press).

WOODRUFF, CALVIN W.
1966 "An Analysis of the ICNND Data on Physical Growth of the Pre-School Child," in *Pre-School Malnutrition, Primary Deterrent to Human Progress*, An International Conference on Prevention of Malnutrition in the Pre-School Child, National Academy of Sciences–National Research Council Publication 1282.

WOOTEN, E. O.
1908 "The Range Problem in New Mexico," College of Agriculture and Mechanic Arts Agricultural Experiment Station Bulletin no. 66.
WOOTEN, E. O., AND PAUL C. STANDLEY
1915 "Flora of New Mexico," in *Contributions from the United States National Herbarium*, vol. 19, Bulletin of the United States National Museum, Smithsonian Institution.
WRIGHT, HENRY A.
1974 "Range Burning," *Journal of Range Management* 27(1):5–11.
WYNNE-EDWARDS, V. C.
1962 *Animal Dispersion in Relation to Social Behavior* (New York: Hafner).
YARNELL, RICHARD A.
1959 "Prehistoric Pueblo Use of *Datura*," *El Palacio* 66:176–78.
1965 "Implications of Distinctive Flora on Pueblo Ruins," *American Anthropologist* 67(3):662–74.
ZOHARY, DANIEL
1969 "The Progenitors of Wheat and Barley in Relation to Domestication and Agricultural Dispersal in the Old World," in *The Domestication and Exploitation of Plants and Animals*, eds. Peter J. Ucko and G. W. Dimbleday (Chicago: Aldine Atherton, Inc.).

Index

Abandonment. *See* Migration
Acorns, 28–29; effect of drought on, 100
Agriculture: advent of, effect on diet and health, 5; yield estimates of, 46–55. *See also* Cultivars
Agropyron smithii, 190
Allium cernum, 29
Amaranth, 12, 18–19; pollen from, 199–201; protein content of, 119
American coot, 96
Animal foods: availability of, 6, 30–32, 41–42, 67; birds, 32, 78–81, 100, 108, 146; in children's diets, 118; decline of, with drought, 98, 107–108; mule deer, 72–78; pronghorn antelope, 81–83; rabbits and hares, 67–72; turkeys, 78–81; under famine conditions, 100, 145–147
Antelope, pronghorn, 31, 41–42; caloric value of, 83; effect of drought on, 98; locations of, 81–82; population of, 81–83
Antilocapra americana. *See* Antelope, pronghorn
Aquatic species, 96
Architecture, 6, 42–44
Arroyo Hondo Pueblo: abandonment of, during drought, 104, 138, 141–143; location characteristics of, 6, 33–35; occupational dates of, 6; physical structure of, 6, 42–44; ruins of, 42–44; territory of, 35–38
Artifacts from burial pits, 251–255

Banana yucca, 12, 27; drought resistance of, 100; location of, 40; yield estimates of, 63
Bark sheets and strips, 252–253
Basketry, 254–255
Beans, 11, 17–18, 34; land used for planting of, 54–55; protein content of, 116, 118, 119; yield estimates of, 51–55; yield estimates of, during drought, 106
Bears, 32
Beeweed, 12, 21–22; pollen from, 201–202, 239–240
Berries, 28, 29
Birds: as food, 32; small, as famine food, 100, 146; turkeys, 32, 78–81, 108, 220

Birth rates, 139–141
Bouteloua gracilis, 190
Buckwheat, pollen from, 205–207, 241
Bulrushes, 100
Burials, 147–151; artifacts from, 251–255

Cactus: banana yucca, 12, 27, 40, 63, 100; caloric values of, 61–63; cholla, 26–27, 99, 190, 210–214, 242–243; drought resistance of, 99, 106; fruits from, 25–27, 99; hedgehog, 12, 25, 99; locations of, 40; pincushion, 25–26, 99, 209, 242; prickly pear, 26, 61–63, 99, 106, 190, 214–215, 242–243; yield estimates of, 60–63
Calories: from antelopes, 83; from cactus, 61–63; content of in foods, 49–50, 171–173; from corn, 49–50, 84–86; from deer, 77, 78; from grasses, 66; human requirements of, 161–164; from pinyon nuts, 64–65; from plant foods, 49–50, 60, 61–63, 84–86; from rabbits, 70, 72; shortage of, in children, 119–120
Cattails, 29, 190; pollen from, 215–217, 243
Ceremony. *See* Social organization
Cheno-ams, 19; high samples of, from alien annuals, 191, 197; pollen from, 197, 199–201, 219, 239
Chenopods, 12, 16, 18–19; pollen from, 199–201; protein content of, 119
Children: calorie shortage in, 119–120; chronic underfeeding of, 125; demographic effects of deaths of, 126–137; diet of, 115–123; effects of varying food resources on, 9, 10; long-term effects of PCM in, 122–123; mortality rates of, 9, 10, 115
Chile, 15, 24
Chimaha, 29
Chokecherry, 28, 100
Cholla cactus, 26–27; at Arroyo Hondo today, 190; drought resistance of, 99; pollen from, 210–214, 242–243
Chrysothamnus nauseosus, 190
Cleome serrulata, 12, 21–22; pollen from, 201–202, 239–240
Climate: contemporary, 88–89; field and laboratory methods of reconstructing from pollen, 192–196; health and demographic impact of, 155; prehistoric, 6, 35, 87–90; as reconstructed from pollen samples, 188–189; temperature, 90–92
Cloth, 253–254
Collecting, of plants, 40–41; for lean times, 94, 99–100
Confidence interval, 249–250
Coot, 96
Corn, 11, 15–17, 34; caloric values of harvests of, 49–50, 84–86; chapolote-derived, 16, 46–47; decline of harvests of during drought, 97, 98–99, 105–106; land used for planting of, 50–51; minimum yield of, before abandonment of village, 108–109; pollen from, 217–218, 243–244; protein content of, 116; yield estimates of, 46–51, 84–86
Cottontail rabbit: caloric value of, 70, 72; hunting of in lean times, 108; population of, 31, 69–70
Cottonwood: bark of, in burial pits, 253; buds, 29
Coyotes, 32
Cryptogams, 248; loss of, 191–192
Cucurbita pepo, 11–12, 18; pollen from, 202–204; yield estimates of, 51–52
Cultivars: beans, 11, 17–18, 34, 51–55, 106, 116, 118, 119; pumpkins, 18; squash, 11–12, 18, 51–52, 202–204; yield estimates of, 46–55, 84–86. *See also* Corn
Curlew, long-billed, 96
Currants, 29, 100

Cycloloma atriplicifolia, 21
Cylindropuntia, 26–27; at Arroyo Hondo today, 190; drought resistance of, 99; pollen from, 210–214, 242–243
Cymopterus purpureus, 29
Cyprus esculentus, 100, 190

Datura, 204, 240–241
Death rates. *See* Mortality rates
Demographic effects of childrens' deaths, 126–137; in growing populations, 133–134; implications of, 138–141; time range of, 138
Demography, impact of food on, 8, 9–10
Dental abnormalities, 122
Descurania pinnata, 29
Diet, 11ff; change in composition of, 111; deaths related to, 8–9, 152; deterioration of, with advent of agriculture, 5; difference in among individuals, 110–111; diseases caused by, 121–122; during famine, 100, 112, 114; during lean times, 111–113; meat in, 30–32, 41–42, 67–83; protein in, 112–113, 115; of young children, 115–123; weight loss due to, 113–114. *See also* Animal foods and Food base
Disease, 121–122
Drought: abandonment of pueblo during, 104, 138, 141–143; community-wide responses to, 100–103; decreases in population through, 105; demographic effects of, 126–143, 154–160; effects of, on animals, 98, 107–108; effects of, on children, 125–126, 134; effects of, on plants, 97–98; major, 95–98; minor, 95; regional approaches to, 103–104; responses to, 92–93, 98–100

Echinocereus triglochidiatus, 12, 25, 99
Emigration. *See* Migration
Energy: calorie content of foods, 171–173; human requirements for, 161–164. *See also* Calories
Entomophilous species, 196
Eriogonum, 205–207, 241
Ethnobotanical pollen, 196–198; from beeweed, 201–202, 239–240; from buckwheat, 205–207, 241; from cattails, 215–217, 243; from cheno-ams, 199–201, 239; from cholla cactus, 210–214, 242–243; from corn, 217–218, 243–244; from jimsonweed, 204, 240–241; from *Opuntia*, 242–243; from pincushion cactus, 209, 242; from prickly pear cactus, 214–215, 242–243; from squash, 202–204, 240; from sunflowers, 207–209, 241–242; from turkey dung, 220; from basins, 218–220; from unidentified sources, 244–246
Ethnographic information, 13–14
Eurotia lanata, 191

Family: average size of, 43; changes in, as cause to abandon residence units, 44; migration of, after drought, 142; nuclear vs. extended, 44
Famine: internal management of, 100–103; psychological effects of, 102–103, 114; physiological effects of, 113–114
Famine foods, 100, 112, 114, 144–146
Farmers, nutritional stress in, 5
Farming: amount of land for, 35–36, 42; of corn, caloric values from, 49–50; fields for, lying fallow, 58–59; growing season for, 92; land, amount used for, 52–54; land available for, during drought, 105; new methods of, caused by population dips, 159; types of land for, 38–39; yield estimates from, 46–55; yield estimates from, during drought, 95, 97

Fat, 86
Fauna. *See* Animal foods
Fertility: effects of malnutrition on, 114–115; rates of, 137–138
Fiber cloth and strands, 252, 253–254
Fields: fallow, weeds from, during drought, 106–107; number of lying fallow, 58–59
Floral remains. *See* Plant remains and Food base
Food base, 6, 10; of animals, 30–32, 67–83; corn as, caloric values of, 49–50; famine foods, 100, 112, 114, 144–145; human responses to, 7; during major drought, 95–100; during minor drought, 93–95; mule deer as, 72–78; plants as, 11–29, 49–60; pronghorn antelope as, 81–83; rabbits and hares as, 67–72; trading of, during droughts, 103–104; turkeys as, 78–81; weedy annuals as, yield estimates of, 55–60; wild sources as, 84; yield estimates of, 46–86
Food production, shift to, from food collection, 5
Food shortages: archaeological evidence of, 144–155; community-wide responses to, 100–103; faunal evidence of, 145–147; major, 95–98, 114; malnutrition during, 120–121; minor, during early Pueblo period, 93–95; regional approaches to, 103–104; responses to, 92–93, 98–100; weight loss due to, 113–114
Food stress. *See* Food shortages
Food supply, redistribution of, among community, 110–111
Forage range, 40, 42
Foxes, 32
Fruits: from cactus, 25–27; from cactus during drought, 99; from trees, 27–29
Fulica americana, 96

Game: changing population of, 67–83; depletion of, 98; effects of, on indigenous vegetation, 34, 35; quantity available during drought years, 107–108; quantity of near Arroyo Hondo, 6, 30–32, 41–42, 67; used for starvation food, 100, 145–147. *See also* Animal foods
Gathering, 40–41, 42
Gavia, 96
Goosefoot, 18–19; effect of overgrazing on, 191
Gophers, 32, 108
Grains. *See* Seeds
Grama grass, 190
Grasses, wild, 24–25; cool-season, rarity of, 190–191; grama, in Arroyo Hondo today, 190; Indian rice grass, 12, 40, 65–66; mutton grass, 190; needle-and-thread, 191; squirreltail, 191; as starvation food, 144; wheatgrass, 190; yield estimates of, during drought, 98, 100
Grazing, effects of on vegetation, 34, 35, 190–192
Ground cherry, 12, 23–24
Growing season, 92

Hares, 31; caloric value of, 70, 72; hunting of in lean times, 107–108; population of, 67–70
Health, deterioration of with advent of agriculture, 5
Hedgehog cactus, 12, 25; drought resistance of, 99
Helianthus, 12, 22–23; effect of overgrazing on, 191; pollen from, 207–209, 241–242
Hunter-gatherers, nutritional stress in, 5
Hunting: characteristics of, during drought, 98, 107–108, 145–147; impact of changing animal populations on, 66–67; of mule deer, 74–78, 145; of pronghorn antelope, 82–83; of rabbits, 69–70, 72; territory for, 41–42; of turkeys, 78–81

Immigrants, increase in population from, 44, 137, 142
Indian rice grass, 12, 24–25; caloric value of, 66; locations of, 40, 65–66; present rarity of, 190; yield estimates of, 65–66
Insect pollination, 196

Jackrabbits, 31, 42; caloric value of, 70, 72; population of, 67–70
Jimsonweed, pollen from, 204, 240–241
Juncus saximontanus, 100
Juniper, 28, 190; increased density of from overgrazing, 192
Juniperus monosperma, 28, 190

Kochia scoparia, 191

Lagomorphs, 31, 42; caloric value of, 70, 72; hunting of, in lean times, 107–108; population of, 67–70
Lamb's-quarters, 18–19
Lepus californicus texianus, 31, 42; caloric value of, 70, 72; hunting of in lean times, 107–108; population of, 67–70
Long-billed curlew, 96
Loon, 96
Lycium pallidum, 29

Macrofloral materials. *See* Plant foods
Maize. *See* Corn
Mammals. *See* Animal foods
Mammilaria, 12, 25–26
Marriage, 158
Meat. *See* Animal foods
Mentzelia albicaulis, 29
Mice, 31; as famine food, 100
Microfossil, plant, 246–247
Migration, 138; during drought, 104, 138, 141–143; effects of, 141–143
Mortality rates, 132–133, 143, 138, 151; of children, 9, 115, 125, 126, 143, 147, 155; of elderly, 8, 114
Mule deer, 30–31; caloric value of, 77, 78; effects of drought on, 98, 108, 145; hunting of, 74–78, 145; location of, 72; population of, 72–78
Mustard, tansy, 29
Mutton grass, 190

Needle-and-thread, 191
Neolithic period, population increases during, 5
Numenius americanus, 96
Nutrients: decrease in, during lean times, 112, 114; human needs of, 7–8. *See also* Stress, nutritional
Nutrition: biochemical and physiological aspects of, 7; cultural and ecological factors of, 8; disease caused by under-, 121–122; human requirements of, 7–8; inadequate, 114; inadequate for children, 116–123; societal factors of, 8. *See also* Stress, nutritional
Nutritional stress. *See* Stress, nutritional
Nuts, 27–29; acorns, 28–29, 100; pinyon, 12, 27–28, 40, 63–65, 100

Oak, 28
Odocoileus hemionus. *See* Mule deer
One-seeded juniper, 28, 190
Onion, wild, 29
Opuntia. *See* Prickly pear cactus
Oryzopsis hymenoides, 12, 24–25; caloric value of, 66; locations of, 40, 65–66; present rarity of, 190; yield estimates of, 65–66

PCM. *See* Protein-calorie malnutrition
Phaseolus vulgaris, 11, 17–18, 34; land used for planting of, 54–55; protein content of, 116, 118, 119; yield estimates of, 51–55; yield estimates of during drought, 106
Physalis, 12, 23–24
Pigweed, 18–19; winged variety of, 21
Pincushion cactus, 25–26; drought resistance of, 99; pollen from, 209, 242

Pinus edulis, 12, 27, 28; bark of, in burial pits, 253; increased density of, from overgrazing, 192; location of, 40
Pinus ponderosa, 190; bark of, in burial pits, 253
Pinyon nuts, 12, 27–28; caloric value of, 64–65; drought resistance of, 100; locations of, 40; yield estimates of, 63–65
Pinyon pine, 12, 27, 28; bark of, in burial pits, 253; increased density of, from overgrazing, 192; location of, 40
Plant collecting, 40–41; forage range, 40, 42
Plant foods: archaeological remains of, 13–15, 175–183; caloric values of, 49–50, 60, 61–63, 84–86; fruits, wild, 25–29, 99; miscellaneous, 29; weedy annuals, 11–12, 18–24, 40, 55–60, 97–98, 191; wild, 11–12, 18–29, 40, 59, 60; wild grasses, 24–25, 40, 65–66, 98, 100, 144, 190. *See also* Cultivars
Plant microfossil, 246–247
Plant remains, archaeological, 13–15, 175–183. *See also* Plant foods
Plants, wild, 11–12, 18–29; caloric values of, 60; locations of, 40, 59
Poa fendleriana, 190
Pollen: as analytical tool, 13, 188ff; from beeweed, 201–202, 239–240; from buckwheat, 205–207, from cactus, 25, 26–27; from cattails, 215–217, 243; from cheno-ams, 19, 199–201, 239; from cholla cactus, 210–214, 242–243; from *Cleome*, 22; from corn, 16, 217–218, 243–244; field and laboratory methods of reconstucting climate from, 192–196; from jimsonweed, 204, 240–241; from *Opuntia*, 242–243; from pincushion cactus, 209, 242; from prickly pear cactus, 214–215, 242–243; from squash, 202–204, 240; from sunflowers, 23, 207–209, 241–242; transportation modes of, 196–198; from turkey dung, 220; from unidentified sources, 244–246
Ponderosa pine, 190; bark of, in burial pits, 253
Population: balance between food supply and, 6–10, 108–110; of Component I, 46; demographic characteristics of as seen through burials, 147–151; demographic effects on after deaths in children, 126–133, 134–138; demographic effects on after deaths in children, and with a growing population, 133–134; dips, archaeological evidence for, 153–160; effect of decline of adults in, 138–141, 153–154; effects of drought on, 105, 154–160; effect of one-year drought on, 134; estimated from number of rooms, 43–46; family size, 43; fluctuations in, 154–160; increase of through immigrants, 44; increases in after shift to food production, 5; as influence on amount of land and resources used, 42, 49–51
Populus, 29
Portulaca retusa, 12, 16, 19–21, 97
Potherbs, 19
Prairie dogs, 31, 145–146
Precipitation: contemporary, 88–89; effect of on weedy annuals, 60; influence on bean farming, 52; influence on corn farming, 48, 51; prehistoric, 6, 88, 89–90, 93. *See also* Drought
Prickly pear cactus, 26; today, 190; caloric values of, 61–62; drought resistance of, 99, 106; pollen from, 214–215, 242–243; yield estimates of, 61–63
Pronghorn antelope, 31, 41–42; caloric value of, 83; effect of drought on, 98; location of, 81–82; population of, 81–83

Protein: in children's diets, 115–120; content of in seeds, 118; in diet, 112–113, 115; long-term effects of inadequate, 122–123; requirements, 165–169
Protein-calorie malnutrition, 9, 156; in children, 119–123; mortality rates from, 125; as seen in skeletal remains, 151–153
Prunus virginiana, 28, 100
Pumpkin, 18
Purslane, 12, 16, 19–21, 97

Quercus, 28–29; effect of drought on, 100

Rabbit brush, 190
Rabbits, 31, 42; caloric value of, 70, 72; hunting of, in lean times, 107–108; population of, 67–70
Raiding, 104
Rainfall. *See* Precipitation
Rats, 31; as famine food, 100
Reptiles, as famine food, 100
Rhus trilobata, 29
Ribes, 29, 100
Rocky Mountain bee plant, 21–22
Rushes, 100
Russian thistle, 191

Salix, 190
Salsola kali, 191
Scirpus olneyi, 100
Seasonings: acorn meal, 29; amaranth, 19; chenopod, 19; chile, 15; ground cherry, 24; juniper berry, 28; wild onion, 29
Sedges, 100, 190
Seeds: from cactus, 25–27; from chenopods and amaranth, 18–19, 201; from Indian rice grass, 25; protein content of, 118; from purslane, 19–21; from Rocky Mountain bee plant, 21–22; from sunflowers, 22–23; from tansy mustard, 29; from trees, 27–29; from wild plants, 12; from winged-pigweed, 21; yield estimates of, 55–60; yield estimates of during drought, 106–107
Sitanion hystrix, 191
Skeletal indicators of nutritional stress, 151–153, 155
Skunkweed, 21–22
Social organization, 157–160
Soil, 34; for corn growing, 48; formations of, 38–39; loss of fertility of during drought, 97
Spores, 247–248
Squash, 11–12, 18; pollen from, 202–204; yield estimates of, 51–52
Squaw bush, 29
Squirrels, 31, 146
Squirreltail, 191
Starvation foods, 100, 112, 114, 144–146
Stickleaf, 29
Stipa comata, 191
Stockpiling, 92, 93–94
Stress, nutritional: community-wide responses to, 100–103; of farmers vs. hunter-gatherers, 5; induced by climatic factors, 93–94; major, 95–98; minor, 94–95; regional approaches to, 103–104; responses to, 92–93, 98–100; skeletal indicators of, 151–153, 155
Summer cypress, 191
Sunflowers, 12, 22–23; effects of overgrazing on, 191; pollen from, 207–209, 241–242
Sweetening agent, yucca as, 27
Sylvilagus: caloric value of, 70, 72; hunting of in lean times, 108; population of, 31, 69–70

Tansy mustard, 29
Temperature. *See* Climate
Trading of food during droughts, 103–104
Tumbleweed, 191
Turkeys, 32; hunting of in lean times, 108; location of, 78; pollen from

dung of, 220; population of, 78–81
Twine, 251–252
Typha latifolia, 29, 190; pollen from, 215–217, 243

Vegetation: today, 188–192; effects of grazing on, 34, 35, 190–192; prehistoric, 6, 87, 189–190; as reconstructed from pollen samples, 197ff. *See also* Plant foods

Warfare, 104
Water: for irrigation, 38–39, 48; sources of at Arroyo Hondo, 6, 33–34
Weapons, 104
Weedy annuals, 11–12, 18–24; caloric values of, 60; effects of overgrazing on, 191; locations of, 40, 59; yield estimates of, 55–60; yield estimates of during drought, 97–98
Wheatgrass, 190
Wild grasses, 24–25; cool season, rarity of, 190–191; grama, today, 190; Indian rice grass, 12, 40, 65–66, 190; mutton grass, 190; needle-and-thread, 191; squirreltail, 191; as starvation food, 144; wheatgrass, 190; yield estimates of during drought, 98, 100
Wild onion, 29
Wild plants, 11–12, 18–29; caloric values of, 60; locations of, 40, 59; yield estimates of, during drought, 98, 100, 106–107; yield estimates of prickly pear and banana yucca cactus, 60–63; yield estimates of weedy annuals, 55–60
Willow, 190
Wind pollination, 196–198
Winged-pigweed, 21
Winterfat, 191
Wolf berries, 29
Wooden artifacts, 255

Yucca baccata, 12, 27; drought resistance of, 100; location of, 40; yield estimates of, 63

Zea mays. *See* Corn.